Letters from the Horn of Africa 1923–1942

In Memory of My Father without whose letters there would be no book.

Letters from the Horn of Africa 1923–1942

Sandy Curle, Soldier and Diplomat Extraordinary

Edited by Christian Curle

Pen & Sword
MILITARY

First published in Great Britain in 2008 by
Pen & Sword Military
An imprint of Pen & Sword Books Ltd
47 Church Street
Barnsley
South Yorkshire
S70 2AS

ISBN 978 1 84415 845 4

A CIP catalogue record for this book is
available from the British Library

Typeset in 10pt Palatino by Mac Style, Beverley, East Yorkshire
Printed and bound in the UK
By Biddles

Pen & Sword Books Ltd incorporates the Imprints of Pen & Sword
Aviation,
Pen & Sword Maritime, Pen & Sword Military, Wharncliffe Local History,
Pen & Sword Select, Pen & Sword Military Classics, Leo Cooper,
Remember W   Publishing

For a col   contact

47 Church S   , England
E

Contents

List of Maps		vi
Foreword		vii
Acknowledgements		ix
List of Acronyms and Abbreviations		x
Glossary		xi
Introduction		xiii

Chapter 1   Young Officer, 1919–21   1

Chapter 2   First Footsteps in East Africa, 1923–5   9

Chapter 3   An Administrator in Meru, 1925–6   36

Chapter 4   By Foot to the Northern Frontier, 1926–8   47

Chapter 5   Administrative Officer in Somaliland, 1929–30   75

Chapter 6   Consul in Abyssinia, 1930–2   91

Chapter 7   Survey of the Gum Arabic Areas of British Somaliland, 1933   112

Chapter 8   Boundaries and Walwal: The Run-up to the Second World War, 1933–5   117

Chapter 9   On the Border of War: British Somaliland and Fascist Italy, 1935–6   151

Chapter 10   Quiet Life as a District Officer in Tanganyika, 1937–9   179

Chapter 11   Back to the Army, 1939–40   205

Chapter 12   The Raising of Curle's Irregulars, 1940–1   233

Bibliography   253

List of Maps

1. The Horn of Africa pre-Second World War   xv
2. Rhineland: With the Army of Occupation on the Rhine, 1919   3
3. In Kenya, 1923–1928   13
4. British Somaliland and Ethiopia: Administration 1929–1933   79
5. British Somaliland and Ethiopia: Border Disputes, 1933–1936   120
6. Tanganyika: Administration, 1937–1939   181
7. Northern Kenya and Southern Ethiopia, 1940–1941   235

Foreword

By Field Marshal The Rt. Hon. Lord Inge KG GCB DL

This is a 'great' read because it brings to life how the British Empire provided resourceful young men with great responsibility at an early age, and how the great majority of them rose to that challenge.

Sandy Curle was commissioned into the Gordon Highlanders in 1918 and served in the Army of occupation of the Rhine. However it was clear that peacetime soldiering did not appeal to his adventurous spirit which was inspired by stories of Empire and challenges in faraway places. In addition promotion to Captain took sixteen to eighteen years. Thus after five years Sandy Curle volunteered for service with the King's African Rifles and was stationed in Jubaland, then part of Kenya. Aged only twenty-three he found himself in command and the only European in the town. He thrived on the responsibility and being stationed in remote and isolated locations.

When aged only twenty-six he took command of Mandera Station on the Ethiopian frontier with orders to assist the civil officer who was daily threatened with death. The description of the six-week trek with his platoon, their wives, children, 220 porters and forty pack animals makes life seem dull by comparison. He clearly enjoyed living with his men, their families and mules in a small area and facing a situation where border raids were a constant threat.

After leaving the Army and joining the Colonial Service in 1929 he served in Somaliland. This was the period when the Italians were expanding their influence in Ethiopia.

He later became a Political Officer, an Assistant Commissioner on the British Somaliland/Ethiopian Boundary Commission, and as a Political Officer ran a series of agents in Ethiopia during the period when the Italians consolidated their hold on the country.

Just before the war his final posting was in Tanganyika as a District Officer supposedly to allow him to lead a quieter life and to get married, but war was soon to break out and he rejoined the King's African Rifles. He enjoyed being back in the Army and relished the challenge in training the recruits from the various and very different tribes. He formed 'Curle's Irregulars', though their official title was 'The Second Ethiopian Irregulars'. The unit had some 300 men selected from Ethiopian refugees and were trained to be a highly mobile 'irregular' force. He even chose his own officers!

He was awarded a well-deserved DSO and to quote from his citation:

'Their success has been outstanding and shown the highest standard of discipline, fine fighting spirit and pride in themselves which his company derived from his personal influence and incessant care. Wherever they operated they won the admiration of all. No situation had been too difficult and no enterprise too bold for Major Curle to tackle personally and it is his own example of courage and endurance that has produced such efficiency.'

He was also awarded the Military Medal of Emperor Haile Selassie I and at the end of the campaign was promoted Lieutenant Colonel.

It is therefore not surprising that in 1966 Sandy Curle was one of the twenty-five veterans who were invited back to Ethiopia by the Emperor to celebrate the 25th Anniversary of the Liberation. Amongst the guests – and the names speak for themselves – were Wilfred Thesiger, Sir Laurence van der Post, Colonel Hugh Boustead and the son of the late Major General Orde Wingate.

Acknowledgements

To begin with I am very indebted to Professor Peter Garretson from the USA, who was a childhood friend from my Ethiopia days, for his continual encouragement and help. He had known my father and knew his story was one that ought to be told. Of course there are several others: Lady Richard Percy, Doctor Richard Pankhurst, Doctor Thomas Crump, Doctor Sylvia Auld, Mr and Mrs Michael Voggenauer, Mr and Mrs John Sears, Mrs Rachel Bradley and Mr Hugh Mitchell, whose father served alongside my father in Jubaland in 1925. For help on matters military I would like to thank Major R.N. Sweeting and Captain T.G. Usher.

I am very grateful to Patrick Rafferty for his photographic work and to David Langworth for his mapping skills. He has shown great determination in pinpointing some of the obscure places mentioned in the text.

I must thank Henry Wilson and Bobby Gainher from Pen and Sword for making my dream become a reality. I am very grateful to Field Marshal Lord Inge for writing the foreword which my soldier father would have been very proud of.

Last but not least my husband for his unfailing confidence and patience in my endeavours.

List of Acronyms and Abbreviations

ADO	Assistant District Officer
APS	Army Postal Service
CO	Commanding Officer
CSM	Company Sergeant Major
DC	District Commissioner
DCM	Distinguished Conduct Medal
DO	District Officer
DTs	Delirium Tremens
FO	Foreign Office
GHQ	General Headquarters
GOC	General Officer Commanding
HE	His Excellency or High Explosive when referring to bombs
IO	Intelligence Officer
KAR	King's African Rifles
LG	Lewis Gun
MC	Military Cross
MM	Military Medal
MO	Medical Officer
MT	Motor Transport
NCO	Non Commissioned Officer
NFD	Northern Frontier District
OC	Officer Commanding
PWD	Public Works Department
QM	Quartermaster
RAMC	Royal Army Medical Corps
RASC	Royal Army Service Corps
RHA	Royal Horse Artillery
RFA	Royal Field Artillery
RSM	Regimental Sergeant Major
RQM	Regimental Quarter Master
SAA	Small Arms Ammunition
SCC	Somaliland Camel Corps
Temporary Gs	Temporary Gentlemen
YMCA	Young Men's Christian Association

Glossary

Askari	Guard or private soldier
Balambaras	Ancient Ethiopian title for a commander of a fortress
Baramids	Water tanks
Baraza	Parliament, meeting or open-air gathering
Blackshirts	Equivalent of Hitler Youth
Boma	Enclosure for Livestock or Fort
Buna	Roasted coffee
Charpoy	Common Indian bedstead
Chokra	Cook's boy
Dejazmatch	Senior court official or General
Dubats	Italian irregulars
Duka	Small shop
Enteric Fever	Typhoid
Fatigues	Daily routine jobs
Fitaurari	Formerly a military one, title of leader of advanced guard
Grazmatch	Formerly military title for leader of left guard of army
Habash	Colloquial term for an Ethiopian, from the Arabic
Illaloes	Irregular Soldiers
Intama	East African name for Sorghum
Jock	Scottish regular soldier
Koboko	Rhinoceros hide whip
Koran	Muslim Holy Book kept in a cloth bag
Lij	Literally 'child', courtesy title for children of the nobility
Makuti	Plaited cocoa nut leaves
Manyatta	Temporary Pastoralist Shelter
Ngoma	Dance or celebration
On the square	On parade
Provost Sergeant	Army Equivalent of Police Sergeant
Shamba	Farm
Shifta	Bandit, Ethiopian term
Zareba	Encampment surrounded by cut thorn bushes

Introduction

On retiring in 1958, my father, Sandy Curle, inherited a writing desk from his father within which, to his surprise, were bundles of his letters, written home regularly from 1919 to 1956 – like so many he had never kept a diary. Sandy's mother had died when he was a small child. The close bond between the rather austere, conventional father and the adventurous son reveals itself in these frank and at times amusing letters. Sandy's sister Jane kept house for her father. On the outbreak of war she joined the ATS. The arrival of the almost weekly despatches must have been a big event. Sandy's disciplined upbringing, Sandhurst training and many interests enabled him to make the most of all the varied situations in which he found himself.

Born in Edinburgh in 1900, Sandy was brought up there. His father, who had come from a family of lawyers in the Scottish borders, had been the first secretary of the Royal Commission on Ancient Monuments of Scotland and then director of the Royal Scottish Museum. His father was also a dedicated archaeologist with several publications to his name. Another lifelong interest was gardening. As a boy Sandy had accompanied his father when he was working on inventories of the ancient and historical monuments of some of the counties in Scotland, one summer holiday being spent bicycling round sites in Dumfriesshire. Sandy had inherited and acquired from his father a real feeling for antiquities. His mother was from the Scottish Borders from a family who over generations had seen service in India, China, Tibet and Africa. Sandy's maternal grandfather had been an officer in the Bengal Horse Artillery, while his great uncle, General Sir Harry Lumsden, had raised and commanded the regiment of Guides in India. Many a holiday was spent in his late mother's family home which was filled with memorabilia of faraway places, about which many a yarn was told. Sandy's imagination must have been stirred by all the tales of making war and keeping peace in foreign parts in the Victorian Empire and beyond.

Like boys of his background, Sandy was sent to prep school in Edinburgh and then away to Repton in England. The boy did not enjoy school and found learning difficult, however, after joining the Army class, he got 100 per cent in a tactics question and passed into Sandhurst at his first try.

Sandy was a prime example of the 'Caring Side of Colonialism'. At times he was a tough taskmaster but with a discipline that the Africans understood and appreciated. It was a relationship of mutual respect. Many who had served with him kept in touch for years after – he was in touch with his platoon sergeant from his days in Jubaland in 1923, up to 1956. Sandy was captivated by Africa and its people and the varied characters from all other nations and walks of life which formed the kaleidoscope of the Dark Continent. My mother was always fearful that her husband would want to spend the rest of his days there but he had roots in his beloved Borders of Scotland. After thirty-five years of a varied life, he was able to buy back the stable courtyard of his mother's old family home, where he embarked on meticulously filing the letters. With great forethought he was able to find several negatives of the original photographs to accompany the files, realizing what a unique record they were of a varied life in far-flung corners of the Empire. The collection was left to Rhodes House at Oxford but with the proviso that I could work on them first. Sandy's varied life as soldier, colonial officer and diplomat unfolds before us in the pages that follow.

The Horn of Africa: Pre 2nd World War

Khartoum

ERITREA
Asmara
E R I T R E A (Italian)

Red Sea

YEMEN

ADEN PROTECTORATE
YEMEN

Aden

Gulf of Aden

ANGLO-
EGYPTIAN
SUDAN
REPUBLIC OF SUDAN

Blue Nile

FRENCH
SOMALILAND
Djibouti
DJIBOUTI

BRITISH
SOMALILAND
Hargesia
SOMALIA
Somaliland Republic*

Addis Ababa

ETHIOPIA or Abyssinia
(Ind.)
(invaded and occupied by Italian forces from
1936-1941 to create Italian East Africa
together with Eritrea and Italian Somaliland)
DEMOCRATIC REPUBLIC OF ETHIOPIA

O g a d e n

disputed boundary**

I T A L I A N   S O M A L I L A N D

SOMALIA

White Nile

Lake
Rudolph

(BRITISH EAST AFRICA)

UGANDA   KENYA

J U B A L A N D

Mogadishu

Kampala

Lake
Victoria

Nairobi

ceded to Italy 1925

RUANDA-
URUNDI   RWANDA
(Belgian)   BURUNDI

Indian

Ocean

TANGANYIKA
TANZANIA

ZANZIBAR

Lake
Tanganyika

Dar es Salaam

Map showing states and territories governed by the
major Colonial powers Britain, Italy and France from
the Mid 1920's to 2nd World War together with their
present names.

* The former area of British Somaliland declared independence from
Somalia to form the Republic of Somaliland in 1991 but it is not
internationally recognized.

** The international boundary line agreed between Ethiopia and Italy
(formerly Italian Somaliland and now Somalia) is now not recognized
by both countries in dispute over the territory of the Ogaden.

0 miles   200   400

CHAPTER 1

Young Officer, 1919–21

On passing into Sandhurst, Sandy was enrolled into the Emergency Course in January 1918, and on 20 December of the same year he was commissioned as a Second Lieutenant in the Gordon Highlanders. Sandy had chosen the Gordons as their recruiting area was Aberdeenshire where his mother's family came from; at the start of the First World War he had three cousins in the Regiment.

And so we come to Sandy's first letter home, written as they all were to 'Dear Daddy'.

Botanic Gardens, Chanonry, Old Aberdeen 14 February 1919

I arrived at Aberdeen all right and found the Hotel very comfortable but a trifle expensive. I had to report at the Headquarters of the 3rd (Reserve) Battalion at King's Street and was sent in the end to H Company at the above address where I found a very undesirable looking room, bare boards and walls, no fires, with camp beds up round the rooms and a few equally undesirable looking Officers about. Our anteroom is very bare, and the food bad meat and I should say very badly served. There are two regular captains, one Captain Meish son of the Colonel and the other an ex-prisoner who was in the battalion before the war. There is one regular subaltern who I have not seen as yet. The only work each day is PT for the officers of whom there are twenty four. One is free every afternoon from 12.00 am till the next morning. This afternoon I went to see Aunt Mary at Murdan and stayed for tea. [She was the widow of General Sir Harry Lumsden who raised and commanded the regiment of Guides in India, and was responsible for introducing the wearing of khaki. The home in Aberdeen was called after the Headquarters of the Guides in India.] The house is full of rubbish and early Victorian art such as highly ornamented chairs and of course very uncomfortable.

I hope to get transferred to the depot as soon as possible where they are forming the regular battalions again; I simply couldn't sit here doing nothing; everyone is praying for something to do.

I have never seen such a city for crowds of loafers about and one can't move for them. I saw thousands from my room in the hotel just loafing in the streets like unemployed. The trams are excellent; one can travel for three quarters of an hour solid for half a penny at a good speed and with less noise than in Edinburgh.

I think this is all.

P.S. I am the only regular in the company; the other regular has just left while the other captains are in the neighbouring company.

April 1919 saw Sandy joining the Army of Occupation in Germany. His stepmother booked a hospital bed for him as when sent abroad the chances of coming home wounded were so high. After travelling from Scotland by train, crowded in a first-class carriage, Sandy reached Dover and marched to Shaft Barracks at the bottom of the cliff where the shaft for the channel tunnel had been started.

His first letter home from Dunkirk was on Young Men's Christian Association [YMCA] writing paper.

On Active Service.

WITH THE BRITISH
EXPEDITIONARY FORCE

Dunkirk
Wednesday.

8 April 1919

We have been in rest camp here for two days. We had a most lovely crossing, dead calm, but my platoon had to unload the ship at the end and then march three miles up to St. Pol rest camp. The town has been badly bombed; indeed the cathedral got a direct hit. We got up the line today across the war area.

Sandy was able to visit Dunkirk the next afternoon and have tea and drinks in a café. He found that it had all been knocked about by the war.

On Active Service WITH THE BRITISH EXPEDITIONARY FORCE
53rd Gordons Army of Occupation

We have at last reached Rhineland only to find we are to be disbanded shortly.

We left Dunkirk Rest camp at 4.30 am instead of 12.30 pm and went up through Bailleul, Armentieres, Tournai, Braine-le-Comte, Charleroi, Namur and Liege to Zulpich. It was frightfully exciting seeing all those places.

At dusk we approached the old front line and as we were ten in a *bosche* cattle truck from Berlin with our valises, a coal stove and straw, we saw out all right. We had our haversack rations which included bully beef and Maconochie's tinned meat and veg. First we came to bomb holes along the sidings and farms; then we came to shelled houses, all roofless and deserted in towns such as Armentieres which is a big town like Edinburgh in size. All the windows were smashed and roofs broken by shrapnel with only a very few indeed demolished.

After that we came to the desolated area, all shelled and no grass or greens; all trenches with the wire up for miles. Then we saw the old front line of 1916–1918 and no-man's land and on behind the bosche lines and networks of railway for small arms ammunition [SAA]. The railway had just been repaired right across the battlefield. Wire et cetera was all salved and collected into dumps beside the railway. We saw a Chinese labour corps cleaning up.

On the way up we saw a man ploughing with a cow or mule among the shell holes. The Bosche had blown up all bridges on the railway and smashed with explosives the lines at every other join from Beaujeux to Isieres; after that they had all been prepared for demolition but had not been blown up. At Luttine there was a siding; about seven lines of rails absolutely bombed to bits by our aeroplanes. Outside the station by the side of the railway were the remains of a whole truck twisted to bits. It had been carrying ammunition and was hit by our aeroplane. At five other places we saw the remains of SAA trains blown to bits. The whole line was inches deep in bits of shell and whole cases of gas

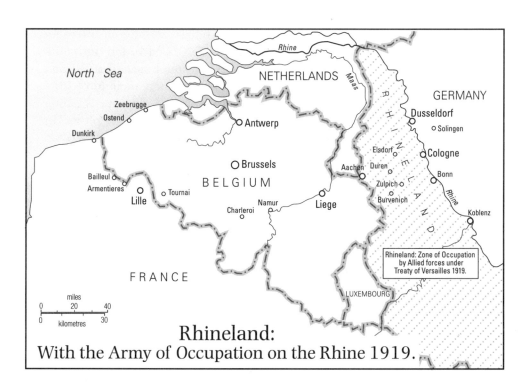

Rhineland:
With the Army of Occupation on the Rhine 1919.

cylinders. At all large stations as far as Namur which were out of shell fire, the aeroplanes had absolutely knocked the sidings and sheds to bits. At Chisehun we saw a whole large dump of shells, guns et cetera which had been collected from the country round and in some areas the shell cases were lying as they had been left. All the houses along the line were numbered by the Bosches and the number of men billeted there written up. At Basolly we saw some men of the Indian cavalry who were in billets there. At Pont-a-Celles we saw a canal with women filling the barges. At Charleroi we saw trains full of returned loot. We got out of the train at Zulpich and marched to our billets at Burvenich where I am in quite a good house, but we mess in an old inn of which the landlord is a farmer; eggs for breakfast every morning. He has cows, goats and horses; all most beautifully clean. One of the sergeants was in a house and was talking about the 51st when the old Frau told him that it was that division which had killed her husband.

It is very warm here with sun.

Sandy soon found that he had profited from two years in the bottom form for German at Repton as one of his jobs was to go to each house in the village to arrange for accommodation for the men.

53rd Gordon Highlanders Army of Occupation
British Expeditionary Force 1 April 1919

Many thanks for the letter which arrived today.

Our Company mess is in a very nice old farm house; we have an anteroom with a piano and a mess room. We get eggs at one mark each, and fresh milk daily with cream for our porridge. Our billet is in the house of a German Captain who is returning soon. We behave like policemen; men doff to one in the streets; you make your landlady make your bed, do your washing and generally lick your boots. We go into exactly what rooms we please. In fact in the town our motto is 'Remember France and Belgium'. A German Colonel of the Deaths Heads Hussars [German Cavalry Regiment] lives here and his house is another mess. They have commandeered his best bedrooms, bathroom, drawing room and dining room and they make him produce his wines for their use. He has his photo stuck up with the Kaiser and Hindenburg, all outside a big Schloss. [Field Marshal Hindenburg was chief German strategist in the First World War.] For a pound of English money we get two marks. Every coin is paper of which I enclose a few. I have not seen a paper since we left Dunkirk so could you please send the old Times out by twos as soon as you are done with them and keep a note of the cost. I hope it won't be very much trouble but one does miss a paper. Cigarettes here cost a penny each, chocolate three marks for half a usual sized bar and boiled sweets a penny. I also have some *bosche* soap which is like clay mixed with monkey brand which won't wear down. Every house here has a telephone and all have electric light even in the pig sties, but as for the sanitary arrangements the less said the better; they are appalling. An open drain runs down one side of the main street and all the buildings have a midden in the back yard. The people here do nothing on Sunday but go to church in one endless stream from 6.00 am onwards. My platoon sergeants are billeted in a house with a Hun Sergeant-Major who talks a little English; he was in the line for over three years. All men have to be in their houses by 9.00 pm when a drum is beaten. You should see them run.

Sandy's letters home were, as is still usual amongst the young, not quite as frequent as the Parent would have wished. On one occasion Sandy received this note:

If you have such a thing as a letter knocking about in your pocket you might just send it on as a favour.

Your affectionate Father Alex O. Curle.

Sandy found that the officers were given generous leave, but that they had to walk as there were no motor vehicles, just horse transport. Each Company Commander had a charger and the Battalion had an officer's mess cart. Sandy and his friends often used to go to Cologne which involved walking to Duren, a distance of 3km, and catching a train on which they travelled free of charge. On entering Cologne they passed the opencast brown coal workings. This coal was made into briquettes and used in the stoves in the houses. Some clever soldier found that if a lighted briquette was put into an oven it left a brown ash which could be used as khaki blanco on web equipment, spats and so on. Sometimes the trains were stopped and all the German civilians were searched for army supplies – if found with any they were arrested. Sometimes Sandy and friends would take a chance on getting a 'Lorry Hop', which involved walking to the main road and getting a lift on a RAF lorry or tender. They would be set down in the cathedral square in Cologne and had to jump from the back of the lorry onto the cobbles (bad enough but with a kilt on it was even worse). They could get a good lunch at the Ewige Lampe Hotel which was run as an officer's club by the Expeditionary Force Canteens (forerunner of the NAAFI) but the bar was bad so they always went to Joe's Bar at the Dom Hotel where the speciality was champagne cocktails. Joe, the barman was of vague nationality. The bar had a good atmosphere and was regularly frequented by the Mayor of the town.

Sandy was already developing an asset which was to stay with him for the rest of his life – namely an immense interest in people regardless of

5

their rank. The Joes of this world made an amusing change from fellow officers.

In May 1919, Sandy was granted five days leave to go to Brussels to look for the Belgian refugee family who had been with his family for some months in 1914–15. He succeeded in finding them and they showed him all round the city before he went on to Ostend and Zeebrugge. Along the dunes there were the remains of fortified concrete German pill boxes – the dining room of the hotel in Ostend still had a concrete pill box in its bow window. Although Sandy was able to travel free with a leave pass, nobody else in the Battalion had thought of going on a few days leave in Europe at that time. Indeed that trip was the first of many independent trips which he made in Europe over the next sixty years.

Sandy next found himself at Esdorf where he was attached with his platoon to the Carabiniers (a British Cavalry Regiment) to help them groom their horses. There was very little to do. The company mess was in the house of the manager of the sugar factory and the cushions were all emblazoned with patriotic slogans such as 'Unser Flagge immer flott Schwarz' (a naval hymn from the war, 'Our flag always streaming' emphasizing the fact that the ship is speeding about so much keeping things under control). In addition, one had a battleship flying the flag which was somewhat out of date. At one point Sandy went out with a .303 rifle in the forest nearby and shot a roe deer. His hosts were overjoyed when he gave them some of the meat as they had not seen such fresh meat for ages. Being a well-disciplined race they had not thought of poaching in the state forests. In June, Sandy found himself with the Battalion at Solingen where he was billeted in the house of a justice, while the Jocks (a Scottish soldier) were all in civilian billets or with working-class families. The houses mostly had privies down the garden with electricity laid on.

On 22 June, the unit 'Stood To' (on alert) pending the signing of the peace treaty. On that day Sandy was to hear 'Deutschland Uber Alles' (the old national anthem 'Germany rules everything', although during the war it was taken to mean that Germany ruled the world) being played in a house in the street. The matter was of course passed to the military police.

The Higher Command of the British Army of the Rhine ordered that Sandy's Battalion should be sent for an outing up the Rhine on a steamer. After embarking at Cologne, they chugged slowly up the river past Bonn as far as Andernach, just short of Koblenz. A lusty brass band played Teutonic airs and the sun shone as they passed castles, villages and a huge sign advertising the Appolinaris springs. Sandy found it all lovely but unfortunately the Expeditionary Force canteens had provided a bar to which the tougher officers adjourned. The result was that when they disembarked on their return, the Company Commander and the Second-in-Command had to be returned to the railway station in a horse cab. Their brother officers covered up for them and it never came out, but Sandy was extremely proud on this occasion to march the Company headed by the piper from the quay to the railway station. It was the first time that he had commanded a company.

The Rhine trip had made a lasting impression on the young Sandy who was determined to repeat the trip again, which he finally did in 1954; alas then there was no live band, only a tape recorder played when they passed the Lorelei and it poured with rain. Living in a village, as Sandy had, gave him a great interest in Germany and he frequently visited the country in his retirement.

The Battalion left the Army of the Rhine on 14 August 1919 and went to Leeds on strike duty. One day they had a deputation of senior citizens who asked to see the Company Commander to explain that they were the fathers of young girls who lived in council houses adjoining the parade ground – they asked that the Highland soldiers should be prohibited from sitting on the wall in their kilts.

A posting to the 2nd Battalion in Dublin followed in October. They were stationed at Collinstown aerodrome which was about 4 miles out of Dublin. Discipline was strict and they had to attend classes in Highland dancing under the Pipe Major. As long as the officers were 'On the Square' they could only dine out of mess once a week. Dublin was a 'Jarvie' or 'Jaunting car' ride away, both horse drawn. Sandy and friends used to go to a certain restaurant where the patron invariably sneezed into the bowl where he was mixing the salad, and there was a bar where cider and ginger ale would be served from a champagne bottle.

After a further move to Lichfield, Sandy was very relieved to be posted to the advance party of the 2nd Battalion who were to go to Silesia. However, after hanging about in Cologne for ten days with the value of the mark falling rapidly, the move was cancelled and they returned home. Sandy was then sent on a grenade course at Hythe which he passed with distinction. His next move was to Scotland.

HM The King's Guard, Ballater, 26 August 1921

Many Thanks for the waders; they will be the very thing.

I have got the best job going this time. We only go on parade two mornings in the week just to superintend. The remaining mornings we play golf, tennis and get up when we like. We have to turn out and meet all royalties arriving at the station; so far only the King and the Prince of Wales have arrived.

We got a command yesterday morning to dine at Balmoral at night so we attended in our full dress mess kit. We went by a hired car to the castle and were shown into the most appalling drawing room; very early Victorian, statues and tartan chairs and decorated clocks and paintings of dogs and

Prince Albert shooting were all we saw. The Ladies and Gents in Waiting, five in all, stood round the fire till the Royal Family came in; Princess Mary, The Prince of Wales, Prince Albert and Prince Henry. We were introduced to them all and shook hands with them. We then went into dinner. I sat between one of the Ladies in Waiting and Prince Albert while the Queen was next to Prince Albert with Alexander on her left. We had a very nice dinner of six courses, champagne et cetera. They all talked away and tried to make us as much at home as possible; after dinner we all drew up our chairs round the King and chatted. We then returned to the drawing room and talked away for about an hour when the Royal family withdrew and we went through to have a drink before leaving when all the Princes returned to join us. We left after about half an hour and each of us was given a huge cigar to smoke on the way home. We are going out fishing this afternoon. We are awfully bothered by awful old fogies with daughters who try and get us to all their dances and bun fights as we are apparently a great draw. We have so many people after us for poodlefaking that we refuse most of this and prefer to fish and golf instead.

I have just had a very strenuous weekend fishing without any success and was out all Sunday afternoon paying calls and have just spent a day with Sir Victor Mackenzie grouse driving at Glen Muich, 160 brace and am off for another day tomorrow driving again. I have just received another Royal Command to attend a 'Gillies Ball' on Wednesday night.

Yours in great haste.

Sandy danced the 'Flirtation Polka' with Queen Mary at that Ball.

However life as an officer in peacetime must have begun to pall for the adventurous young Sandy and so he followed in the footsteps of his ancestors and went abroad. He always considered himself lucky though to have soldiered in Germany in the armed occupation, in Ireland, in Glasgow and at the regimental depot for two years. He always looked back on the Gordons as a very happy regiment with the result that nobody left so promotion for most subalterns was running at sixteen to eighteen years. Also the pay was not very generous and unlike some of his fellow officers Sandy did not have much of a private income. The conventions of officer life must have irked him to a certain extent. His commander once told him that his red car was not an appropriate vehicle for an Officer. Like so many officers in Highland Regiments Sandy was always extremely proud to have been in such a company and that feeling of camaraderie with fellow soldiers never left him. To him it was the finest freemasonry in the world. The tartan and the various distinctive items of the regimental uniform welded the officers and other ranks into a body intensely proud of their regiment, its traditions, history and uniform. On retiring in 1958 he was thrilled when his soldier servant from thirty-seven years before arrived on his doorstep having hitched a lift out from the local town, some 7 miles away.

CHAPTER 2

First Footsteps in East Africa, 1923–5

In 1923 Sandy applied and was seconded to the 3rd Battalion King's African Rifles (KAR). His uncle had been with the 4th KAR, while other relatives had been in the German East Africa campaign in the war and gave him some idea of what to expect. The Colonial Office produced a magnificent pamphlet on what clothes to take. The form was to take your mess kit and your home service one with you; tropical kit was all made by the Indians in Nairobi within a day and was ridiculously cheap. There was no question of a course of injections in those days.

Sandy travelled out on a Union Castle boat, first class, which stopped at Marseilles, Genoa, Port Said, Aden and then Mombasa.

Reflecting on this career change forty years later, he was to remark: 'In the army one was always prepared to move and it didn't involve anything particular. You took everything for granted. In those days you see we had the Colonies. You went out there and you were the master. One was much more one's own boss, running one's own show.'

NAIROBI.

Nairobi, Kenya, 16 May 1923

I landed in Mombasa on the 13th. There was no quay and the ship anchored out in the stream so you went ashore in a small boat. There were numerous customs and immigration examinations during which you have to produce to be stamped all your guns and rifles which meant opening up the wooden case and also unpacking. I eventually got them all registered and caught the special boat train. The first class carriages are appalling to our notions, wood and bad cloth and distemper. They have no racks but a bunk folds down from the sides so that four people can sleep; you take your own bedding and it gets covered with red dust and so do you, as on the way up you pass through a district which is all red with it. The journey took twenty-one hours and as it was the rainy season and cold, the country looked very nice; grass and shrubs standing about 5ft high and a few native kraals about with huts et cetera. We crossed the game reserves and it was rather like a zoo; we saw all sorts of animals; ostriches, zebra, buck and some bigger beasts.

On arrival at Nairobi I left my luggage at the station, lunched at the New Stanley Hotel and went up to the mess and reported. One's mode of conveyance is a rickshaw and one boy shoves, the other pushes behind, all with bare feet. The roads in town are good but owing to the rains in parts they are about 2ft deep in mud. The town is rather like some of the 'Film Towns' but there are no salons and it is very obviously just sprung up.

The mess is about a mile out of the town on a hill, a wooden building nicely furnished while the officer's quarters are bungalows adequately furnished quite close to the mess. The Commanding Officer [CO] is a Major Durham, the Adjutant is a ranker and a large number of temporary officers are still kept on which of course has the usual result of making the place like a pub and everyone stands drinks in the mess but I think they are all on their last tour and are being replaced as soon as possible. My Company Commander, a Captain Kerr, comes from Edinburgh and fishes the King's water on the Dee when he is home on leave. I had heard of him from our gillie at Ballater.

The master tailor meantime is making me more jackets at 10s and trues and shorts at 5s; very cheap indeed. The nights are cold as at home here and as yet mosquitoes don't bother us and no one uses a net. The day time, although there is no sun just now, is not hot but we have to wear a topee always till 5.00pm. My uniform is shorts, drill tunic and blue brown boots and a topee with a square 1in in scarlet cloth. The only non commissioned officers (NCO's) who are white are the company sergeant majors, (CSM), the regimental sergeant major (RSM) and the regimental quarter master (RQM) making six in all. Here there are only one and a half companies; the others are out on the Jubaland border and up the Northern frontier by the Nile and Abysinnia. I expect I will be here about three or four months and then go out into the blue for about a year and a half.

KAR, Nairobi, Kenya, 23 May 1923

I am getting well settled down now and thoroughly enjoy the change of life. I was given leave to get my kit till Saturday and during the interval I went to a place called Thika, 30 miles away with some friends who I had met on the boat. They were waiting to go up to Uganda. We stayed in the Blue Posts hotel which consists of a central building and grass huts all round, dotted about; they are the rooms. The roads are all in an awful state; 3ft of mud with ford cars stuck in them, dead oxen, and wagons bogged down while such traffic as can move just makes a new road round. I went out after snipe and got three but ought to have had many more; they are bigger and easier hit than the home species.

They have corporal punishment here and the Provost Sergeant [Army equivalent of Police Sergeant] administers the '*Koboko*' (or *shambook*) [a whip made of rhinoceros hide] on the square quite close to the company office and as a result the screams of the victims are somewhat disturbing in the morning.

I have engaged a black boy as personal servant; he gets 30s a month. He rejoices in the name of Mwatu. His tribe is the Makonda who are hunters; his teeth are filed to a point so that he can eat meat easier. He is a cheery sort of soul to see when you wake up. I can't talk much to him yet but can make him understand essentials. I also have an orderly who assists the boy and is one of my men. All the soldiers have their heads shaved and they keep them so by using the tops of cigarette tins sharpened up on stones.

It rains every day at 4.00pm in the afternoon for certain and some days of course in the morning as well; not English rain but real tropical storms and as a result, hundreds of bridges are washed away. Someone shot at a monkey through the roof of my room so it leaks at times. All the roads are in a terrible state. There are no stone pavements in the town at all and very few of the roads are metalled, mostly just beaten down earth which is excellent in the dry season. One day last week the lowest temperature was 54°. The highest in the sun 123° and we had 6ins of rain. There are roses and great bushes of geraniums outside the mess door but when the hot weather comes they will dry up. We have a brass band which plays all the latest tunes et cetera; it even has '*Ta Bouche*'. [This was a popular French song of the time by Maurice Yvain.] All the instrumentalists are Africans with a British Bandmaster.

We have just finished a small 'War' against the Masai. I think in December we killed four in a battle and we have been keeping order since so the party of about sixty came in a day or so ago and of course were in absolute rags, officers included, having been torn on thorns in the bush and the whole lot had to be refitted.

KAR, Nairobi, Kenya, 7 June 1923

I am quite settled down here now and like the place very much indeed; the only trouble is that three quarters of my work is clerical and it would have been done at home by NCOs and as the men can't read or write one becomes a clerk. They have cut down our white NCOs so now we have only two in the

11

Battalion. The RSMs, RQMs and the officers have to do all the clothing books et cetera.

The majority of our recruits are Kavarondos, Nandis or Kikuyus and we only take them fresh from the wilds, always dressed in a blanket only or a skin when they first join. We have also a fair number of ex-bosche askaris [guards or private soldiers], who have joined us as they look upon themselves as warriors and will fight for anyone who pays them. The bosche had the local populace of his territory properly drilled into militarism. [There had been fighting during the First World War between British and Germans all along the border. Kenya bordered on what had been German East Africa and then became Tanganyika; it is now Tanzania]. The Masai are a people like the Irish; they never enlist at all.

We all went to the Levee at Government House on the King's birthday, Hindus and Africans all mixed together.

The mails are very irregular indeed here; sometimes we get two within a day of each other then none for three weeks and just now our cable is broken between here and the UK and we get no news at all in the local paper (East African Standard).

KAR Nairobi Kenya 14 June 1923

I am leaving Nairobi next week and going out on detachment to Gobwen which is on the River Juba about 12 miles from Kismayu and almost on the equator and on the borders of Italian Somaliland. [Gobwen was, until 1924, in the province of Jubaland, which was part of Kenya.] I shall live in a house alone but there is one other Officer there who is in command and also lives in his own establishment. Unfortunately there is not much shooting as shooting goes out here; but quite a lot to home ideas. I have added a hammerless twelve bore shot gun to my magazine; quite a good make. I paid £3-10s for it and it will come in useful on safari when these weapons get knocked about and it would be foolish to take the good gun out on the trek. I have also got a 9mm rifle which a fellow gave me who is going home. I have got 500 rounds of shotgun ammunition and a 1,000 rifle cartridges, soft nosed and copper nosed

I shall be leaving complete with my establishment; ie one cook, who rejoices in the name of Angussi who gets paid £2 a month, my boy Oboyu who gets £1-10s and my orderly or soldier servant who looks after the guns et cetera. I have been on a week's leave getting supplies. I have taken enough supplies to last six months including a 7lb tin of some cheap sweet which won't melt, rations of all sorts, tinned stuff, champagne and brandy in case of fevers; you never open it except as an emergency. Also an assorted case of whisky, gins and vermouths. I got three month's advance of pay to buy the supplies.

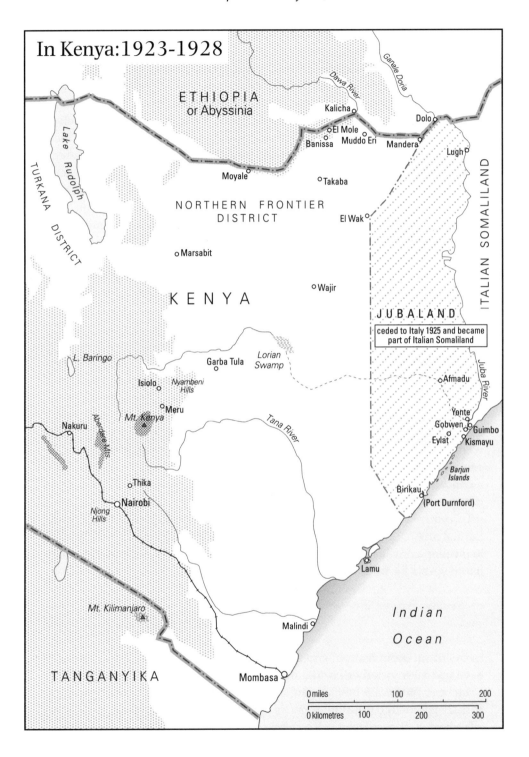

In Kenya:1923-1928

ETHIOPIA
or Abyssinia

Ganale Doria

Dawa River

Kalicha

Dolo

El Mole
Banissa   Muddo Eri   Mandera
Lugh

Lake Rudolph

Moyale   Takaba

TURKANA
DISTRICT

NORTHERN FRONTIER
DISTRICT

El Wak

ITALIAN SOMALILAND

Marsabit

KENYA

Wajir

JUBALAND

ceded to Italy 1925 and became
part of Italian Somaliland

L. Baringo

Garba Tula

*Lorian
Swamp*

Afmadu

Juba River

Isiolo   *Nyambeni
Hills*

Meru

Tana River

Yonte
Gobwen
Eylat   Guimbo
Kismayu

Nakuru

Aberdare Mts

Mt. Kenya

*Barjun
Islands*

Thika

Birikau
(Port Durnford)

Nairobi
*Njong
Hills*

Lamu

Mt. Kilimanjaro

Malindi

*Indian

Ocean*

TANGANYIKA

Mombasa

0 miles   100   200

0 kilometres   100   200   300

I will be pleased to get out of Nairobi although it is a nice place with lots of tennis and very healthy. I would prefer to be at an out station where you are your own boss more or less. I think there six Europeans within 20 miles of Gobwen while there are a lot of Italians across the river in Italian Somaliland. There is no white doctor within 300 miles on our side, only an Indian one 12 miles off and one native dresser at Gobwen, so the officers do doctor's work. I haven't the faintest idea of any medicine at all so I pity the poor patients, if I do kill one, I sign the death certificate myself always, so it doesn't matter. I will be able to get you all sorts of Somali things for the Royal Scottish Museum as we have dealings with the local chiefs. There is also a rare beastie called a 'Gerenuk' [long-necked gazelle].

I have only once been on parade since I have been out; you spend all the time in an office doing clerical work.

I never wear a tie here; my usual, kit out of uniform, is stockings, a local type of boots price 24s, shorts, a cricket shirt and a coat, and a hat like the cowboys wear only in grey known as a 'double terai', very comfortable in town or club and thank goodness we are not worried by convention. The boys wash one's uniform with a stone every time you wear it, as a result it becomes white and starched.

I wore my kilt for a mess ball the other night. I have never had such a surprise in all my life. I never worried to find partners; they all wanted to be introduced, I got fed up in the end with it. It is apparently a great novelty here, especially with the pre-war jacket which fits one very well, better than the taily affair.

The next mail comes out the day I leave here so I won't get the letter for another month perhaps.

Crocodiles abound at Gobwen for shoes or suitcases. Anxious enquirers please note.

Can you please send me out 'The Times Weekly', 'The Daily Graphic' Empire Edition and 'L'Illustration' so as to keep my French up. Debit the cost of same to me please. Also any old magazines of any sort would be most useful as one has to spend the middle of the day in the house.

KAR, Nairobi, Kenya, 11 July 1923

I am still sitting in Nairobi and shall be only too glad when I get off at last. I have had all my clothes packed up now for a month ready to go. [As Sandy wrote years later: 'On first landing in Africa, imbued with a spirit of efficiency and accustomed to time tables one is apt to get a rude awakening'.]

We have had here last week a circus, a huge concern on its world tour; it is of course always crowded with Indians and natives who look on the Indian elephant, quite a small one, which does tricks, as quite a deity. We have also had a concert party called 'The Futurists' on for a week; they are also on a world tour. They were very good indeed and helped to pass the time away.

The Navy are at Mombasa at present and a lot of them came up country for shooting. We entertained several of the Officers in the mess [Sandy's grandson who was in the Navy did exactly that in 1988].

Football matches here are a great attraction and everyone goes to watch them; they never start till 4.45 pm. It seems very funny at first to see the natives in their skins, bangles and ankle rings watching the game. One side of the field is usually reserved for Europeans the other for natives and Goans.

We had sports here last week for the askaris or troops; we had a spear throwing competition in which of course they excelled; one man threw about 60yds and in the high jump the winner jumped his own height. The great difficulty is to keep everyone from entering as they all want to go in everything.

There are quite a nice lot of people in Nairobi and everyone keeps a sort of open house which is such a change after the UK. No one worries what you wear at all. And of course the KAR are gradually getting a better name and one gets asked out more and more when they see you are a regular soldier; the mess still of course gets a dud cheque or so for mess bills from some Officers just to remind us that there are still some Temporary Gentlemen left. [Temporary Gentlemen – a term used for wartime officers.] All the officers practically have a shoe in various farms of sorts round about and so have an additional interest in the country; one or two have fruit farms, another coffee and another sisal which eventually becomes hemp for ropes and twine. It seems very funny to think that there is hardly a white man out here who has been twenty years in the country.

I have been to one or two local hops here as one has to go out or else life would be unbearable as there is nothing else to do of an evening; they always go with a good swing and everyone is out for a cheery time.

Mombasa Club Kenya 15 July 1923

I have at last got out of Nairobi only to find that my boat doesn't sail till Monday 16th now so I have to spend two days in this town which is damp and very hot and as most of my clothes are packed up in one of the fifty small boxes I have, I am reduced to very nearly pulp. The boxes are about 2ft by 2½ft which hold about 60lbs each so that it can be carried on the heads of porters; as I left Nairobi with 170lbs in the 50 boxes it was no fun having to get them all out of the guard's van.

The hotels are not very good and the club is worse; I have got a room luckily on the top floor of the Manor Hotel. There is no such thing as windows, the whole of one side being always à la veranda. You are never supplied with a blanket as you never need it; all one wants is a mosquito net. Your own boy always looks after you in the hotels in this country and does your washing luckily. My whole entourage are living in the police barracks where there is a hut for KAR detachments, luckily quite close to the hotel. My native soldier orderly had never had boots on before till we left Nairobi. I have never seen such a pathetic sight, one would think he was shot with lead; he was just able to drag one foot along after the other.

I went out for a swim yesterday with several other people; we bathed inside a coral reef with coconut palms on the beach. The sea was very warm and as we bathed after 4.00 pm the sun was not too hot. There were lumps of pumice stone such as one buys in Boots for 3d along the beach.

There are some very picturesque old streets here, narrow with balconies and mosques and the old fort, now a prison, called Fort Jesus with some old guns still in it. [It was built by Vasco da Gama in 1593–5. At that time Mombasa was the capital of the Portugese possessions in East Africa.] It is very funny here on Sunday in the evening if one walks down the main street you hear all religions practising, Roman Catholic next door to Church of England and lastly Hindus or some patent breed.

In all these places one meets the inevitable Scotsman; lawyers from Edinburgh, Glasgow shippers and the great majority of the staff of the banks are Scotch. One fellow I was introduced to asked me at once if I was connected with Curle and Erskine [the family law firm in the Borders].

Detachment 3rd KAR, Gobwen, Jubaland, 23 July 1923

I reached Gobwen on the 18th after a varied journey. I left Mombasa on Monday and boarded the SS *Cetriana* [not the *Tuna* as was planned] which is a little bigger than a trawler and used to be in the Leith-Norway trade; as you can imagine most suitable for the tropics. It is owned by an Indian. I had a state cabin in front of which there were numerous Arabs, Indians and Somalis, sprawled out with their luggage. They were being carried as deck passengers. The Captain is a native of Inverness; the chief Officer is a Persian. [The ship regularly collected cattle from Kismayu to take to Zanzibar.] Myself and the District Commissioner [DC] who was going to Kismayu fed with the Captain and the Persian. The meals when we were able to take them were excellent. We left at about 5.00 pm and, after a rough night in which I suffered as usual, we put into Lamu for the day. It is a wonderful old place on an island; the streets are only 5ft wide and practically all the houses built of stone with beautiful carved doors, most wonderful work. It is also the place where Allan Quartermain landed. [Allan Quartermain featured in Rider Haggard's novel *She*. The author's brother was British Vice Consul at Lamu in 1884–5 and is thought to have provided much of the background for some of Rider

Haggard's famous novels. Lamu is generally thought to have been founded by an Arab sheik in AD 694 but it may well date back to Phoenician times. It was at one time a Persian colony and was once a rival of Mombasa thriving on the trade in slaves, ivory and spices.] The people are almost white in colour and the women wear two sticks in their head-dress which is about 2ft in height which gives it the appearance of a sail. [The old inhabitants were people of mixed Persian, Arab and African blood. This headdress was known as a 'Shirraa'. In the past, it would have been carried by slaves over free women.] They still sew the dhows with coconut fibre as opposed to nailing; it is a very funny idea and very seaworthy.

We lunched with the DC of the district and set sail in the afternoon. All harbours here are guarded by the most terrifying reefs of coral. The next morning we reached Kismayu where a heavy sea was running. I put off in a dhow to the shore; very rough indeed, boats bumping about at the ship's side in a most alarming fashion. There is no pier so one is carried ashore on a chair carried on the shoulders of four Arabs. At Kismayu there is a club of sorts which chiefly supplies the whites up river with books. There are only two whites there now. [Kismayu was the main town for Jubaland.]

After I had seen my kit ashore and loaded onto two ox wagons, I set out for Gobwen on a mule at midday. The road or rather track runs for 9 miles across sand dunes and scrub. It took about two and a half hours to get there. Gobwen is situated on the edge of the Juba River and also at the beginning of a flat desert. The village consists of about eighty huts, all wattle and daub. Three stone houses and tin huts surrounded by barbed wire form the camp. The two officer's houses are perched on a sand dune right over the village and 100ft or more up. I am in a wood and mud hut with concrete floors which belongs to a commercial firm who rents it to the government; two rooms, a verandah and the cookhouse are outside. The bathroom is in a lean-to with a cement floor. When the water from my twice daily bath flows out of a pipe into the sand, snakes are attracted and come up the pipe. They are very easily killed with a *koboko*. I just slash them and break their backs.

At present owing to the rains all is green; the sea lies 2 miles off separated from us by dunes. The village is at present practically under water and the streets are always full of children, cattle, goats and camels of which there must be hundreds as all transport uses them. All our water which is sold for 1d a tin comes from a well a 100yds from the sea shore on donkeys, the river being tidal.

Opposite us is Guimbo, in Italian Somaliland, with houses of stone; a great contrast to our shanties which are full of wind, sand and bugs. There are some terrible species in that line; a cockroach the size of a dessert spoon, hornets, scorpions, mosquitoes galore, flies, ants, white and black; in fact everything except the domestic wasp. Some vile beast has already devoured the string and glue binding a new fibre shaving brush, a stick of first class shaving soap and some Birds custard so nothing is safe unless in tins.

I live on 1s a day. Whole chickens are 9d if dead, 1s if alive; draught oxen 12s and meat 1d a pound. Fresh fish, milk and fruit are available but there are no vegetables at all and none will grow. [Sandy being a natural gardener soon proved that they could.] Eggs are thirty three for 1s. I wish I could make angel cakes and then I would live on them. I buy fresh limes, 200 for a shilling and make my own lime juice. You buy a monkey for 1s alive from up the river.

I have been out shooting every day since I have been here but the game is very scattered just now. I dragged my Officer Commanding [OC] out my second day here; he is the most awful waster I have ever struck. He has been here a year or so and thought he better show me he knew where the game was. He had no gun and no cartridges. We got four whistling teal, I believe they call them, brown with a speckled breast. I got a grand left and right. We fired at sand grouse, bustards et cetera but didn't hit. The next day I also got him out, lending him the gun I bought the other day and cartridges; however after four hours walking he went off to cadge a drink at a *shamba* [farm]. I went on home and got a dik dik [small deer about the size of a large hare] and fired some shots at jackals; as I only had my shotgun I didn't kill. I went out again today for four hours but only fired one shot. My OC said he had an attack of fever coming on? I have since not enquired after his health.

The great beauty is that in Africa, on detachment, you always have your own house and eat meals alone. One is completely cut off from all outside news which is rather a blessing in some senses and a nuisance in another. We get mail twice a month. Across on the Italian side we get some quite nice leather goods. I believe that most of the leather in Rome, wallets, cushions and such like comes from Somaliland; it is goat skin which is tanned.

I have an excellent cook who buys everything. I have a cup of cocoa at 6.00 am, parade 6.30 am–7.30 am and then 8.00 am breakfast of fish and scrambled eggs with tea and scones, no butter obtainable and tinned jam. There is Musketry from 8.30 am–10.00 am. From 10.00 am–2.00 pm it is too hot for parade. Lunch at 1.00pm consists of fish, meat with tinned veg followed by tinned pears or dates and bananas or dried pudding and coffee. No tea. Dinner is at 7.30 pm with soup, fish, fruit as above and coffee. The best drink is home made lime juice and a dash of Plymouth gin. I find vermouths here are no use at all; whisky is too warming. I am selling a case to the Indian shopkeeper here and keep the rest for visitors; we do have some who come down the river in canoes from the Northern Frontier District [NFD] of Kenya and Abyssinia.

We have had several more shooting trips, sand grouse and guinea fowl falling victims to our prowess. The OC has just purchased an old box body Ford car which he considers very useful for going down to the lines, about 300 yards and intends going out onto the plain to shoot in it which if I give him a tin of petrol may be very useful.

If you could let me have the descriptions or names of birds and nests you want for the museum I will probably be able to get them but of course here they have no names; practically all just birds; jays, parakeets, canaries, sparrows, larks and orange breasted birds of sorts. My orderly eats small birds as I have found him gloating over whole nests of fledglings on the doorstep. He uses them to make soup with I believe.

Can you please get some pyrethrum powder or crystals in any form and send me a good size tin as it is the only thing which keeps the bugs away from the clothes, also a supply of fumigating candles (after measles breed) and a spray of disinfectant for the walls to keep flies off. In Aberdeen we used to have to spray the cookhouse once a month and render a certificate. Here when we really want it we can't get it for love or money out of the government. A native village is not exactly an eau de cologne distillery, I am only too thankful I am up the wind from it.

One has to do all the carpentry in connection with the making of targets et cetera and as well as repair any rifle or Lewis guns that go wrong and a 101 other little jobs which at home would be done by the men themselves or the workshops.

Detachment 3rd KAR, Gobwen, Jubaland, 30 July 1923

I have got settled down at last in this place in spite of the bugs and am getting to know the ways of the beasts better now. The Islam xmas took place last week so we had the usual holiday and a band of Nubian women and children chose to arrive at my house the day after and do a 'Ngoma' [a dance or celebration] which being interpreted means to make an awful row on drums of sorts. I could not get them away so I had to present them with about 5lbs of sugar and tea which they accepted and went but later they brought my gift back and said it was not enough so I just kept it and they ended by getting nothing. [Nubians came from the Sudan and had been slaves of the Egyptians. On being freed by the British, they were enlisted in the KAR.]

We had a terrific wedding in the village recently. *Ngomas* commenced on Monday round the bride's house and continued till Saturday when there was a feast. On Sunday morning a government Ford, lent by the Provincial Commissioner to the bridegroom, arrived, decked in muslins of all sorts, and collected the bride. Then on Sunday night the fun began at intervals of about ten minutes between 9.00 pm and midnight when they let off cartridges and bullets as is the custom with Mohammedans. The whirr of the bullets and shot falling was not at all comforting

The village has several rather curious workmen who sit in their respective huts and ply their trades; one is a silversmith who makes silver bangles and anklets. You give him a certain number of silver coins and he turns out a bangle of that weight. He makes wonderful stuff with only a crucible and a mould or two. Another man makes stools, like the one in the smoking room at home, with leather stretched across it; another makes *charpoy* beds [the common Indian bedstead].

I was in Kismayu to get some fresh veg off the Italian passenger boat which was in but they had used all theirs up and were living on tinned stuff.

We have a Swedish Mission in Kismayu with a branch here; as usual without exaggerating, the home of rogues. We don't count the Swede in charge as a white man.

The time of day here is our one great difficulty as of course there is no post office so we go by the sun and as no one has a reliable clock, we got about an hour behind last when we came to check it.

I am feeling extraordinarily fit in spite of the change of climate, sand and so called bad water one has to put up with; as long as one can get some exercise here it is quite OK. The only crab is the awful loneliness of the job never seeing another white man except one's brother Officer who by the way has got fed up and not been out shooting with me again. One gets used to it sooner or later and on the whole far better and more interesting than soldiering at home in a cut and dried manner with everything being done for you. It is such a grand change from convention and fences, walls et cetera and being able to go as far as you can see over the whole country.

The great blessing here is we always have a steady wind in off the sea in the form of the monsoons but at midday even that won't keep one cool.

Detachment 3rd KAR, Gobwen, Jubaland, 16 August 1923

We have not had a mail since I came here [about a month]. There has only been one out. We have had no papers or news of any sort since 13 July from Kenya and since 14 June from the outside world so we are a bit behind hand. [SS *Cetriana*, which Sandy had sailed on from Mombasa to Kismayu, had actually sunk off Kismayu]. The *Cetriana*'s cargo is slowly being washed up along the coast. We got some soap here yesterday in a horrid state and I hear they are trying to salvage the three bags of mail off her but unofficially as of course she is the property of the underwriters.

We have still got the rains on but expect them to cease soon. They don't much matter as you are soaked through and dry again in five minutes.

We had the Italian Resident to dinner one night, the OC Post and myself between us. My boy of course had to do it all. As the Resident, Signor Fazioli, talked French and Madam a little English, things went off all right; they apparently liked our whisky as they all have been over once or twice at sundown with their doctor who is a doped looking individual who always wears the same uniform and very occasionally has a shave. He has fifteen medals including three the same. One bright Italian walks about with a lap dog he calls 'Lion', about 6ins in height. He wears his braces outside his shirts and always carries a town walking stick. Our men think that he is a woman and nothing will convince them that he is not. They are not used to seeing their officers with lap dogs and white clothes all day long. The same gent told me he never shot at all here, it was too dangerous. He also writes with rose tinted and perfumed envelopes; a true descendant of the Roman Legion.

During the war the government had a light railway near Kismayu about 3 miles long over sand hills to the road where motor cars could go. As soon as they ceased to use it daily the local wandering Somalis took the rails to make spears.

I will probably be going out on patrol shortly for a month or so to a place called Afmadu, a 100 miles or so inland; it really devolves into a shooting trip for the Officer but is ordered by the Commissioner to show the flag so to speak as the Somalis have been rather troublesome in that quarter. Each officer is encouraged to spend ten days a month out 'Becoming acquainted with the area in which we are stationed'. This enables us to take advantage of the excellent shooting which abounds here.

Gobwen is a grain distributing centre as dugout canoes come down daily from Gosha full of maize, loose in the bottom and camel safaris also arrive daily; it costs 5s for two bags to buy now and is all stored in native mud huts near the river. Later it sells for as much as 15s for the two. A camel costs a shilling a day to hire here for baggage use. The bush is thick with meat camels and herds of all sorts just now; the former feed on thorns. I saw two huge prime camel kidneys, a veritable breakfast for a *Bosche* at 2d each.

Later. A telegram has come by wireless from Nairobi ordering the OC Post to return by the first boat to Nairobi and to hand over to me and they are sending a native Officer to take the place of a British Officer, so once he goes at the end of week I will be alone in the post with half a Company. I think I get extra pay of £50 per annum as long as I am in command of half the company but it will be very lonely with no one within walking distance except the Italians. Anyway I get a nice stone house to live in overlooking the river and away in the distance we see the sea.

The Italian boat comes in tomorrow so I hope to catch the mail.

Detachment 3rd KAR, Gobwen, Jubaland, 22 August 1923

The OC left at the beginning of the week and the native Officer who is to assist me arrived some days before. He is an excellent fellow who speaks English well and has about twenty-six years service. He originates from Cairo. [His father was a Captain, or the equivalent in the Army in the Sudan, which was commanded by Hicks Pasha and defeated at the Battle of El Obeid by the Mahdi in 1883. Sandy kept in touch with him up to 1956.]

I have moved into my new house now; it has four rooms and the windows of course never have glass in them. It has concrete walls and floor, an iron roof with *makuti* on top [plaited cocoa nut leaves] and Japan cotton for a ceiling. There is an 18in air space round the outside walls between the roof and the wall for coolness. There is a large verandah which faces the mouth of the Juba and Guimbo. I found a large crab in my room one day and frogs in my boots daily but I still like the place.

I have had my work cut out the last week taking over all the stores, buildings et cetera and am trying to put things square again. I am going into things pretty closely and have refused to take over the OC's water cart as the thing is rotten anyway. He has left me his gramophone records and about £20 of stores all mixed up in an open box. He said he couldn't be bothered to take them. He has left his car with a degenerate Italian Baron in exchange for a gold cigarette case. I will make a few changes in personnel and in the state of the buildings.

All the Europeans from the farm near here have been sacked and have left. Law suits are pending for slander and breach of contract so the whole place is in an uproar. A son of one of the company's owners has come out to manage it. One of the Somalis said they would cut his throat if he didn't pay them their back wages. The result is that the chap is scared to death out there and appears to be helpless. He talks with a fearful Lancashire accent and can't speak a word of the language. He has been in an office most of his life and is already down with fever and he hasn't been in the country a month.

We had a grand shoot when Major Durham from Nairobi visited the Detachment last week. We got eleven and a half brace of sand grouse in half an hour before breakfast. Major Durham told me he thought I would quite likely remain here till Jubaland was handed over to the Italians as I was able to speak French. [Jubaland was to be handed over to Italian Somaliland under an agreement made with Italy in 1915.]

We are after ivory smugglers, but as Gobwen is the centre of the traffic, we can't get them since they know every movement you make.

All the steamers with mails arrived within three days of each other. Most thoughtless.

Detachment 3rd KAR, Gobwen, Jubaland, 1 September 1923

Many thanks for the letters and papers which I got today, some from 20 July [NB. it was now September]. Thanks also for the books from Thins which are the very thing for reading at meals and I can't tell you how much I appreciate them out here in common with all papers.

We were quite gay last week as the Italian Resident, Senior Fazioli at Guimbo, asked us across to dine on Saturday night and of course we went. We had a terrific feed including spaghetti and various olive oil soaked dainties. We've also been over once or twice for a drink and he to us at sundown. I prefer his wine to whisky here. They are our nearest European neighbours being about a mile and a half away.

I expect Gobwen has gone back since your friend, Colonel Elliot was here; all the government bungalows having gone and there being only four Europeans in Kismayu and ten in all Southern Jubaland. I don't often go into Kismayu as it is quite a ride across sand and coral on a mule and nothing to do when you get there.

The village is now filled with cattle, from the Somali camps on the plain, trekking to the river to water and then back again. There is a continuous stream all day long.

I am getting on OK with my Swahili now and manage to explain all I want. The language of the district being Somali, the natives don't all understand Swahili. Across the river they understand hardly any as the Italians make them learn Italian and that includes all cooks, boys, soldiers and so on as it is too much trouble for the *dago* to speak Somali.

The native soldier is very nice to deal with. They regard themselves as warriors and they work very well indeed and very hard. On fatigues they are wonderful. They are always very smart on parade or on guard. They get issued with their rations once a week on Mondays hence Tuesday is our bad day as they always overeat if possible.

The river is drying up now and the monsoon is changing and as a result sand is drifting all over the place; in your bed, in your food, in clothes, in everything possible and to add to which the sun fairly burns down. It is almost overhead at midday. If you wash anything it is dry in an hour and a half after sunrise. Ink becomes a horrid paste at once. [This accounts for these letters being written in pencil.] Soap is hard and dry. The mosquitoes have all gone now and one need no longer sleep under a net. My house is rapidly falling to pieces and, as all the wood is hollow with bugs, it is no longer sun proof so I have to wear a hat all day long at meals and reading and writing. My verandah has 1ft of pampas grass stuff on the roof in addition to the iron so it is alright.

I have been employed as interpreter between the Italian Resident and the British DC in Kismayu, neither of whom can talk nor write a mutual language. I have been translating, with apparent success, long screeds of French written by the Italian into English and vice versa as well as attending at some of their interviews to interpret. [Sandy had a very good ear for languages. He must have just picked up Italian while out there and during a family holiday in Italy].

Detachment 3rd KAR, Gobwen, Jubaland, 7 September 1923

We are expecting to go out on patrols soon as caravans of undesirables are coming down from the north with illicit ivory which they take across the river to Guimbo where our friend, the Resident, gives them 24s a lb for it while our Government won't buy it. As tusks weigh from 30lb - 300lbs you soon see the reason. I have to go in and confer with the DC in Kismayu soon and get the question fixed up.

Here in Jubaland we are eight officers short. Captain Hussey Macpherson of the Camerons who was attached to the 3rd KAR died last month up in Turkana of cerebral malaria, but as he was slightly mad before he left here and he got a touch of the sun here as well, no one was surprised. Captain Baron von Otter, a Swede, who had been out here since 1913 also died of blackwater fever at Lodwar.

The crocodiles have been very active with men of late. Three natives were eaten last week while one was saved through someone near hearing his screams and catching hold of his legs and pulling him out. His whole forearm had been bitten through by the croc and on the other hand his fingers were all skinned. He was brought to us to bandage up and send on to the Indian sub-assistant surgeon, who as usual was overcome by fear and said he couldn't amputate as he might kill the man and would we get the Italian doctor to come across. When the doctor arrived we found that the man had fled. He was finally found having walked 9 miles into Gobwen. He got his amputation in the end.

I wouldn't soldier at home now for anything. I much prefer African military life; no social functions to worry you and clothes don't matter. One is always on active service out of Nairobi according to government reckoning.

Detachment 3rd KAR, Gobwen, Jubaland, 5 October 1923

I have been lucky again not only having got command of the station but also I am in charge of the civil office as well and that means the whole civil population comes under me. I have no legal powers over the civilians as far as prison is concerned. It is great fun; I hold two orderly rooms a day, one for the soldiers and the other for defaulting tax payers. My second day in the office, some natives stole, during the night, our sandbags from the range, so I held a 'Baraza' [meeting or open air gathering] of all the headmen of the village and told them that the culprit or the bags must be returned in three days. The time limit expires tomorrow when if they are not returned I have got permission to take the cost of new ones off the headman's pay.

I am kept working twelve hours a day sorting out the clerical work in connection with pay and clothing as well as musketry and training of NCOs and Lewis gunners. Once I get things organized, I will have a lot of time to myself. The native Officer who as I have said before is an excellent fellow does all the spade clerical work. He is really a far whiter man than some whites.

I am still as fit as can be and I am so brown that you wouldn't know me. What without sweets and drinks between meals and eating plain food and half what I do at home, I couldn't be fitter.

Kismayu, Jubaland, 20 October 1923

I am down with enteric fever [another name for typhoid] and was evacuated here on 16th. Luckily it is not bad as I was inoculated not long ago. I am under the charge of a white doctor who was passing through and has stayed on. Don't worry, it is not really that bad and I am well looked after. I have had my blood examined and there is no trace of malaria. [Sandy was first seen by the Indian Sub-Assistant Surgeon who looked at the rash and pronounced that it was the prickly heat of Africa. Mercifully a Singhalese doctor with Cambridge degrees was passing through the very day that Sandy became ill. The doctor was bringing a patient with appendicitis down the Dawa River from the Northern Frontier. Sandy was delirious when he was moved by car to Kismayu; he thought he was arriving in Aberdeen. The first night there it poured with rain, the roof leaked and Sandy was soaked, but it had the effect of bringing his temperature down. The doctor stayed to look after him for a week.]

Kismayu, Jubaland, 27 October 1923

I am still in bed and living on a milk diet but am feeling much better. I expect to be up in about a week and return to Gobwen to recuperate before returning to Nairobi to take some leave. It is most annoying getting this typhoid enteric affair just as I was getting into my stride and had got such a great chance.

An Officer arrived to carry on temporarily; the ass is bringing his wife. I expect she will either die or return on the first boat; the bugs et cetera, not to mention the sand and awful heat are hardly suitable.

My Gobwen house is all packed away. While here, I am living in a room in the police house with my own boys, cook and soldier servant.

A thousand thanks for vegs [obviously tinned] which all arrived safely. Now I lie in bed and look at the petit pois and haricot vert with longing and the Dorset butter makes my mouth water.

Kismayu, Jubaland, 2 November 1923

I am getting on well and am allowed up on the verandah all day and am on solid food again. The tinned veg comes in most useful. It is delightfully warm here and the house I am in is on the sea shore so there is always a breeze and being a stone house, it never overheats.

There were a couple of murders last week near Gobwen; a blood feud between Somalis. They had a set to in broad daylight with spears. They are going to hang the murderers in the market at Kismayu; a public affair to warn people.

There is a large dhow trade here. Some of them have square sails made of matted grass and look just like the pictures of Roman galleys. The fishing boats have outriggers which are hollowed out of a tree.

The shore has always about six beds on it. When white ants get at the woodwork, the natives take the bed into the sea and leave it for a few days. After it is soaked in salt water no bugs will touch it. They never get washed away or stolen. The native children run about naked and are in and out of the sea all day long.

I had a long-winded letter full of advice from Aunt Elize. I wish you could tell her to shut up and not write rubbish about malaria and mosquitoes and wearing shorts. Mosquitoes here don't bite or appear till the sun goes down. One always changes for supper. I usually wear a cricket shirt and an old pair of tartan trews.

Kismayu, Jubaland, 5 November 1923

Tomorrow I return to Gobwen to convalesce so as to be strong to stand the journey to Nairobi. I am very weak on my legs but feeling stronger daily.

Things at Gobwen are in a bad way as for three weeks there was only the native Officer in charge and he can't do sums so the rations of course are all muddled up. It is the fault of the CO for having only one Officer at the post and I merely laugh. When I was ill any stores which were short were written off as lost and no one was responsible.

When the British Empire exhibition comes off, you ought to go and see the Jubaland exhibit; the spears and knives are not mere tourist trophies as we see men with them walking through Gobwen daily.

Next followed a period of recuperation in Nairobi for about six weeks, which culminated in an excellent fourteen days shooting in the Ngong hills. Sandy lived in great style in a government tent with his two Somali boys and a cook. A buffalo, warthogs and bush bucks were shot. It was 14 miles from Nairobi but only once did Sandy hear another sportsman.

Sandy then left by train to collect army reservists for training.

Attached 5th KAR, Meru, Kenya, 1 February 1924

We had a very hard month's work training our reservists and practising for the Presentation of Colours which was last Saturday and went off very well. The Governor came to dine with us on the Thursday before. On the Saturday afternoon we had sports and an 'At Home' followed in the evening by bonfires and native dances. Each tribe had their own bonfire and danced their own particular dance round it. All our ex soldiers with over fifteen years' service were allowed to come free to Nairobi so we had about 300 veterans who marched past. Some of them had the 1888 Egyptian medal and star and eight other war medals. Two or three had eight clasps to their African General Service medal. We reckoned they had been in fifteen small wars. Some had got the the Distinguished Conduct Medal (DCM) and the Military Medal (MM) in the late war. One old fellow had served for a few years in the German army and had the Iron Cross on, mixed up with his British medals. The native Officer who took the Regimental Colours had fought against us at Omdurman in the Dervish forces but had joined our army after as our rifles were better. [The battle, in which Kitchener defeated the Dervishes, was in 1898.] Yet another Sergeant had served in the Turkish army for three years, the French for three, the German for six and is now in our 5th Battalion. He is Sudanese by birth.

However, Sandy couldn't wait to get back to Gobwen.

Detachment 3rd KAR, Gobwen, Jubaland, 21 April 1924

I have at last got back to Gobwen. I came up nearly three weeks ago by the Italian steamer to relieve Mackay who was sick and returning to Nairobi so that is three officers invalided in a year from here which is pretty good going.

I went up to Yonte with Major Fowler who was out inspecting to visit the old Sudanese soldiers' shambas and met some wonderful old men. Each man has a small plot of land which he cultivates and they live under the mango trees. One or two were in the original company of 200 soldiers which were recruited in the Sudan and were landed at Mombasa and trekked to Kisumu. Some of them have fought in fifteen wars and can tell you the name of practically every officer they have served with. They even asked after Lugard. They dated from about 1897. [Lugard was a soldier, administrator and author (1858–1945) who had journeyed widely in East Africa.] Their wives can all fire the Maxim gun because when they moved in those days their wives went with them. They considered that the days of 'Beebee Victoria' had been the best as she gave them nice clothes; the little red coats which they wore made everyone respect them. 'Kingie Edward' had taken their nice clothes away and 'Kingie George' took even more away. They are always sending me presents of bananas and limes, the former on great stalks which I hang on the verandah till ripe. We walked out and came back down the river in a canoe, breaking our journey to poach on the Italian side. We chased a herd of oryx, saw two lions and some wild pig.

I have secured a very good cook, a Somali. He can cook Italian dishes very well; macaroni is his speciality. I got a dozen bottles of bianco secco from the Italian boat which, as I got it duty free, worked out at about 5d a bottle. I find it the best thing to drink here, of course diluted with water. I also got some spaghetti which is the best stuff you can get for these parts as it doesn't go stale and is not affected by the climate.

I am being waited on by my orderly at meals now and the housework has to be done by another askari. Their ideas as regards knives and forks and other things are crude; such things of course being unknown in their own homes. Their ideas of Europe are also very undeveloped. Quite suddenly one asked me how it was that during the war the soldiers had marched for days and days from German East Africa to Portugese East Africa without getting to Europe. They can't understand how everyone is white in England and all the soldiers are white and there is no tribe to do the work of sweeps.

I have to do the sick parade as before so am kept fairly busy. Both my boys are down with fever and an average of six per cent of the men are down daily with malaria. I have a woman patient or two from the lines as well to see so my medical knowledge is growing daily. Do I prescribe aspirin, quinine or salts?

Detachment 3rd KAR, Gobwen, Jubaland, 7 May 1924

We have had a very poor mail service of late; only one boat last month taking mails home so I am sending this from the Italian side and it will get home much quicker.

I got quite lost with Easter and thought it was a week later much to the annoyance of the mission boys of which we have a few. They were the only people who really worried.

The rains have just broken but only about 2in have fallen. It is slowly getting cooler now but it is still pretty hot or at least at home you would reckon it is. The exercise question comes in as it is too hot till 4.30 pm and always dark at 6.30 pm so we have rigged up a punchball and skip every evening.

I have got one of the 5th KAR Officers staying here waiting to take the annual rations up river to Serenli but there is no hope of that for some weeks. Major Fowler is coming from Nairobi to inspect us and we will have a small shoot. I think he is coming mainly to get out of Nairobi. He is also bringing me a subaltern [Hugh Mitchell] to assist me which is a good thing. I am going into Kismayu to meet the Major and have a day's fishing tomorrow. I start at

4.00 am and get there at 7.00 am; even then it is pretty hot but one can bathe on arrival.

I have started a farm or rather shamba by digging up two acres. I have planted mealies, pumpkins, melons, beans, kale, tomatoes, cucumbers, red peppers and about an acre of maize. They are all coming up like fun especially as the plot covers an old village or cemetery; once they get down they grow like smoke. You would like the ground for an allotment as it is stiff with old bits of pot but nothing interesting. The great trouble is that the earth is always so hot; peas won't even sprout but rot off. If one wants to grow pawpaws you just have one for breakfast and plant the seeds at night; they always grow. Three weeks ago it was just bush. I have bought a cow and a calf for 45s; a first class looking animal who yields about three pint of milk a day. I have two Muscovy ducks now and expect to get some eggs from them soon. I have had a wattle and daub hut built for them.

The whole attitude of the inhabitants has changed and the Somalis are becoming very insolent; however they don't worry us as we don't deal with the civil people at all now. We did have some shooting last month as some inquisitive person came too near the house but a volley or two soon made them run. We periodically put the wind up them, with noticeable effect, by suddenly having a route march at 3.00 am; they then wake up to find the lines deserted.

We have had periodic reports that the Somalis will cause trouble when we hand over to the Italians. The natives are very worried chiefly because they have seen the differences between the two methods of rule and vastly prefer ours. The Somalis are backed up by petty chiefs who know they will lose their power and salary as the Italians rule by hereditary chiefs and they will import them. The trading Arabs and Indians will lose heavily because the cattle, which is the chief worth of the country, are worth only half the value in Italian territory. The great cattle trade is with Zanzibar and they think this will be taxed and the existing British boats will put the freight up in order to encourage trade in Kenya. One large tribe of Somalis has already sent all their stock away into Kenya and only left a few goats and milk cows which they intend to sell later.

I have found an Arab sweetmeat called Halva which is like Turkish delight in a way but not so sweet; it is a good substitute for sweets and is made locally.

I have just had a message to say that all the Arabs are coming to do a *ngoma* or dance at my house tomorrow. That means I have to buy an ox for them to eat; 40s's worth, only a 1d a pound.

Detachment 3rd KAR, Gobwen, Jubaland [No date]

The Governor came to Kismayu to have a look round and the Provincial Commissioner asked us to come in to guard him as they expected trouble; so when they had a meeting of Chiefs we formed a Guard with rifles et cetera, fully loaded and prepared for any trouble but all went quiet. The HMS *Colombo* arrived at the same time and added to the moral support. We went on board and replenished our supplies from the canteen and drank iced beer. The Captain and two of the Officers were in camp at Yonte and spent the time shooting; we took them across to the Italian side and showed them some game and they fed with us on the way out and back.

There is no more word of the Italians taking over yet. I see a lot of hot air in the papers still about the fertile land. There is no fresh water in Kismayu. All rainwater is collected in tanks and the ration is three buckets a day. There is no made road in the whole province, only clearings in the bush and the surface depends on the soil. The only European farm growing cotton has gone bust. Thirty other farms all the way up river were all abandoned before the war or in 1919 so the Italians are welcome to the country.

I have applied to get home on leave next May rather than January as the climate and things to do at home in February and March are nil while in June-September I will get shooting or fishing even if it is in a hotel in Caithness or elsewhere. The social functions will all be over I hope; life out here does not tend to make one like these social affairs at home.

Detachment 3rd KAR, Gobwen, Jubaland, 14 July 1924

The Mohammedan New Year is on just now; a feast lasting a week during which one is supposed to sling out coins to all and sundry who ask. Each community comes and yells and dances at you. In fact the whole populace turn beggar. I attended several dances in the village; among others one at the devil remover's hall which consisted of a band of tom toms and a red flag on a pole in the centre at the foot of which was a small brazier burning incense and dope. The so called possessed ones revolve in circles round and round for hours keeping time to the music and they reel round and when their feet give out they go on their knees. When they can proceed no further a 'chucker out' of sorts puts their head in a bucket of water and then puts their nose in the doped smoke and they carry on. The whole thing is most weird. It is certainly a commercial speculation. One poor fellow thinks he has six devils in him so he pays about 1s per devil per night for their removal.

I have been very fit and have not been down with fever once yet though Mitchell [the Subaltern] was in bed for five days. The place is alive with mosquitoes and sandflies; if we didn't go away for a few days or so every month we would be ill at once as I was before and the fellow who followed me also.

Detachment 3rd KAR, Gobwen, Jubaland, 30 July 1924

I have just arrived back from an elephant hunt but unfortunately never got a shot. I had a guide with three donkeys. We moved about from puddle to puddle over the country drinking rainwater. I got hold of a 'Boni' or Bushman. ['The Boni are a tribe of aborigines who are dwarfs, somewhat similar to those found in the Congo forests, but they are very shy, hiding themselves in the thick jungle and seldom coming out. These people are nomadic hunters and live entirely on the game they shoot with their poisoned arrows.' See Wightwick Haywood 1927.] This little fellow dashed about with his bow and arrow and shot at and hit several animals but failed to kill any.

We have heard nothing about the Italian question for ages; our last papers were full of the King of Italy's visit to London and they are now over two months old. We have no communication with the Italian side now as the new Resident has not returned our official call; he is an appalling outsider. We are selling all surplus stores. As a result we have got about £50 for our Company funds and propose having a huge feast before we leave, killing about five oxen.

Detachment 3rd KAR, Gobwen, Jubaland, 8 August 1924

We only got one mail last month and I got six letters from home all together, as well as the veg from Fortnum and Mason which are jolly good, especially the plums. We have rationed ourselves to two a day after lunch. Many thanks indeed for them.

The sand grouse are coming in every morning to water now; a continuous stream of twos and threes come over high from 7.00am to 8.00am. Every Friday we have a straf [original war slang of 1914]; this morning Mitchell and myself got twenty-six brace in the hour. It is too expensive on cartridges to do it every day, although our average worked out at three to one.

We have had no rain now for some time and as the sun is straight overhead, all grazing has dried up; my cow too has dried up. All the European seeds planted in the shamba are in a very bad way in spite of abundant water. We have picked some groundnuts and a melon to date while cows and baboons get the best of our mealies.

Detachment 3rd KAR, Gobwen, Jubaland, 2 September 1924

I had only a short trip out last month but quite the most exciting I have had. I left Gobwen with four donkeys; two were loaded with water. I couldn't manage a tent but as there was no fear of rain, it didn't really matter. My destination was a place called Eylat which consists of a clearing in the dense forest and a pool of water which you can smell a mile away, as something like 2,000 cattle had watered there daily. When we arrived the majority had left. We had no sooner pitched our camp when a Somali came up and said that a lion had killed one of his cattle and he had driven it off with a spear. We told him to erect a *boma* [enclosure for livestock, or fort] near the corpse and that after we had eaten supper, we would come along as we had already travelled 20 miles. I duly started out as soon as possible with an orderly and a guide. After going for about an hour, we heard low growls on the road in front so fired a Very light [flare fired from a pistol] and saw a huge lion bound into the bush about 10yds off. We then got into the *boma* which was about 2yds from the corpse and waited. In about half an hour, a lioness came out of the bush and sniffed about, horribly close to our cover. We could not get a shot without having to move and risk a noise, so we just waited and in due course it came into my field of vision at about 5yds. As there was no moon, I had to chance to luck and let bang. There was a terrific roar and the brute jumped over the boma and promptly died. The lioness was a huge beast and is known to have killed about thirty cattle. It had fat on it like a cow. The rest of the trip I got nothing but followed rhino and elephant.

We celebrated the event by a weekend in Kismayu. I took the rod and hired a dhow for two days but only caught small fish. Next month I hear the big fish come in so I have arranged to go. I can't find out what breed of fish they are but it gives one good sport from all accounts.

I also visited old Kismayu and collected some pots. It is a most extraordinary place as the sea has encroached and as a result whole skeletons are lying about. The roads are paved with pots; some like the green celadon bowl at home and some blue and white. I also found some beads. I have a representative collection to bring home.

We have no further news of the Italian cession but we won't move out till at least parliament ratifies the treaty and in all probability not for some months. The Boundary Commission will get to work first as there are all sorts of complicated questions to be settled about tribes and grazing as the intended line will cause one large section of Somalis to spend half the year on each side owing to the water and grazing. As all the Somalis are nomadic and move where there is grass, it will be a difficult job for the Italians to keep them in.

Blackwoods has arrived and also the Times which is a very nice change after the Daily Graphic which we have been reduced to of late. It really is an awful rag; it regards night clubs as 'The waiting room to the madhouse'.

Before catching his ship for home leave Sandy was given permission to go on a dhow trip.

The Buffin Bird as depicted in the crest of the club (below) was the emblem of Jubaland.

JUBALAND CLUB,

KISMAYU.

4 March 1925

I hired a small open dhow at Kismayu. The plan was to sail from Kismayu to Lamu via the Barjun islands which are a string of narrow islands about 2 miles off shore and extending for about 70 miles. I embarked in the time honoured fashion by being carried from the beach to the boat seated in a chair on the shoulders of four men.

There was the *Nahoda* or Captain with two of a crew and two small boys. In addition I had with me my boy, a Somali, my KAR orderly, a Sudanese ex-soldier and a local guide. Two travelled before the mast with the kit while the remaining seven persons myself included were behind the mast. There were rations for my party for fourteen days, my valise, table, chair, suitcase and chop boxes.

It was delightful sailing before the north east monsoon which was nearing its end. We were in calm water sheltered by the string of islands. The glare from the sun off the water was trying but the blue sea which was quite shallow left a lasting impression of peace on my mind.

Three nights were spent camping on various islands amongst the villagers. The inhabitants belong to the Barjun tribe who are light skinned and claim descent from Persian settlers. They were in occupation of the islands long before the incursions of the Somalis on the mainland in the last century. Their villages were all sited on the landward side of the islands and thus hidden from the eyes of slave traders in former times. There are ruins of stone built mosques and many stone tombs on the islands and on the mainland. Thorn trees, palms and baobab trees clothe the islands. A little millet and sim sim [sesame] was grown.

The *Nahoda* had been in a great rage as his wife was living with a Chinaman on one of the islands. However on arrival presents were exchanged and everyone calmed down. Fish including turtles and sea slugs (*bêche de mer*) were plentiful. It turned out that the Chinaman had been sent by the merchants of Hongkong to teach the islanders the method of preparing the slugs for market which was a complicated affair involving men, women and children. The process involved boiling and drying before sending them in sacks to China where they were considered to be a great delicacy. [Sadly the trade, which went through an Indian agent in Zanzibar, stopped when the Communists took over Zanzibar in the 1960s. William Travis in his book, *The Voice of the Turtle*, published in 1967, describes the islands and mentions the Chinaman who was still remembered.]

The sail had been giving trouble as it seemed practically rotten. The *Nahoda* who was responsible for the gear of course had no spare canvas or rope and was forced to cut the tail off his shirt to patch the sail!

We turned west up the Birikau creek and a short way up sighted the remains of the old stone KAR house where Port Durnford or Birikau village used to stand. The whole region had been populated by Arabs before the abolition of slavery. Inland I came across an old fortified stockade built of palm tree trunks on end in the ground to make a perimeter breastwork. In this the Arabs and their slaves took refuge from the marauding bands of Somalis.

Whilst camping further up, a thunder storm broke away to the south. All night long there were sounds of elephants moving southwards towards the rain, guided by the thunder and lightning. In the morning I could see that the paths had been beaten flat in the night by the elephants. The rains were coming after the long dry season. The dhow then had to be punted up till we could go no further.

We sailed out of Birikau into the open sea, no longer enjoying the protection of the islands. We kept close to the mainland and happily it was not too rough as there was not much free-board. We suddenly sighted a small boat, loaded with men, women and children. When we drew close to them, they told us that their dhow had sprung a leak and was beached near Ras Kimboni and that they were afraid of the Somalis and hoped to reach the Barjun Islands. On finding the wrecked dhow on the shore, the *Nahoda* was able to take some rope and canvas to repair his shirt and our sail. The dhow had come from Muscat.

Next day, with our sail patched, the *Nahoda* decided to take a short cut from the open sea across the reef into the sheltered waters of the Lamu archipelago. The wind suddenly dropped and the bow of the dhow rose up on a huge wave and then crashed down into the trough. A following sea broke over the boat. The crew wailed like hell to Allah. As if by a miracle, a gust of wind caught the sail and carried the dhow over the reef just grazing the coral into calm water. The vessel was waterlogged, the crew and passengers frightened to death and soaked and the kit, camera, bedding et cetera were all swilling about in sea water. We at once baled out as quick as we could and got some buoyancy back into the ship and took the sail down. We made for the nearest small village and put ashore and dried out our belongings. We camped for the night beside the sea close to the pier.

Soon after dark a large dhow which belonged to the village arrived from Mombasa with drums beating, bugles sounding and the crew dancing and singing. [The crude bugles were made from conch shells which belong to a mollusc found in tropical waters.] The bowsprit was decorated with numerous flags on short sticks. As they neared the shore the whole village joined in. Torches lit the scene. It was one of the most enchanting spectacles I have witnessed and a good end to an eventful and hazardous day.

Next morning we sailed into Lamu reaching the anchorage at the same time as the coasting steamer which I had to catch in order to get to Mombasa to get my ship home.

Coincidentally in March 1944, Sandy's wife and four-year-old daughter, Christian, crossed from Aden to Djibuti in a dhow. Having been stuck in Britain throughout the war they got a passage on the first passenger ship through the Mediterranean to Aden, where they were told that there was no way a civilian lady could get a passage to Djibuti. Undaunted, they proceeded by dhow which at least would not have attracted Japanese submarines. There was no engine so if the winds failed the trip could be long, but the dhows had a great reputation of always arriving in the end. The captain lent them his bed in the poop and looped a rope between the edge of the bed and the awning to stop the child falling overboard. All through the night there were scuffling noises as the crew foraged under the bed for their provisions; bits of dried fish would appear which they always wanted to share. The steersmen stood quite close to the bed singing away through the night with a small oil lantern to enable him to read the compass. There was often a following sea. At night at least there was relief from seasickness, lying watching the giant mast swaying backwards and forwards across the galaxy, which gave a break from the constant reading to the child of *Orlando the Marmalade Cat* by Kathleen Hale, and eating tinned sardines and condensed milk. Three days in a dhow with a four-year-old child did not quite have the enchantment which Sandy had experienced nineteen years previously.

CHAPTER 3

An Administrator in Meru, 1925–6

 UNION-CASTLE LINE

S·S "GASCON"

off Port Said

6/6/26.

We have had a most amusing voyage so far. We stopped at Gibraltar and I went ashore with my cabin mate, who is in the Buffs, to his mess. I had to begin with been in a cabin with two other blokes but I complained at once and got shifted in with this other soldier. At Marseilles I went to visit my friend, the restaurant keeper, but he was away; nevertheless we fed royally with 'Rose Champagne Veuve Cliquet 1911' and caviar et cetera. We only stopped for one night so I could not get to Arles. We reached Genoa on a Sunday morning. I left for Turin and went round to call on the General. [Sandy and his father had met him whilst holidaying at Courmayeur in Italy]. He lives in a large house, off the Corso Pesciere, with huge gates. I handed my card to the concierge and two minutes later the General came rushing down the drive with his arms in the air and would have embraced me if I had been smaller; as it was we walked along arm in arm. [This greeting was obviously very different to the reserved behaviour of genteel Edinburgh.] All the family were there including the other daughter who is very good looking and the son who is a waster. He asked me if I was at Doncaster for the St. Leger. [Sandy and his family were not at all horsey minded!] The General wanted me to escort his son to the east as he does nothing at home and apparently worries the old boy. The family had to go out to tea but the old man, glad of an excuse, took me out to see the sights.

We went to the mediaeval village which was most interesting and after called on his cousin who lived in a lovely house with very fine pictures and ceilings and also who kept very good whisky. I went round to dine in the evening; a typical Italian meal with very good wine; much better than anything at the hotel. There was a butler and footman who both wore white gloves. After dinner we danced. We then went up to see the General's room which was full of old furniture with arms and heads round it. He has a very fine Mouflon head [wild sheep]. I left Turin at midday the next day and he came to see me off.

We reached Naples on Friday. Four of us hired a car and went out to Pompeii, lunching there and returning in the afternoon. Never take a car there; the roads are fearful and it is much cheaper to go by train. We passed Stromboli and through Messina by day and also past Crete. We are due to reach Port Said on 7 October.

We have a cheery clique on board; two soldiers, four political cadets going out for the first time, all public school men, and we have a table together. The other passengers are a very mouldy lot; a few very nice men who are administrators, hunters and planters. There are three or four people on board who I have met out east before, otherwise no one I know. I bought a medicine ball before I left home and we have exercise every morning and evening. I have also got the ballbearing skipping ropes so I manage to keep very fit. The feeding is good but we shall run out of salad tomorrow and then we shall get grapefruit for breakfast.

We reach Port Sudan on about 12 October and Mombasa about 24 October stopping at Port Said and Aden with cargo for all of them.

Detachment 3rd KAR, Meru, Kenya, 3 November 1925

I am hugely in luck. I arrived at Mombasa on 3 October, glad to get off that infernal boat at last and found my boy awaiting me at the customs house. We spent a night in Mombasa and went up to Nairobi arriving on Saturday. I reported on Monday and was told I was for Meru which lies north of Mount Kenya and if possible was to start on Tuesday so I did. We left by a KAR motor lorry, spending two nights on the road, going by the most beautiful country past flowing rivers in deep gorges with wonderful vegetation and even wisteria growing in the trees with dates and bananas alongside. What a change of scene from Gobwen. I just slept on the road where the lorry happened to stop at 6.00 pm.

Meru used to be the headquarters of the 5th Battalion but, as the 3rd and 5th are now amalgamated in Nairobi under a new CO, this place is now only a company station. We have one company at Wajir and half a company at Marsabit and Moyale.

I am employed as a sort of clerk as this company is just being formed. All books et cetera have to be made out. The Company Commander takes the parades while I do the clothing, stores, rations and transport. All the stores and rations arrive here by motor lorry and are sent on by ox wagon to Marsabit and the things for Wajir go to Garba Tula where they are then sent on by camels. We act as a sort of advanced depot, sending out porters and convoys to the posts. We deal in hundreds of porters who each carry a load of around 60lb. Each man is allowed one porter and if he is married two; NCOs more still. The porters and men all have to have their rations carried so it is no sinecure here. The other posts are near Lake Rudolf but we don't deal with them.

All men coming down have to wait at the end of the camel safari while we send porters out to collect their kit and bring them in and from here we send them by porter to Nairobi.

We store a lot of the boundary commission stores here. They are starting from a place called Wajir and are going north. They have ordered 300 copper '*Baramils*' or water tanks for camels at £12 each.

We are always having people passing through here; at present, Cook, a subaltern in the Black Watch is waiting to get a car to Nairobi as he is going on leave. We are expecting three Officers in from up country any day now.

I have a very nice mud house, wattle and daub with a grass roof (full of white ants and rats); a fine place. We had a lot of rain last week but my mud house kept it out well. I have a fire every evening in my house. I have had to get an askari's great coat from the stores to wear as I have left any warm clothing in Nairobi.

I have an excellent garden with carnations, roses, dwarf chrysanthemums and a hedge covered with blue convolvulus. All English veg grows here and very well indeed. We live on brussel sprouts, french beans, cabbage, potatoes et cetera while my tomatoes are huge. There is a kind of dwarf loganberry which is fine eating. I am busy superintending the laying out of some cuttings. The whole place is grass and trees. In the morning there is an 'Easterly Haar'. In fact though it is on the equator, it is almost like England with wonderful scenery looking away north over small hills to hot deserts.

There is a golf course here, well kept up and tennis courts. The civil have an office here and two assistant district commissioners, one a fellow, Wise who I was at Repton with. In addition there is a man collecting labour, a doctor and a Public Works Department [PWD] foreman who at the moment has Delirium Tremens [DTs]. There are two missions here. There is also a very nice fellow who is a game warden and comes up in the evening for a drink in my house. One of our own 3rd KAR Officers is here now on his way down from up country. I was at the Royal Military College with him. He has got his elephant, each tusk was 30lb.

Zammarano, who wrote that book you sent me 'Hic Sunt Leones', was on the boundary commission and several of our people met him. He was quite a nice fellow but Italian countesses have been chasing him in cars over half the colony causing a fearful nuisance and bringing their inevitable continental amorous entanglements even to the frontier. He had to pay £160 in car hire alone the other day. He has now been recalled to Rome.

This company is supposed to be moving to a place called Wajir near the Lorian swamp in the NFD in several months' time; 1st class shooting district.

They have recommended the African General Service medal be granted for the Jubaland show so I may collect one. They are awaiting approval of the War Office.

Fortnum and Mason sent me a booklet about 'Joy Parcels' which sound very good and appear to suit our wants here if anyone wants to know. Their 'Sweets Parcel' and 'Entrée Parcel' or 'Hors d'Oeuvre' appear the best but for heaven's sake don't send a Stilton cheese.

We have two mails in a week and out and they go by runner to Nyeri and thence by car to Nairobi.

Detachment 3rd KAR, Meru, Kenya, 19 November 1925

I got back on Monday after a strenuous weekend. I left the lines on Saturday morning at 10.00 am and after hard going reached a camping ground at 3.00 pm. I had four pack mules and a porter. I shot a zebra and a waterbuck that evening and then returned with a temperature to bed; however I sweated it out and was woken next morning and told there was an elephant near. I rushed out and saw a solitary bull about 500yds off with about 50lb tusks. I ordered breakfast and detailed two of my scouts to follow it while I fed. The country round was quite open and easy shooting. After a hasty breakfast, I set off and about an hour later came to some thick bush and found my two scouts held up by buffalo; however we chased them off and followed the tracks of our friend. We caught sight of him under a tree at about 11.00 am. As I approached, to my horror we found not only buffalo but also two rhino nearby. The buffalo cleared off, frightening the elephant who went with them. We went off again and this time we met the buffalo who cleared off. We then met the rhino who refused to move and was snorting as if to charge so I let her have one and brought her down through the shoulders and finished her off with a close up in the brain which lies just under the ears. Next a year old bull calf who was hanging around came at us so I blotted it also in one and handed in his horns to the game department. All this firing had disturbed the elephant and we heard it clearing off. The front horn of the rhino measures 20in by 7in and the back one 2in by 7in. On returning to camp we saw four herds of buffalo and four more rhino.

It has rained here; 19in in eighteen days so you can imagine our climate is not African.

I have been laid up with a poisoned foot for two days but it is alright again now. Jiggers and rats are the chief pests here. [Jiggers are the maggots of a type of flea which lay their eggs under human toenails. The secret is always to get an African to get them out with a sterile needle as they are brilliant at doing it; far better than any European.]

Detachment 3rd KAR, Meru, Kenya, 27 November 1925

Many thanks for the Fortnum and Masons boxes; they had some excellent delicacies in them. One prefers and enjoys far more expensive delicacies than plum puddings et cetera.

I have been laid up for a week with a go of flu and luckily missed the General on his inspection. This place is a snare as in spite of all the fruits, from apples to beans, it is cold and damp at nights with an easterly haar which sometimes envelops us in the mornings. Someone is always ill here. I will be glad when we shift to the warmer zone at Wajir.

We had a wonderful view of the total eclipse of the sun; we were right in its path. All the followers of the prophet dashed off to the mosque to pray as soon as parade was over as they regard it as the evil eye.

Our detachment at Marsabit have just had a good show; they struck a large party of raiders, who were Abyssinians out for loot and elephants, and all armed with French '*Fusil Gras*'. The detachment was close to Lake Stephanie on patrol and opened fire with a Lewis gun killing fourteen; we had three wounded, all as a result of ricochets. A similar party looted 8,000 camels from the locals up there, killing and murdering numerous natives as well about three months ago. The party we caught were apparently trying to enrich themselves likewise; they are not poor ignorant natives.

Detachment 3rd KAR, Meru, Kenya, 11 December 1925

Many thanks for your letter and for the £28 worth of multiple stores. I have not got much news. Things are very dull here and as I shall be alone at Xmas, I see no chance of getting out of the '*Boma*' for my intended shoot.

I have bought a pony for £10 and a shot gun for £7-10s, both of which I will sell again in due course. I intend to try a little mild polo with the pony first.

I have been playing a lot of golf recently. Mitchell, who does my shopping for me in Nairobi, got a lot of old clubs and sent them up to us for which we were heartily thankful as there is not much to do here of an afternoon.

Please order the 'Sketch', 'Nashes Magazine' and the 'Weekly Times' to be sent out to me as at the moment we are a bit short of papers. Also I had ordered two books from Orrs; perhaps you could jog their memory: 'East African Game and its Spoor' by Captain Stigand and 'Sarcasm Art'.

Detachment 3rd KAR, Meru, Kenya, 26 December 1925

Many thanks indeed for the books from Thins which arrived today, also for your letters. I have heaps of literature now to last the year.

I had planned a trip out for fourteen days shooting but as the Company Commander's relief turned up at the last minute, I had to put it off, as the new fellow is taking over. He is a very decent Captain in Royal Field Artillery (RFA) who has served in the Mespotamian war, ridden at Olympia in jumping competitions and is also very keen on shooting.

I have got my new house and garden very nice now but white ants are the trouble. They attacked my mantelpiece the other day but only went for the 'Manual of Military Hygiene' luckily and left all other books alone.

I have planted bananas all round but the donkeys which bring up my water will eat the tops off which rather cramps the style. We have two apples ripening not to mention pineapples. We have strawberries twice a week in mess; home grown. Owing to pests, we can never let them get quite ripe, worse luck. My roses are coming on well and so are the chrysanthemums; the soil is so fertile that they never seem to stop flowering. The soil is all rich red.

If I am up country longer, I will increase my allotment home to £20 as I am being very economical, there being no shops here. I pay for my cartridges out of the profits I make reselling guns and rifles which I have bought cheap.

I have also gone teetotal almost as usual. The local Indian trader offers us 'Gilbeys Spanish Red Port' at 7s a bottle while among the liqueurs are cherry brandy, invalid port and also claret; these wines alone would upset most of us I think.

We expect to have a war soon in the Mandera district as the Civil Administrators have taken over with forty police where we had three platoons of a hundred men and even then we couldn't stop the raiding. It is the topic of conversation these days and the poor fellow who has gone there is regarded as a martyr. The powers that be won't listen to people who have been there and no inspecting Officer dared visit the place when we were there as there is ten days on the road with no water at all in order to get there.

The bird's nests are coming with this letter addressed to you at the museum; the eggs are inside their nests. Please send me an egg blower as I nearly burst my lungs on these. I will look out for some wild flower seeds for you. I haven't been able to get out so much since the rains stopped.

Detachment 3rd KAR, Meru, Kenya, 14 January 1926

I am getting rather fed up with Meru though it is supposed to be the best station in Africa; it is not a healthy place at all and one always has aches and pains. I much prefer the coast on the whole.

Our Company moves to Wajir in March I believe and from there we have patrols and all sorts of jobs including the Boundary Commission escort which I daily hint to Officers that I want.

The Colonel and Inspector General are due here soon to inspect us.

Two of our men at Moyale ran amok and shot a British civilian who was there buying horses. A Doctor up there ran into a raiding party of Abyssinians. He shot one, wounded four and captured a lot of rhino horn and ivory. Again our mail runners were shot at near Wajir so we are all expecting a bust-up soon and will be quite happy as our troops are now quite well trained.

I have got a platoon of two sections of Somalis and two sections of other natives; being the only one with Somalis, I will get all the bush work going.

As was expected, a number of tribes are leaving Jubaland now [Jubaland had been ceded to Italy in July 1924]. The Italians have controlled all prices which are much cheaper than ours and a system of measures does away with any chance of swindling. As a result all who can are taking their English money back too Kismayu where the exchange for the lire is low and they gain tremendously. The Italians had brought more troops than there was water for and they were forced to send a lot away.

Father must have been expressing concern at the gay abandonment in which Sandy mentioned killing Abyssinians:

Detachment 3rd KAR, Meru, Kenya, 1 February 1926

The Abyssinians whom we have to shoot up are not defenceless natives but are all armed with 'Fusil Gras' and they are mixed up with the outcasts from Kenya, Uganda and the Sudan, all of whom shelter in the Lake Rudolf corner. The cause of all the raiding is that the Governors of the Abyssinian provinces have each to pay tribute to the King every year so they send out raiding parties in order to get it.

The Italians have had a very bad knock indeed in Italian Somaliland; three warships loaded with troops have been sunk and two aeroplanes crashed. Then the native troops mutinied and refused to embark after the wrecks. A tribe of Somalis revolted [the Mifertain Revolt]. They will soon find that they will have to use European troops to quell the rising; already half the country has become quite independent and the Italian losses are very large. We have troops standing by in case it spreads to our territory. Owing to censorship nothing has come out. Also I hear they have had a serious knock in Tripoli; the Arabs have completely routed them as far as I can gather.

We have had an outbreak of raiding in Turkana and a small war is in progress there but we have had very little news of it.

I was out after duck yesterday at a crater lake close to here. It was a fascinating spot surrounded by high sides, about 300 feet, wooded and with a pond thick with water lilies in the bottom. There were thousands of duck but they wouldn't come over the guns and wouldn't rise off the water except in two's or three's; they never seem to leave the place at all and are never shot at.

We are going out for a week's camp to a spot on the Siolo River, about 30 miles from here for a change.

Detachment 3rd KAR, Meru, 16 February 1926

We had a most successful trip down to Isiolo where we repaired the musketry camp we have there. We left Meru at 2.00 pm one day and marched with our pack mules till 6.30 pm when we camped beside some water, going on the next day from 7.00 am till 1.00 pm. We had a camp of houses built of grass and bamboo, neither sun proof or rain proof.

As the men were employed on fatigue, I got leave from Friday to Monday and set off with three mules, shooting towards the Gaso Nyiro River following the Siolo for water. The first day I shot a zebra and sent the meat straight back to camp on two mules which I had specially brought. I pushed on the next day, shooting very badly and missing a good oryx and impala, both after a good stalk. I pitched my camp near some loofah trees, which produce a long seed pod which makes a powerful native beer and at the same time provides sponges for Europeans when treated. This area is the favourite hunting ground for the rich parties which come out from home. I saw the remains of Colonel Denver's camp. I think his father, Lord Denver, shot the 'Mangy Lion' of Dicksons. [Dicksons was the well-known gunsmith and fishing tackle shop in Edinburgh.] I soon saw that in order to get game I had to get off the beaten track so on the Sunday I went to the west side of the river Siolo and moved towards the Guero, shooting an impala for meat. Soon after I saw a quantity of vultures over a kill so as I thought it might be a lion, I stalked it and suddenly came on five Warderobo natives with a female buffalo they had just killed with a poisoned arrow. I got them tied together with strips of leather by the neck and we took all their bows and arrows and marched them back to camp and so home to Isiolo. I sent them to the DC and he tried the case giving them a month in gaol each. I was able to get from them two fire sticks and a special arrow which they use at very close range to puncture the neck of a cow when they want to drink its blood and not kill it. [The Warderobo, also known as Dorobo, were the earliest surviving inhabitants of Kenya and are probably related to the Bushmen and Pigmies.]

The next morning I returned to camp and at 3.00 pm moved to Meru with a day on the road. While going along we saw a snake chasing a rat, moving like lightning. We also heard elephant shoving a tree down while we were halted in the forest.

Yesterday my game scouts reported that there was a large elephant in the forest so in the afternoon we went out and looked round and saw a large herd of cows and calves, about sixty of them, 500yds off. Through the glasses we could see every movement. We saw them suddenly put their tusks up in the air, some picked a little dust up and scattered it to test the wind; then scenting something they moved off. It was only five miles from the lines and in the same clearing where we always see rhino; truly 'A Haunt of the Greater Pachyderms'. I also saw a large herd of giraffe quite close to Meru; over forty of them were spread out and feeding over about a mile. They were a most wonderful site but as it was 6.00 pm it was too late to photograph.

We have done away with Lewis guns which is a good thing as the African can never become really efficient in the use of them as they are too complicated and their transport and their SAA costs such a lot that they have been scrapped and we have rifle grenades instead now; a far more dangerous toy for 'John African' but equally useful and far simpler.

We have trouble with troops in camp always, as if one has an Islam orderly to cut the throat of the kill, the Abyssinians can't eat it as they are Christians and so vice versa. When I shot the buffalo I took out an Abyssinian as well as a follower of the prophet; I let the Abyssinian cut the throat first and he said his phrase and did the deed, but the Islam seeing so much meat being wasted followed at once saying the Abyssinian hadn't cut deep enough so he plunged his knife in after to ease his conscience and as a result all were happy. The pagans who eat anything and the local Christian mission breed also were satisfied.

The 450 is an excellent weapon. I have only hit one animal which I have not killed and that was a rhino. With it to date, I have killed a lion, a buffalo and two rhino. It is just right for dangerous stuff. I am buying another rifle, a 256 bore with a 28" barrel which will replace my 305 for soft-skinned game as the latter is held together by a match to keep the sight steady and tied together at the hand guard with goat skin; it is a good friend but it is finished I am afraid.

I hear now there is a good prospect of our pay being raised next month as we have in this colony to be treated the same as the civil Officers by order of the colonial office.

Detachment 3rd KAR, Meru, Kenya, 22 February 1926

Many thanks for the books; the elephant book is an excellent publication full of interesting information. The food parcels arrived yesterday and in spite of being in biscuit tins which were bashed in they were in excellent condition inside except the 'Chocolat Cerises aux Cognac' which have melted and there is only the outer core of chocolate left. For sending out here each thing must be tinned or else it is just wasted. The paté is alright as there is a tin inside the jar.

We move in about six weeks time to Wajir; it will take us nearly a month to get there; sixteen days by ox wagon and ten or so by camel with no water on the road. I will be glad to get away from here; it is a damp place and too near civilization. You can't help finding old camps with sardine tins.

We have had no excitements during the last week at all except one corporal lost his rifle the day he was promoted. His men apparently hid it so the native Officer was sent for and he suggested we should hire a witch doctor from the village who would examine the case and prepare a potion or else try the boiling water or red hot iron test and he would be bound to find the thief. However we refused to allow this. The next day the corporal whose rifle had been stolen came to the orderly room and said he had prepared a drink for his section; 'It was just like tea, perfectly harmless and wouldn't kill anyone or send them mad but if the guilty one drank it he would instantly become as drunk as if he had taken whisky'. Provided his section would drink this concoction we said it was his affair if they died but of course they all refused so we are no further on with the case.

Our new Colonel is rushing things along at a fearful pace; he has never had any experience of Africa before and as a result we are landed in the soup. Four of our lorries are smashed and our stores which were sent on 12 December 1925 are still on the road, so if things don't improve in three weeks time, there will be an awful mess up when the rations arrive.

Could you please order for me from Paris, and debit my account, 'Les Oeuvres Libres'; it comes out monthly in book form and each one contains about six stories in French of course. [It was published in paperback and contained unedited stories.]

Detachment 3rd KAR, Meru, Kenya, 9 March 1926

At last we are getting a move on and two platoons move up country as soon as we can collect porters. It takes 220 porters and our 30 animals to move us to a place called Garba Tula where we change over to camels to travel to Wajir; a week with each mode of transport. As soon as we get to Wajir, I leave with my platoon, as soon as camels are available for Mandera. It will be a trip of fourteen days, ten of which are without water. On arrival there I have to assist the Civil Officer who has been landed there and is daily threatened with death. He has already been shot at and several of his men killed but our arrival will calm things and we are sure of some fun. I have a platoon of thirty men with a Sudanese Sergeant; one section of Somalis from Northern Somaliland, one of Somalis from Jubaland, one of Wakambas, one section of all sorts and two Somali NCOs. [The Wakambas, also known as Kambas, were famous hunters. Many became soldiers and policemen.]

45

I am looking forward to the trek and expect to be at Mandera for several months and then take a turn at Wajir. There is quite good shooting on the way in the animal line and plenty of sport in the raider's line as it is just on the boundary of Abyssinia. I have a year's stores with me; lamp oil and everything downwards; flour, sugar, tea and everything except meat and milk. I hear a rumour that I have been recommended for my Captaincy in the KAR but I am not paying much heed to it; if I am landed for Nairobi I would much sooner go without it.

Letters are bound to be erratic as we have only one mail a fortnight and during the rains, no movement is possible. There is also a shortage of hard cash on the frontier as the traders deal in our money and take it into Italian territory with them as the *dago* coinage is looked upon as tin while ours is everywhere.

CHAPTER 4

By Foot to the Northern Frontier, 1926–8

S andy was now detailed to take command of Mandera station in the NFD of Kenya on the Abyssinian frontier.

Detachment 3rd KAR, Wajir, Kenya, 5 April 1926

I have at last reached about half way to my destination. We left Meru on 14 March 1926 with some 220 porters and about 40 pack animals; we did 2 marches a day of about 10 miles each. It is a fearful job with conscripted porters. As you can imagine it involves slave driving to move some of them along and in addition they have to carry their rations for the return journey.

After crossing the Nyambeni range of hills with any number of rivers and cool springs on the road, we went down a steep hillside with forests and creepers to the hot arid plains. We crossed about 5 miles of high elephant grass with elephant tracks through it and found a river bed where we hoped to get water; it had gone dry so it involved an extra march to get water which was a bit of a trial as we had to do it by day and during the hottest part. We then had 30 miles of bad going to do to reach a place called Garba Tula where we had to change onto camels and meet our relieving platoon.

We stayed three days at Garba Tula where there was a KAR staging camp with a house for the officer. The water is drawn from a hole in the dry river bed. We then pushed on but the rains broke at our second halting place and we were delayed for a day as the camel is useless in mud. The country from now onwards becomes drier with bush and occasional patches of grass. Vultures, guinea fowl, gerenuk and oryx are the only game found, with an occasional Grant's gazelle.

We plodded on, two marches a day; 3.00–7.00 am and 4.00–8.00 pm; our fifty-two camels having to be unloaded at each halt. We had a small herd of goats which are driven along behind us and slaughtered every other day for the meat ration. The men are also accompanied by their women and children; the latter are usually attached to camels by some means or other. The Somalis are excellent working with camels and sing while loading. We passed close to the Lorian Swamp and found a lot of rain pools on the road, so instead of having to make use of our '*Barramils*' which are attached to camels and hold 10 gallons, we accomplished with discomfort a long waterless stretch of six marches. Two hours out of Wajir we got this well water which is excellent for Africa and comes from wells about 30ft deep cut through the rock at some distant age. The water is slightly epsom saltish.

The next morning we reached Wajir which is just a cleared bit of bush with barbed wire lines and officer quarters, civil administration offices and a well, all in the square with a central keep with a sentry on the roof. The officers' quarters are a disgrace; of course there are no doors or windows to be had and everything is just home made: tables and bookcases made out of old ammunition boxes. They would be excellent quarters for two officers but with four or five of us to reckon on, it is awful being herded together; no boys near as they have to live with the troops. The houses are stone and lime built and all has to be blasted by us and the lime burnt; it takes six months to put up a two roomed cottage. However in due course we will get better quarters I hope.

There is no fever and very little sickness indeed here. Among the men there is beri-beri at present but so far no deaths have occurred. Nothing will grow except melons and we have a large quantity of them. We get a very little bush spinach.

The people and the country are just the same as Jubaland except the water is better. There is practically nothing to do as you are in the middle of a desert and are supposed to be escorted about. There are six shops for native trade outside the wire and several hundred civil huts.

I leave tomorrow at 3.00 pm for Mandera [it is on the north-eastern corner of Kenya on the border of what was then Italian Somaliland and Abyssinia]. The women and children will stay here till things are quieter on the frontier. I will travel for fifteen days, along the boundary most of the way. I will be there for three months or so and then return to Wajir. The mails take at least a month to six weeks to reach Nairobi and run irregularly; if possible they go once a fortnight. About seven days or so out from here we strike El Wak and there the water is concentrated epsom salts so I have to fill up here with water for the whole trip.

The DC who is at Mandera is a fellow Pease who I believe comes from Northumberland. He has already been shot at and we have to ensure that he is reasonably safe in future.

I have an *askari*, an Abyssinian, who has served in the Italian forces in Rome and Tripoli in the 112 Regiment and he speaks fluent slang Italian.

This vicinity is the key to promotions as with its hundreds of wells all close together, one can control the natives of any tribe by holding their wells and they would soon submit.

The rains have just broken here and we have had a heavy shower lasting about three hours (probably our ration for six months) and as houses here are constructed to keep out the sun one suffers rather after a shower. It is funny to see all the children being washed in puddles. The men and women wash their clothes in the puddles too.

The other Officer is a fellow Murray, who was educated at Eton, and is staying on here; he is a Gunner normally but has served a lot in the colonies and is an excellent fellow. The other fellow who is going down to Meru is a Welshman and a very nice fellow and a Sahib [Indian term of respect]. The fellow at Mandera now who I relieve is a Gunner and also a Sahib. The DC here who has just arrived is very keen on game and wrote the Xmas article in the Field on big game. He has two ostrich chicks and two cheetah cubs which are delightful pets. The ostriches are unwell and have had to be given castor oil but still don't look any better.

The chair with the cover which Jane made is a perfect boon at halts as is the gramophone; all the men love sitting round listening. Harry Lauder is universally popular and a special favourite especially when he laughs on the record. [He was a famous Scottish singer and entertainer in the early to mid 1900s].

I am very glad to be out of Meru and back in country one understands again and already I feel ever so much better than I did in civilisation although to the 'Poodle Fakir' and 'Lounge Lizard', this post and life must be a sort of hell on earth; that type usually takes to drink here and is only too pleased to answer for you if you want to go shooting.

The marrons glacés which I opened last night were excellent and we enjoyed them for desert. Being in sealed tins they travelled well and were 'Fine Eating'. To give you some idea of the handling one's stores get: boat from home, train to Nairobi, motor to Meru, porter, donkey or mule to Garba Tula and camel to Wajir. The tins of peaches are reduced to pulp always through the constant shaking.

Detachment 3rd KAR, Mandera, Kenya, 26 April 1926

I at last have reached my destination after going for six weeks exactly, trekking hard. I have had varied sport on the way along and my game book includes ten gerenuk and sixty one vulturine guinea fowl. I shot 'A la Continental' browning the herd for food and succeeded in getting seventeen in one shot. At one spot I shot four duck of a type I don't know; in addition two snakes, two iguanas, two Grant's gazelle, one oryx, one hyena and four dik dik.

We had no trouble from water at all so instead of having seven days without any, we had rain water nearly every day. I only twice missed my bath as we got lost and held up in bad country through not knowing that the Jubaland

Boundary Commission had not cut all the boundary. We came along from El Wak where there are wells, 40ft deep, and they go round corners, so unless you have fourteen persons, it is impossible to draw up a drop of water. We followed the Jubaland boundary as far as Durasa and thence to Fino. The Boundary consists of a cutting through the bush as straight as a die; every kilometre is marked and every ten there is a cairn.

It is a large attractive 'Boma'; mud houses, well made with their 'Zareba' [encampment surrounded by cut thorn bushes] all round and barbed wire. We look away across Abyssinia towards the Dawa River which is only one and a half miles away. The water here is excellent and plenty of it but the one weak point is that it is one and a half miles off and has to be carted by camels in tanks twice daily.

I have struck quite a good season as the river is so high that no raiders can cross. Since January there have been four raids and four police have been killed and three wounded. The KAR platoon we are relieving caught up the tail of the raiders and killed twelve just about a fortnight ago.

There are twenty nine police here and a DC. We live together and run a mess, but as our nearest Englishman is 232 miles away, we are not likely to have many mess guests.

We have a fit leopard about fourteen days old which runs about the house like a large kitten, a cheetah, two gerenuk, and an oryx; they all run loose round the 'Boma' and go down to the river to water with the syces and the stock. The young leopard is known as Balambaras which is an Abyssinian title [ancient title for the commander of a fortress]. I've just got a dik dik but the leopard will probably eat it. They play about together in great style all day.

Camel's milk is a great luxury here and I was able to have rice puddings made out of it; it sounds horrid but isn't really.

The platoon I am relieving has a Corporal in it who was wounded at Verdun and has the Croix de Guerre and another French decoration with a ribbon like the Legion of Honneur which they gave their native troops. [Verdun was a major French battle in France in 1916.]

There is a mail going down in a day or so with the platoon which I have relieved so I will send another letter then when I have got settled in more.

Detachment 3rd KAR, Mandera, Kenya, 1 May 1926

Many thanks for the book 'Havash' (by Brevet-Major W. Lloyd Jones); it has caused us much amusement and the author is a windbag of the first order and we know too much about the life to appreciate his doings.

We have had heavy rain since I arrived and it is fairly cool now, about 75°F at dinner at night and by day when the sun is out it averages over 101° in the office.

The local tribe the 'Gurreh' are a worthless lot. They murder each other on an average of five a week. [The Gurreh were a nomadic tribe of Galla extraction. Gallas are a very large tribe in Abyssinia but they are now known as Oromos.] We shall spend our time later on chasing the raiders who come down from the north-east and raid their stock. At present the raiders have all returned north as they can't cross the river owing to the floods. They have had twenty killed this year already and are fearing more counter raids from us.

The houses are built of palm tree trunks with '*Makuti*' roofs; they are not sun proof or rain proof and one has to wear a hat indoors. They have their usual quota of snakes and scorpions but one can avoid them. There is no furniture, only home made or camp furniture.

The Police are a rotten lot and five of them are in jail awaiting court martial for throwing away their arrows and equipment when attacked and running, leaving two of them to put up a fight which they did right well killing several raiders. This was about a month ago. I have known a number of them at Kismayu before. They arrived here in January, forty strong and are now reduced to about twenty six through being killed, wounded and sick.

In the event of a patrol being wanted, we get mules from the DC and beat off as fast as possible with a little water and dates.

How I envy you going to Courmayeur. I often long for the nice cold water of the springs and rivers. I hope the General [Italian family friend] will be in good form and that you visit the Chamoix Solitaire and sample their excellent lunch.

Detachment 3rd KAR, Mandera, Kenya, 10 May 1926

I am still stuck in the '*Boma*' here and don't see any chance of having much fun up here. There is practically no shooting to be got close at all.

The Abyssinians have been collecting tribute from people on our side of the border; if we meet with any when out we are to shoot them on sight. They are allowed to carry guns for self-protection which are mostly Fusil Gras 1874 and Austrian 76 with no sights on them. Some of them are brass bound. SAA is very scarce; two or three rounds is the average. It costs an Abyssinian dollar for two rounds or a camel for about thirty rounds. Of course they have no uniform.

We had two of their roughians here yesterday getting a pass and taking nine lion skins as a present to their *Fitaurari* or local governor. One of them produced an old watch of which the main spring was broken and asked the DC to mend it for him and he would pay handsomely for it but we couldn't help him. The other one was a bit of a hunter and had killed a rhino at some time as he wore a small silver cross in one ear lobe and the hairs of the giraffe were worn as a necklace. If you have killed an elephant, you wear a gold button suspended from your ear and if you have killed ten rhino you wear a cross in both ears.

There is very seldom any money here; everything is done by barter in camels, goats, sheep, cartridges or rolls of cloth. The payment to the men is made on signed chits to the one and only shop who in turn brings them to the DC who issues him with a draft on some station down country where he has an agent who sends him up more stuff. The troops are never on full rations owing to the distances and the bulk, but we are not too badly off now.

We have practice alarms twice a week on Thursdays by night and on Saturdays by day so that everyone in the '*Boma*' knows their station in the keep, women and children included. We have a few horses which come from the Somalis south of here.

Detachment 3rd KAR, Mandera, Kenya, 21 May 1926

We have had no mail for a month now and heard today that the bridges are all down and the road impassable near Meru and the Lorian. Your last letter was dated 21 February 1926; we may get our mail in about another month. As usual we have to go on short rations; we have actually in our store enough tea to last us three years, sugar for a year and lime juice for a year and a half but nothing else except the local grain, a brand of millet which has to be hand ground.

I shot a 44in Red Mamba in my house a day or two ago behind a chop box; a bright vermilion beast and he is only found in Jubaland and the neighbouring districts.

We have had several bad cases of fever among the troops and the house buzzes with mosquitoes all day long but are not bad by night. I have not been worried by any signs of fever yet; it is not as bad as South Jubaland for mosquitoes.

The Italian DC next door to us in Italian Somaliland, the Marchese della Stuppe, who I wrote to, to get permission to shoot in their territory, wrote a very nice letter back saying that officially he couldn't give me leave but he would tell his police not to worry about me in their territory and to assist me, which was very decent of him. .

I have sent a huge packet of feathers to Smith, the tackle makers at Ballater and ordered him to make a hat spray and send it to Jane. We get good clear honey bought in at times but it tastes much stronger than English honey and almost as if there was a touch of beer in it; I hate it personally.

Detachment 3rd KAR, Mandera, Kenya, 27 June 1926

Am just opening a month's mail. Many thanks for the papers and specially for the £100 for investment but don't send valuable documents here as they won't accept responsibility beyond Meru as they have to do 500 miles from there by a runner who is shot at occasionally and floods, ants and everything attack the mail bags.

I am just back after twenty nine days safari; we didn't get any '*Habash*'. [Habash is the name given to Abyssinians in that part of the country. It is from the Arabic word 'Habashire' meaning a muddle as the Abyssinians are a conglomeration of races.] No excitements but we did cover 400 miles; as I have covered 1,000 miles since the middle of March and only spent a month in a house I am very fit indeed. I had with me twelve men, five mounted on mules and the remainder escorting fourteen camels, three of which carried water. I had a pony. When we halt for the night we always adopt a plan with myself in the centre, men round the outside, our milk goats in a small *zareba* and camels alongside but down wind. We did 20 miles a day. On the way we passed no less than four old KAR '*Bomas*' which had been abandoned through fever.

At Muddo Eri there is a rocky river bed with springs in the sand; a delightful spot with green grass. It was here that a police post was wiped out by the Abyssinians in April. We found the remains of a policeman up a tree in a grass mat. Anyway we sewed up a few of his bones in some '*Murduf*' [cloth or skins] which we carry for trading goats for meat rations and gave him a decent burial firing a volley over him.

On nearing Terkali country, we collected two guides from a *manyatta* [temporary pastoralist shelter]. The guides dare not go alone or they would be done in so you have to take two. At Terkali the country is very thick bush about 10ft high. We got news that three shiftas or Abyssinian soldiers, who have got out of hand, were making for Golga so we pushed on to try and catch them at the water but missed them. We camped beside some large rocks and got our water from holes or cracks in the rocks; not quite fresh but still liquid though green in colour.

We reached Sakurar the next morning; it is the site of an old KAR boma which is still standing; it is on a hill about 4,000 feet up and surrounded by deciduous trees for miles; as they were just turning brown the view was very pretty indeed and it was cold at night. However we pushed on soon to Eil Mole which is on the frontier and consists of a pond with a little water in it and some duck and an Egyptian goose swimming about in it. I potted two duck. We then set about preparing a place for a picquet in case any shifta should be in Banissa and make for the frontier as the DC approaches. We had to sleep without mosquito nets as they show up too much in the dark. No shifta came and we moved back to Sankurar and thence to Futtilo. We saw

53

plenty of fresh rhino tracks and several lesser kudu; very nice country; large trees, rocky hills full of caves and lions' dens of fiction and later in the year the robbers and shiftas' dens in reality. An Officer was killed near here attacking a band of shiftas just before the war. There is good water at the foot of all the small hills collected in kinds of wells and above all the district is cold at night; in fact we shivered for an hour in the morning but we had the fires on quickly and everyone was sorry to leave this pleasant district.

We struck across for Takaba; it was vile country and we were short of water. At one place in the march our advanced guard reported a number of vultures in the trees near the road, so we halted and sent a patrol to investigate. They found a lion had just killed a young full grown oryx. It had disembowelled it and buried the insides neatly covering them up. The carcass had then been dragged a 100yds and hidden under some thick thorn bushes. I went to investigate and stayed up sitting over the kill but the lion never came again. At Takaba I met the DC again and also the one from Moyale who was there settling some blood money claims. A man is only worth thirty camels in these parts and one man balances another; further south with the Ogaden Somalis a hundred camels is his value.

Various chiefs sat and killed a sheep and ate '*Buna*' [roasted coffee] and made peace in their own fashion. One chief arrived with a sword; he was a fearful scoundrel. On close examination the sword was made in Germany for export to Abyssinia and was covered with Lions of Judah and pleasant remarks about the Emperor.

The natives in these parts live on camel's milk and its products, eating it sour or as ghee; meat only occasionally; water once or twice a month from the water hole often 20 miles away. They wear '*Murdug*'. Such things as grain, flour, tea or sugar are unknown. The cloth is the medium for exchange; one '*tobe*' [approximately 8yds] is worth 8s and for a *tobe* we get 2 goats. We take out rolls of cloth to pay for our meat ration. Money is useless or unknown. If I want to buy a bow and arrow I exchange *buna* or cloth for it. Milk is never refused to anyone but we make the troops give a little meal in exchange always. They live in '*Manyattas*' following the grazing. The houses are made of mats of Dom palm leaves. These mats are also used for covering up the goods on the loaded camels when on the move. Milk cans are cut out of wood or woven from fibre ropes which are made from camels' hide or fibre and plaited. Cooking pots are about the only imported thing and they don't often use them.

On getting back to the *boma*, we had to stand to at once and be ready to move out again as the Aulihan have started out on a raid and collected a lot of Italian cattle and were en route for us but in due course they turned back and the alarm was false. [The Aulihans are a Somali tribe.]

We have started making cream cheese; the first is a great success and we are going to experiment with a camel's milk cheese next. We merely put curds in a cloth and hang it up overnight but with a mature brand which we are going to try for we will have to use stones to press it.

The DC is putting up a stone house and it is going on well; we burn our own lime and all the tools the masons have are four old nail hammers, three mason's trowels and a shovel but they work wonders. We use government red tape to get the line; string is too expensive and we haven't got any. Luckily the stone is in large flat blocks ready for use as it is found. The masons are Yemeni Arabs who came over from the Italian side. [The house was as good as ever when Sandy saw it over twenty years later.]

The Italians have at last crushed the rebellion in Somaliland not without a lot of trouble. Jubaland is to be administered by Italian Somaliland now. [The two northern Italian protectorates were now firmly incorporated into Italian Somaliland along with Jubaland]. All DCs who arrived with a flourish of trumpets have been retrenched sometime ago and where they had four, they have only one left. As the Government is in mourning the Italian official note paper is surrounded by a half inch black margin; curious idea and waste of money.

You forget that it is not like at home; I have to keep a cook, a boy and an assistant boy and buy all my food stuffs. I can't go out and buy a fresh tin of jam if I run out; it means it has to come from Nairobi by camel et cetera and may take four to six months as heavy loads don't follow the post route. One has to have ample stores of flour, sugar, tea and everything one eats in sealed tins or else weevils, white ants or rain get at it. Bread is made by the cook; you can't send to the bakers for scones or cakes if you run out. As a result initial expenses are heavy. You use your own crockery, knives and cooking pots which cost money even in Nairobi. Once I have paid off these I will be able to put back larger sums of money. [His father had obviously given Sandy a telling off for spending so much on stores.]

I got the French book for which many thanks, also the news of the Fortnum and Mason parcel which sounds good. I have several good curios I have collected during our raids on *manyattas* and have some more coming in. I have run out of films worse luck owing to the rains and dud postal service; I wrote in April for more but they haven't arrived yet.

Detachment 3rd KAR, Mandera, Kenya, 20 July 1926

Many thanks for your letters; I got a mail yesterday with your news about the strike [the first general strike in British history which began on 4 May]. We have had no excitements of late. A stray Abyssinian or so comes over to look for runaway slaves accompanied by two soldiers with long greasy hair, white breeches, an old white coat or even an American khaki tunic, an old blue and white football jersey underneath and a rifle is the usual kit. They look the blackguards of fiction and usually are.

A platoon came up to relieve us yesterday. On the way two Abyssinian soldiers who were on guard deserted with some cash; £350 of it; so we got word and I had to send a section of my Somalis out to catch the brutes. They have not yet returned but the news is reassuring and we carefully told them we didn't want the thieves but only their rifles and the cash. Persons for court martial would be a nuisance here; on top of that just as I was handing over we got news that the Aulihan were raiding so I have sent the rest of my platoon off up the river after them. I follow at once. I will be out patrolling for about two months up and down the river living with the camel *manyattas*. We will be heading for Kalicha. I will enjoy it and we ought to get some fun and shooting.

Detachment 3rd KAR (Kalicha on River Dawa West of Yabicho),
Kenya 28 July 1926

I left Mandera in a hurry following up my platoon. My section caught one of the Abyssinian askaris who ran away with the cash but got none of the money back; the other fellow must have got clean away. The platoon they belong to are a rotten lot and the Officer can't speak Swahili and is a Gunner with no knowledge of Infantry soldiering hence the trouble. They have no shoemakers, tailors or carpenters and take no steps to train any. I have two of each to provide for emergencies which rather surprised them.

I pushed off one morning with my 14 bore erstwhile Hussars and Lewis Gun on a pack mule which keeps pace with us at a canter to visit Kalicha. Now that I have half my men mounted on mules, our range of action is increased enormously. On arriving there we found a huge salt earth plain through which the Dawa River runs. It is fringed with Dom palms and swamps which are breeding places for mosquitoes and tetse flies. Lion, buffalo and rhino abound. Across the river are dried up hills with paths leading down to the fords of which there are six which the Aulihan use. The Abyssinian foothills are close by. The plain was a solid mass of camels; about 3,000, all grazing and going or coming for the water and eating the salt earth which is the attraction. We examined the fords and then tied up in the thick fringe of palms during the heat of the day. I had bought some food in a haversack and got a lot of camel's milk on the spot.

We were all dozing at around 12.00 am when the sentry suddenly sounded the alarm and we saw the whole plain a seething mass of camels, dust and men all making as quick as they could to get inland, yelling, and women screaming and throwing away water pots and even children. All were rushing away from the river. A Sheikh, complete with parasol and a smart but worn Arab waistcoat and a Koran followed by a youth with a board, also joined in the mad rush. We saddled up and sent off a patrol to try and find out. It eventually transpired that the trouble was that one party watering had seen an armed man across the river; they at once thought he was an Aulihan scout and spread the alarm. He turned out to be one of a canoeing party sent across at another ford to make sure there were no Aulihan about while his section watered.

We spent the night in an old *boma* here; saddle for a pillow, horse blanket for a bed and camel's milk for dinner, not nearly as bad as it sounds. The next day we went off to put up a barbed wire fence round the grave of a fellow killed in a mutiny here in 1919. We did the job and came on to Kalicha where I had left my patrol and settled in here.

I expect to be about six weeks in Kalicha post and round about before returning to Wajir. Kalicha is situated about 50ft above the level of the plain on a small projecting spur and so commands an extensive field of fire. The post consists of a low thorn *zareba*, low and wide so it does not interfere with firing, corner breastwork defences and four palm leaf huts, one for each section of the askaris and a house for the officer with of course no door and just an opening for windows. One room of the officer's house serves as a store for the Indian agent of the shopkeeper in Mandera to use for goods he sells to the local tribes here. At first he did a roaring trade, but now the locals have had fines from the DC for various offences, they are more wary at coming. The houses are only for day use. At night no one is allowed to sleep in a tent or shelter. The men sleep round the perimeter of the camp; the Lewis Gunners sleep beside their gun. We are always on the '*Qui Vive*' for raids. Strict military discipline and routine is followed. The day starts with reveille at 5.30 am. There is an early morning parade of PT and games on the parade ground outside the *boma*. This is followed by field work, diamond and square formations and Lewis gun and rifle grenade training. At 10.00 am comes an inspection of the post. All work ceases over the middle of the day. At 3.00 pm fatigues start. There are always improvements to be made in the defences. Crossing places on the river need to be visited.

Fatigues finish at 5.00 pm. The men usually employ the last of the daylight in playing a kind of draughts. It is played with twenty-four pieces; twelve of which are camel droppings and twelve are pebbles. For playing, depressions are scooped in the ground with remarkable speed. Another occupation is shaving each other's heads with razor blades, broken glass or tops of opened tins. Sometimes the men will collect Dom palm leaves to take back to their wives in Mandera to make sleeping mats. Some sit reading. There is always something going on and some excitement; a large crocodile at the ford or a raid rumour.

Sports are sometimes held in the evenings and the local tribesmen join in. Long jump, high jump and spear throwing are the most popular. The locals can never reach the standards of the askaris. The prize is *buna*.

At 6.00 pm daily the flag is hauled down. The mules and ponies are brought back in and inspected for sores. I lie in my long deck chair with an extension and await the Sergeant's report that all is '*Tamaam*' or correct. If raiders are reported in the vicinity or some alarm is raised, 'Stand To' is at dawn and sentries are doubled at night. Two sections mounted on mules are earmarked as a striking force.

The standard of discipline in the units is extremely high. The CO of a detachment is allowed to give up to fifteen lashes in accordance with the KAR. This is hardly ever used up here. In these stations we are far more in contact with the men. One gets to know men much better than at home and vice versa. You know each man by his voice and all about him and his family. I thoroughly enjoy living in the 50yd square with my men and mules.

When the Degodia come down with their camels to water the whole family come along; the children play about and eat Dom palm nuts and herd the camels while the women fill water pots and cut grass for mats or covers for beds. The gallant men folk usually sleep under the trees.

The old men here all talk in parables; it is a sign of wisdom but most tiresome. The local chief, who shows the wounds he got in the last Aulihan raid with much pride, is an absolute expert at the parable stunt. He insists on paying me a visit morning and evening and takes a pride in learning the names of askaris. He always arrives with an offering of milk for my own use from his best camel; this gift game is in the nature of an investment as you always have to return him something like cloth or a little tea or tobacco when you are in camp. On trek it is a right that the traveller must have milk and water.

The Degodia, who are round here now, only crossed over from Abyssinia two years ago as a result of persecutions. They are not accustomed to Europeans at all and often run like fun when they see you coming; men as well as children. They are a mean lot and have no sort of cooperative system like the other tribes. If one man's camels are all raided they don't help him at all; just let him starve; a single stranger or chief from another tribe is never offered hospitality. We had to feed an old man, a Gurreh, who came to us starving as he had been a week with the Degodia chief awaiting a case and was offered no food; the poor old man was absolutely done. They are also bad thieves and often cut the end camel off a string; the leader being in front won't notice it.

On the way up here we camped close to the *manyatta* of the father of one of my askaris; the old man did us well and nobly stumped up a goat to be eaten in his son's honour (he was not a Degodia); jolly decent of him as they value their goats very much.

My stores are almost done here, but I have a fresh lot at Wajir; veg is finished but I have a lot of pickles and they are green so I am eating the gherkins hard. Mustard is finished and also cocoa; flour is done and I am reduced to '*Ata*'. My clothes are all torn with thorns and trousers patched but in spite of all this I never felt better. Camel's milk, goat and guinea fowl are the staple articles of my diet. I can always fall back on dates and rice from the men's rations in due course. The Italians keep nothing at Lugh; we can't get anything out of them.

We get no news from the outside world here at all as we are off the main trade route or track. The Degodia avoid the *boma* as much as possible treating the government with distrust.

I have been up here for three months now and haven't had an answer to any letters I have written to Nairobi. Our last mail from there was up to 25 May so it gives you some idea of the state of the communications in outlying parts of the colony where there are no talkative settlers to create a disturbance. The difficulty of the post here is that from Kalicha we are only dependent on sundry natives who take the letters to Mandera and thence by more natives to Lugh so it is not too reliable.

The medical arrangements have been cut down because no parliamentary commission or settler or anyone who matters ever comes near here. There is one European doctor to the whole Northern Frontier. He is at Moyale, about 200 miles away and is proposing to sacrifice health and comfort to visit Mandera this month. I don't suppose he will get beyond his kind thoughts for us as they are all so afraid of the Dawa valley. The Provincial Commissioner has twice turned tail and openly says he won't visit Mandera till he has to. Although it is very enervating and one can't call it a health resort, it is better than Turkana. There is an Indian Doctor at Mandera but he was ordered to Wajir and the DC refused to send him as we had so many killed and wounded in the year while Wajir had none. They do everything to keep the talkative settler quiet.

At Kalicha I have acquired fame as a doctor amongst the Degodia. My patients for eye lotion include babies of a month old, boys and old men. There is such a rush on my medicine from my small medical box that I have had to send in for more. Patients have included men with lion bites and children bitten by hyenas while asleep. I also have a man with a bullet in his guts; he is beyond me. I only plug the hole up and am sending him to Mandera. [Sandy once cured a man's septic arm with bread poultices. The cook had first to make the bread.]

I have got hold of a bow and arrow and practise in the evenings. The DC is coming up in a day or so and we are having a competition as he has also got a bow. In due course I hope to bag a guinea fowl on the ground with it.

Detachment 3rd KAR, Mandera (Kalicha), Kenya, 21 August 1926 (I think)

I am still out at Kalicha. I had some mild goes of fever last week as a result of mucking about in a marsh, but I caught it in time and dosed myself with quinine so did not have to lie up.

For a change I went off to Mandera and found that the Company Commander was on his way up from Wajir so I stayed a day or so and came on out here with him. He was very pleased with my platoon and is now wanting to get us down to Wajir for the General's inspection in January as we are the only platoon which has got Somalis and decent NCOs.

The birds are extraordinary here but it's not the nesting season yet. I saw a curious little black and white speckled diver with a long beak; it rose to about 12ft above the water and took a stone like dive into the shallow water coming up at once and flying up again; it doesn't appear to swim. There are parrots, black and white crested fellows like cockatoos, brilliant kingfishers, green birds, even blackbirds of sorts; in fact every weird animal with wings and no apparent mission in life. Spur fowl live in our *zareba*. Leopards are heard round the *boma* every night.

We are busy collecting a fine for the DC from the local Degodia; they try all sorts of tricks, childish in the extreme to try to swindle one but we are getting to know their ways. We collect a large number of camels in mass and exchange them for meat ones when they bring them, and returning the surplus when they have paid up their quota. They have not learnt that the Government can always get the better of them and, if they try to evade a fine by taking their stock further up river, it is equally simple to send a mounted patrol to collect it and of course increases the fine accordingly.

I am very fit indeed and have had no sign of fever in spite of having spent the wet season in one of the worst spots for fever. I am thankful I got out of Meru and its damp; I never felt fit there.

Detachment 3rd KAR, Mandera, Kenya, 17 October 1926

I have had a quiet time off and I am alone here as the other Officer has been recalled to Nairobi to explain how he lost the £350 and why he didn't have a proper guide.

I have just spent the afternoon mending a hand mill for grinding '*Intama*' [sorghum], to give you an idea of the various jobs we have to do.

Great road cutting operations are in vogue from Wajir, north to Eil Wak and thence to Mandera, widening existing camel tracks and in course of time a motor will be able to reach Mandera. Rocky hills et cetera along the river render it almost impassable and I very much doubt if it will ever be satisfactory till proper gangs and engineers get at it. The immediate advantage will be that one's kit will not get torn by thorns and have to be repaired each safari. The Italians are likewise cutting roads hard and are connecting Lugh and Mandera so one will shortly be able to go from Berbera in Northern Somaliland via Mogadisco to the Zambezi on roads the whole way. As usual the CO arrived with a flourish of trumpets at Wajir to inspect but when he heard that Mandera lay fourteen days away and an almost waterless trek he cancelled his visit here; we were not very surprised. It is over two years since a senior Officer was up here. They don't like discomfort nowadays; but they air their views on the defence of the Abyssinian frontier all right when they get down country.

We have never yet enjoyed the luxury of full rations; we are usually on half rations as now but the men realize that we do what we can for them and we never have any trouble.

I have started a small *shamba* on the river; eleven of my platoon have taken them up. The Government provides the seed and we offer every encouragement to them to supplement their food supply and avoid beriberi and scurvy. We have recently had a couple of cases. As we get very little rain it is rather a gamble growing in bulk; small plots which can be hand watered do well but rows and rows of beans are beyond watering especially with old tins. The men go in for maize, red peppers, beans (Canadian Wonder), onions, marrows et cetera. We are also starting a banana plantation and, as we have a particularly good brand, we ought to have a large production in a year's time.

I have also started a fish catching exercise. One day a week two Kavarondos, who come from the shores of Lake Victoria and who understand local fish, draw an extra meat ration and proceed to catch fish for the *boma*, usually bearded barbel; they usually get over a dozen but they are poor eating.

To combat malaria I have started quinine parades. Five grains of quinine on Saturday night and five on Sunday morning are given out on parade and each man has to swallow there and then so there is no temptation to sell the magic pills. The result has been that we have only had one case of malaria.

Balambaras, our pet leopard, has had paralysis of the hind legs; the cheetah probably played rather too roughly with him and injured the spine. However he is slowly getting better but it has retarded his growth and made him better tempered. The two gerenuk and the oryx have left owing to the cheetah without a doubt. We have got hold of a lynx as well; a funny little animal as quick as lightning with black ears with a tuft at the end; very playful and always spitting at Balambaras. He is light brown in colour and is obviously of the cat tribe. It has not yet taken to chewing boots or shoes or other household goods. Our young lesser kudu is doing well and we feed it with milk from a football bladder.

I am building a new house for myself; wattle and daub of course with a *makuti* leaf roof, eleven yards by six yards. As all water has to be brought by camel, the daub part of the business takes time. The roof is all bonded with bark torn in strips and soaked in water.

News has just come in that my section has caught the runaway askari and the money intact. I am off at once up the river and hope to have some fun.

The DC is out road making at present and I expect Mitchell up here soon who was with me at Gobwen; I hope it is he who comes up as he is an excellent fellow.

Life on this frontier has its excitements but is really the most enjoyable form of soldiering I have yet struck and is far healthier here than on the Turkana side. Another Officer who left about six months ago has died from blackwater, the result of fever in Turkana.

Can you please get Orr to send me out the following books: 'The Game Birds of Kenya Colony' by Jackson; it will be most useful as a reference book up here where there are plenty of birds about and also 'The History of the K.A.R.' by Lloyd Jones.

Detachment 3rd KAR, Mandera, Kenya, 15 November 1926

I have been promoted Captain now with pay et cetera from 5 December 1925; a nice chunk of back pay. I am one up on my contemporaries at home as when I leave the army I get the rank of Captain but of course I have to return to Lieutenant when I rejoin the Gordons. My pay is now £600 per annum plus local allowances which makes it about £700.

Rain has been scarce here and very local; Mandera of course having had practically none and our *shamba* still less though only 2 miles away. But we did have a good heavy downpour two days ago and the *shamba* got its quota, so now it is coming on well. They must have had good rains in the Abyssinian hills as the river is in good spate with a large volume of water coming down.

Detachment 3rd KAR, Mandera, Kenya, 10 December 1926

A fellow Hughes has been posted here and arrived a day or so ago. I go off on safari for a month on 17 December and expect to get a shot at raiders alright. I will be at Gallicha, up the Dawa about 60 miles from Mandera. All the local tribes are collecting behind us and graze under our guns. We follow the tribes to fresh grazing grounds and are ready to guard their stock. I change about with Hughes after a month and we do month about with our respective Platoons.

It is getting very hot now and dry again but our *shambas* are doing very well. A *shaduf* has been made to help with watering and irrigating. We are getting enormous yields of tomatoes, red peppers and pawpaws. Porcupines are a nuisance. [When Sandy visited Mandera in 1950, the DO asked him for full details of where and how he had organized the garden twenty-four years previously as its fame was renowned.]

I have got some leopard and cheetah skins for Jane. I have seen only one European besides Pease and Phillips between April and December and that was our Company Commander who came to inspect us; we don't have much chance of increasing our circle of friends. I don't count an Italian who we couldn't talk to.

I will drink your health in camel milk on Xmas day in solitary state at Kalicha; I am again reduced to ration rice and dates but my new stores are on the road.

PS. Just off on safari to Kalicha; raiders are out but not as yet after our stock but the Habash.

Very many thanks for the excellent Fortnum and Mason parcel. I will have a jolly good Xmas anyway what with ham and bacon and good tea; it is an absolutely ripping stock of things which I have not tasted for years.

I enclose some more photos of the children of my platoon; could you please send me out four prints of it for the proud fathers.

Detachment 3rd KAR, Mandera, Kenya, 23 December 1926

We excavated one of the numerous burial cairns in the district close to Mandera. It was a large mound of stones 6ft high and 30 across. In the centre we found a curious pot in fragments which we were able to piece together with cement and office glue. We also found that a body had been buried in a sitting position with this pot at its feet; it had some milk or food in the inside at some period. We also found a bronze or copper earring about 2ins diameter close to the skull. It appears to be a Boran type of grave [the Boran came originally from Abyssinia in the seventeenth century]. A stone chamber is made and the corpse put in and roofed over with wood. Other chambers are made round and a vessel with food is placed in each. These pots are unlike anything in use at the present day. [These cairns are common all over the north-east corner of Africa from the River Tana in the south to what was French Somaliland in the north. The local Somalis told Sandy that they were constructed by the 'Madanle' who they maintained were supermen of great stature whose descendants were driven out to the Lake Rudolph area by the Galla. The wells at Wajir and in other areas which are still in use today were perhaps built by these supermen. Their construction is impressive. Sandy had an article published on this excavation in *Man* June 1933, the Royal Anthropological Institute's publication. Sandy's excavation and published account is referred to in Monty Brown's book *Where Giants Trod* on the NFD, published in 1988].

Detachment 3rd KAR, Mandera, Kenya, 10 March 1927

Many thanks for FM parcel, also for the big game book; it is just what one wants here and goes far to stimulate one's interest in the game of the district.

I came in from Kalicha last week; no excitements on the road. I met my friend the Balambaras; he had got a pass to travel on our side of the river as it was safer. He greeted me with a shriek 'Ah Captain Curle' and rushed up and shook me warmly by the hand. I had some cups of sweet tea with him and he wanted to stay and talk all night but I had to get on; he is a nice fellow and an expert looter but being a brother man of arms he looks on me as far superior to the DC, a mere Clerk to his notions. In Abyssinia the only honourable profession is that of a man at arms; it is not a paying one as you only get 8s or so a year plus any loot going.

Unrest has started opposite in Abysinnia. We are now afraid the Reds will start trouble in Abyssinia. Since the war, Minister *Fitaurari* Hapte Giorgis, whose province is opposite us here, has died. It would not take much to start it off as there are two factions now; the Emperor's party and the followers of one Lij Jasu. They had a war in 1919 and, being a fearful mixture of tribes with different languages, they are very liable to be got at by the Reds who would use them to strike at the Sudan.

The Italians are becoming an awful nuisance; they never bother to answer official letters and an ardent patriot destroyed the boundary cairns in front of a crowd of natives and even said 'What, is this not Italy stretching miles West of this?' Their *Banda* or irregular police down south are an awful bother continually looting British stock. Since we shot them not long ago at Eil Wak they mind their own affairs up this end. Mussolini has inspired them with a swollen headedness and they think they are equal in prestige to an Engishmen. The new type of rather low class official, who they seem to have now in Jubaland, spreads anti-British propaganda amongst the natives and thinks he can score off you by not answering or worrying about your letters. The Boundary Commission never wish to see another Italian. They say they have not played the game at all.

Heat here is awful now but I am quite accustomed to it but only three weeks or so till the rains come and then it will be fairly cool again. The river is nearly dried up now; pools remain however all along. There are the usual rumours of raids. We are quite inured to them now; to hear that a party of fifty has crossed the Juba doesn't even raise an 'Oh' from us as they always cry off about half way; the scouts probably exaggerate considerably. On safari one has to sleep with boots on and always with your rifle in bed beside you, ready for any alarm to hop up at once, although there is really no danger, one is always ready so as not to be caught napping.

I shot a wild dog last week; there are a lot about here of all the caracal, leopard et cetera sort. One variety I think is very rare and I am trying to get close to it to study it.

Detachment 3rd KAR, Mandera, Kenya, 17 March 1927

Our latest excitement has been the sudden arrival of the Colonel, the Adjutant and the OC Wajir by car last Friday. We were sitting in the office when all of a sudden the orderly rushed up and said a 'Motor car comes, it goes pouf pouf.' We walked over to the gate expecting to see a bearded Italian but to our surprise found the CO. A huge crowd collected to see this wonderful machine which had done in two hours a two days journey on foot. They had left Nairobi on Monday and had got through without a hitch; the road in parts was very bad; people they met flew into the bush in a fearful state of panic.

They didn't come to inspect but just to see the place and were very pleased with it indeed; we did them well; champagne, paté and lobsters. They stayed two days and then returned. Chiefs and others were driven at a fearful speed round the *boma* for an experience; they invoked their deities.

I will remain up here till the end of my tour as the Colonel says he is pleased with my work and the Intelligence we collect; and as he considers it an important place he doesn't want to change me to Wajir to command the Company unless I wanted to move; as I assured him I was much happier here he agreed to my staying on. We got promises of furniture to be sent up which will improve the place and all sorts of things which we ordered; pictures of the King, tin soldiers for the sand table, cross-cut saws, dyes for making rivers and grass on the sand table and 101 things.

The car news will spread to the Aulihan and I hope keep them from raiding this season. Another party set out to raid us but after much consultation decided to turn back; thirty however went on and fell in with a Habash safari which they shot up only in turn to be counter-attacked and ended up with nine wounded so that has not encouraged them much.

In haste to catch the mail via Lugh where I am sending in to buy some banana plants.

Detachment 3rd KAR, Mandera, Kenya, 19 April 1927

The rain has at last broken here; you have no idea what relief it is. The temperature at once fell from 96° to 76° straight away and we can wear sweaters in the evening. After forty-eight hours the grass began to grow and now all is green.

I have been out on safari to recruit twenty-five Degodia to send to Nairobi for a trial. As I knew most of them it was fairly easy. They were very green when we first got them. I saw one actually take his trousers off when he sat down; as he had been told he must look after his clothing and according to his custom when you have a new robe you never sit down in the earth with it on; you lift it up and sit bare so to speak.

Our local natives have been doing well raiding and have launched two successful raids on the Aulihan in Abyssinia looting 1,400 or so head of stock; the Aulihan have not so far counter-raided. They are in a bad way now as another Somali tribe is pressing them from the north, looting them hard and our people from the south. Some ex KAR askaris, three of them went on this last raid; they got ten head of cattle each and had a good fight, killing six Aulihan and burning the villages.

Our shamba boy killed a python yesterday; it had an enormous bulge in its middle; so I got it skinned and the skin is now drying for shoes for Jane. I think it is enough for a pair. Anyway the bulge turned out to be a rat; tail and legs intact. The brute had demolished it whole, head first.

We got a new supply of stationery up last month so I now need no longer write on the back of scraps of paper and obsolete forms and I have on order some KAR 'Silvian Blue' or some such smart notepaper from Nairobi.

The great drawback to the rains now is the swarms of bugs, beetles, stink ants, stink beetles et cetera which come round the light at dinner and come into your soup; I once got a stink one in a spoonful and they emit a smell like decaying corpses; I did not enjoy the rest of the meal. We have killed eight scorpions the last week round the mess and a couple in my house.

I have written to Nairobi to get them to send up by the next motor car which ventures up a box of orange tree seedlings for the shamba. I don't think there will be a rush here as the first and last lot i.e. the CO and party had a bad trip back; burst tyres, broken springs and short of food.

Detachment 3rd KAR, Mandera, Kenya, 24 May 1927

I am once again alone here as Hughes went off last week to Nairobi to shoot in the Kenya Rifle meeting; an awful waste of public money 1,400 miles to shoot at a Rifle meeting. I don't expect him back till September.

We had a visit from a neighbouring Italian, one Tenente Commino, a Sicilian by birth from Messina. He was in a Bersighian Regiment stationed at San Remo and met at a Dancing a Miss Luke of Glasgow to whom he is engaged. He was involved in a breach of promise with an Italian lady and as a result had to come out to the colonies. He was a very decent fellow indeed. He brought some of his troops with him and we had a shooting competition; we hit the target forty-six times and they hit it thirteen times.

I have been by far the longest of any officer up country and hope to remain so and avoid Nairobi. I have now done over two and a half years on the Juba and the Dawa and only had one go of fever and that I caught in Mombasa which is quite good going; old Africa is not as bad as it is painted as long as one likes the life and has some hobby. One can always keep fit but when one has nothing to do and begin to mope you will always get sick. The fresh veg is the thing here. Pease, the DC, is down with fever now and a lot of flu is knocking about.

I have got up some sets of boxing gloves and we have boxing for the troops along with physical training in the mornings. We have one or two budding 'Sikis'. I don't know much about it but as they know still less it doesn't matter.

The new DC has just arrived along with an inspecting medical officer [MO] to look at the hospital. He is a very young Doctor who is full of medical terms and delights in catching bugs.

The rains down country have as usual upset the post and we have had nothing much for a month. I would like your old copies of the Spectator very much indeed; also could you please send me any Times Supplements when you are finished with them. Also could you please order for me the Army Quarterly (a Service publication with lots of good reading in it).

I am overjoyed to hear that you are so fit and am looking forward to some good walks when I am on leave. I propose to take a low ground shooting in some nice cold spot for a change after here.

Detachment 3rd KAR, Mandera, Kenya, 11 July 1927

Many thanks for the letters, negatives and wee novels which arrived last mail.

I have just come in from Kalicha after three weeks out there, most of which I spent touring about with the Doctor; we examined water holes and swamps and tried to catch mosquitoes but never saw one. We located a large fresh water lake covered with masses of pelican, teal, geese, aigrettes and marabou storks; when they rose from the water their wings made an extraordinary swishing sound. We examined three water holes all of which contained sulphur in varying degrees of smell.

We have had a month of peace; no rumours of war or fear of alarms. An important Commission has been meeting on the question of frontier raids into Kenya from Abyssinia. They will do nothing of course but we may get them to remove one or two of the biggest scoundrels who are notorious on the border; I suppose only to get worse ones in their place.

The Commission consisted of Glenday, the DC, who knows all this district well having been stranded up here during the war, Major Miles, the Consul for South Abyssinia who I know well and two Abyssinian representatives, one the Chief of Customs and the other the Second Judge of the High Court in Addis who speaks French. They are followed by numerous petty officials, soldiery and slaves who included some twenty women, a total of 400 persons. Each official has his tent and their camp is higgledy piggledy over a large area. They travel by day; eight hours at a stretch and the soldiery running along while the bigwigs ride. The head Habash had to have paths cut for him by his slaves lest he should tear his clothing. This vast army has all its own meat stock with it and is I presume exactly like a mediaeval force except they have trumpets and a cornet.

The Habash delegation were given full powers to call for any Official they might want; all those connected with raids on us have refused so the show has become rather a farce but they examine all witnesses and the graves of the slain. I was introduced to the Habash delegation. The whole thing has to go to the League of Nations later on. The Italians' behaviour on our boundary is also being reported to the League.

We found that the local natives had deliberately smashed down the barbed wire fence round the grave of the Officer (which is about 10 miles from here) and had smashed the concrete with stones; we made them clean it up and soundly flogged the first one of the tribe we met and took a heavy fine to teach them. We probably didn't get the right people but the news will spread round. The Solicitor General would probably throw a fit if he heard of our methods of justice up here and summary punishments which are of course absolutely illegal but the only thing which acts up here with the type of natives.

I have been sent up another Officer from Wajir; a very young and snobbish youth who hates safari and the life generally. I think a spell up here will do him a lot of good; he hankers after Nairobi and was quite annoyed because he had missed his bath for three days on the road up; a chase after raiders with only what food you can carry, a boiling sun and no tent would about settle him. I am getting rid of the new Officer at once and will carry on better alone. He is also engaged at home and in addition to his other vices is lovesick.

I am due to go lion shooting with Cimmion the Italian soon; it is sure to be amusing if unproductive.

Detachment 3rd KAR, Mandera, Kenya, 28 July 1927

We have had nothing much doing of late and I have been leading a quiet life in the *Boma* carrying on with the gardening schemes.

We had a visit from the Habash Governor of the district opposite yesterday; he is a big man and used to be the Chief Poisoner to the Empress; a title not entirely a sinecure I fancy in that country. He arrived surrounded by fifty soldiery, more evil looking and certainly dirtier than the usual. Five ran in front of the great man who was mounted on a mule with inlaid bridles. He was completely wrapped up in white cloths with a small black cape with a cowl at the back. Numerous soldiers followed accompanied by slaves who carried a sun umbrella and an enormous cattle horn about 2ft 6ins long full of his *tej* or *arrak* and his cup and a few plates in a basket with leather sewn over it [the local version of a picnic box. *Tej*, which is honey-mead, is the national drink; *arrak* is a grain spirit.] He caused all the soldiery to dismount within sight of our *boma*; he himself rode on to our gate and then dismounted. We asked him into the mess and we had to enter first (as is the custom in case anyone is waiting behind the door) and allot him a seat. He brought his son and *Gerazmatch* who is now in charge opposite, also his Major Domo who stood behind his chair. We produced whisky and the Major Domo poured out his Master a good stiff one, bowing low and was alert to pour a little into the palm of his hand to taste it (as is his job in case it is poisoned) but the *Fitaurari* stopped him which showed that he trusted us or rather Johnnie Walker. The Major Domo is a most useful man all round as later, when the *Fitaurari* found that the whisky was rather too much for him he handed the glass to him to finish off. The *Fitaurari* arrived with a horse as a gift; the DC had to fork out a pistol in return which was handed to the ever ready Major Domo who has to receive it and it is not etiquette for the *Fitaurari* to look at it in our presence. He was a well mannered old boy and obviously well bred. We played the gramophone to him and Harry Lauder was the record they liked best. The *Gerazmatch* proceeded to get rather drunk and objectionable (and in the words of the Interpreter 'I think he is on Sin') but he was kept in his place by the *Fitaurari*. We sent them sardines, fruit et cetera and lent the old man a tent for the day. We gave them an ox which they ate raw according to their custom. They want to build a town opposite us on the Dawa as they don't like the Italians now at all. In fact the whole object of the visit was to score against the Italians who the *Fitaurari* will not visit and he wishes to divert the trade from Lugh to here. He freely stated his wants to us; a tent, a camp bed, a Mauser rifle, a clock et cetera but I fear he will be wanting for a long time to come.

My row last year about rations had some effect as this year we are full up at the expense of stores; several articles have been on the road for seven months. I anticipate it will take ten to twelve months this year for stores to get to us but luckily we have a trading connection started with Mogadishu. Our local shop has just got a safari in with excellent cheap Italian stores; beer which is really good, Asti Spumante, raw sliced ham, Bologna sausage with garlic, spaghetti and excellent tinned fruits. It is a gala day for the natives and we have a special pay out and all the wives appear in their new clothes and fight like cats over them. It is really most amusing the excitement it causes; one interesting point is that the cheap German imitations of native clothes find no sale at all.

The river Dawa is full of alluvial gold; I will send home a small sample of earth and probably your museum geologist could say if it was worth anything. I first noticed it in the *shambas* and there is certainly plenty of it; it may be a paying proposition for someone. The MO at Moyale examined the gold we thought we got in the river and has pronounced it 'Mica'. [Many years later Sandy learnt that the Ethiopian gold mines and surface deposits at Adola do actually lie in the valley tapped by the upper waters of the Dawa River.]

Detachment 3rd KAR, Mandera, Kenya, 30 September 1927

We are still plodding along here without much to excite us. Another *Fitaurari* visited us accompanied by a *Gerazmatch*; both rough uncouth individuals. I managed to get a photo of one of the soldiery with a shield; how you fight with a rifle and shield I don't know; they also had several German-made swordsticks which the more important blackguards carried.

Our *shambas* have been doing very well indeed and we found that lettuce did well, so we have had a galaxy of lobster mayonnaise and salmon from a tin with the first lettuce. Beetroot, turnips, tomatoes and cabbage are good so we are assured of a fresh veg supply. Bananas are coming on also; lime trees are bearing and we have fresh lime juice daily. Our veteran pineapple has actually started a fruit; we will have a great day when we eat it. We have no slugs in our gardens; the worst pests are locusts which only come occasionally. If someone is not always in the gardens we get monkeys and baboons in. The porcupine is a fiend for beans and tomato tops and he appears to be able to get through any hedge. The men are now taking more interest in the *shambas* as they are really producing stuff in sufficient quantities for them.

Communications are no better; it still takes eight months for stores to get up from Nairobi so now we order from Mogadishu and within six weeks from writing we get the goods but not always what we order; I got three tins of raw pig's feet, a more loathsome dish I can't imagine. It must be made for German export.

The awful drought continues but the heat is building up before the rains. The nine cows combine to give a cupful of milk just enough for our tea but not enough for butter making.

I hope this letter will just get down before the rains close up communications.

Detachment 3rd KAR, Mandera, Kenya, 21 November 1927

My relief has now arrived and I leave for Wajir at the end of month to take command of it. I had a letter from the CO saying he was very pleased with my show here or rather the correspondence about it as several Civil Officers have said it was a good show and the Principal Commissioner of the Province quoted Mandera as an example of harmony between Civil and Military. I am having a special runner to take my Xmas mail to Lugh along with this.

Detachment 3rd KAR, Wajir, Kenya, 1 February 1928

Many thanks for your letters. I had a good safari down but on the way as I was moving by night there was an eclipse of the moon which caused much consternation and I had to wait till it was passed before I could get along.

The buildings here are all of stone and are all white washed. The glare and heat is terrific. I have a house to myself which is falling down but move into my new house next week. There is plenty of water from wells in the *boma* but it is somewhat salt although one soon gets used to it. We also have a mess where the two subalterns live; one is a fellow Mallam of the Buffs and the other Jameson of the Seaforths, both excellent fellows.

I have been very hard at it since I came down preparing for our General Inspection. The Inspector General arrived on 25 January en route for Moyale and we did him very well indeed with a ten course dinner for ten people with champagne et cetera. He was very pleased with our Company and congratulated me on the show we put up. Since we left we have done nothing.

We are connected by car road with Kismayu and I have arranged for a constant supply of fresh mangoes and veg to be sent up; close on twelve cars a month come up the road.

I hear the Crown Prince of Italy is shooting in Jubaland; everything was preserved for him from last August and all licences were cancelled; I suppose they have fatted beasts tied down ready for him.

One of the Swedish Missionaries who I knew at Gobwen came up here recently and had a great time baptizing Christians in the lines and singing hymns.

We have now to construct a landing ground for aeroplanes ready outside the *boma* as it won't be long before they reach here.

There is a new Commander who has come from China but I fancy he will be kept at it touring round Turkana, so we don't expect him till June or July. There has just been a tremendous fiasco in Turkana; an Officer of the poodle faking, lounge lizard type went off his head and started to bomb a brother Officer who was visiting him; luckily no one was hurt but the house was knocked about. The next morning he followed up his bombing by firing a hand gun at his pal's house. Luckily the bomb had so frightened the poor visitor that he had cleared off. I expect they will run the fellow for attempted manslaughter.

I will try to get some more seeds for the Botanic Gardens but the country being so dry it is seldom you can see what sort of flower the seeds belong to.

Detachment 3rd KAR, Kenya, Wajir, 9 March 1928

Many thanks for the French novels and the English ones which arrived as I was going out on safari. I have by now read most of them.

I went down to have a look at some water holes about thirty miles north east of the Lorian on the map to see if there was any chance of a Jumbo. I found nothing much so moved to the Lorian; it is a huge reed swamp with the river running through the centre. There is a network of elephant tracks in it and at this time of year there was very little water. The method of hunting is to explore the edge and see if any good size Jumbo has left the swamp during the night; I found that there were not many in and had no luck with following so I tried in the swamp with a ladder made by tying trees together and thus enabling one to get a view of the reeds. I saw a small tusker close but with the licence at £50 and the price of ivory down I only used the UPK [camera] on him.

I struck some elephants however about to come out of the swamp to raid a *shamba* so I waited till they emerged and stalked up close studying the tusks as it was getting darker and darker. They kept hiding one and after half an hour when he was exposed to me I saw that he was a beauty so I wasted no time and let him have both barrels of my .450.

My tusks have just been brought in and are beauties. One is 110lbs which is broken. The other one is 126lbs and is a perfect tusk. It is 9ft in length and 12ft 7ins in girth; 236lbs of ivory in all. It is the best one shot up here for some years.

[The largest tusk was bought by the Indian Community in East Africa and it was used to make a tobacco jar for HRH The Prince of Wales on his visit to East Africa. Apparently the average weight of a tusk is now around 60lb.]

It was very hot on this safari and one could eat nothing only drink tea and eat a few eggs. I returned to Wajir to find that another Officer, one Murray in the Seaforths, was in the *boma* en route for Mandera to relieve Hughes. He is a cousin of the Duke of Athol. However I had a night's rest and then had to set out again; this time by car to Afmadu in Italian Somaliland [previously Jubaland] to fix up with the Italian DC there to return some 2,300 natives who had crossed into our territory and were pushing round the Wajir wells.

On our return we found that Campbell in the Argyll and Sutherland Highlanders who is OC Moyale was en route for Kismayu, also the Provincial Commissioner and his wife arrived to fix up about the move so we are kept hard at it.

Detachment 3rd KAR, Wajir, Kenya, 18 May 1928

I have just got back from Safari. We had a dull and uneventful trip to the frontier. We crossed the Lorian Swamp with some seventy baggage camels, four hundred head of stock camels and three hundred goats. The place was quite dry and a loathsome smell of rotting hippo and fish; the poor hippos were right out of the water, still packed tight together but were dying of thirst. It is an unprecedented state of affairs I gather. Even the elephants were dying of thirst. Some infuriated ones became a danger, several children herding goats being killed. [Sandy's photos of the place and an article were in *Natural History Magazine*, published by the Natural History Museum in London, and in the *Illustrated London News* of 22 September 1928 under the title:

'ANIMAL TRAGEDIES OF THE LORIAN SWAMP: A DEADLY DROUGHT. WHAT DROUGHT MEANS IN TROPICAL AFRICA: FISH DIE BY MYRIADS.']

We went by easy stages guarding all this mass of stock to the frontier. On the way we raided some ivory poachers' villages and got specimens of arrows et cetera for your museum. We got ten outfits and the DC secured ten convictions against poachers at Banane which is shown on the map and where no one had been for years. Round every water pool we found a butt erected to shoot elephant and giraffe from. It was full of wild flowers but as they were all out we couldn't get any seeds. We passed one place only where there had been good rain; that was horribly hot like the hottest house in the Botanics with a vegetable smell. Jameson with another party is pushing out some more Italian subjects further up.

Having got back I am up to the eyes in work getting off acres of correspondence; also we are now blasting to make a new rifle range. I am a jack of all trades here; we use a cigarette tin or two of black powder as a charge and so far have killed no one and blown up tons of rock.

I have a lot of stuff for the Museum of all sorts collected from various natives mostly up on the frontier.

Commenting years later Sandy wrote:

I travelled many thousands of miles with my Somali platoon where there were no roads and only bush tracks. Many nights I slept on my camp bed or the ground with my men all round me. When their time was up every man re-engaged. They trusted me and recognized me as their master. The improvement in communications broke down much of the understanding between the races. In later years how many DOs ruled by the law book and not their personalities?

When in 1955 Sandy again visited Mandera and the Dawa River there was a motorable track, a landing ground and even a post office. Radio communications had arrived.

I feel Sandy would acquiesce with the final description of the NFD by Monty Brown in his book *Where Giants Trod*, published in 1989:

> The Northern Frontier District held a unique place in the story of the East African Protectorate. Peopled by tough, resilient but fatalistic nomads, for a brief period its turbulence was curbed by a small band of white officers, who in their solitudes, guarded their independence with a fierce loyalty, and looked on themselves as a breed apart. Living and working in the vast emptiness of their district they evolved a distinct individuality, self-sufficiency and esprit de corps. Their attitude, which at times from necessity verged on the autocratic, gave rise to the saying that there were two distinct species of government officer in East Africa: the men from the Northern Frontier and, uttered by them with a hint of condescension, the Rest.*

* Brown, Monty, *Where Giants Trod*, Quiller Press, 1989, p. 378.

CHAPTER 5

Administrative Officer in Somaliland, 1929–30

In 1929 Sandy retired from the Army with a gratuity and joined the Colonial Service as a junior Administrative Officer in British Somaliland.

P and O S N COMPANY'S SS *Naldera*, Port Said, 1 October 1929

I had a very comfortable trip to Paris and thence to Marseilles; met some people I knew on the train and fed very well with my friend who keeps a restaurant in Marseilles. I got the address of a wine shop from him and got ten assorted liqueurs for 30s at wholesale prices.

The Boat is one of the big P and O Mail boats; cabin and lounges are very comfortable, but baths and feeding bad. The people are beastly dull. There are none of the cheery party of people we always used to have on the African run; all Indian merchants and a few officials. I met a fellow Spiers who is in the King's Own Scottish Borderers and is going out as ADC to Lord Somers; also a man who used to be in the regiment who is Military Secretary to Lord Somers [Lord Somers was Governor of Victoria and later Chief Scout for Great Britain and the Commonwealth and Empire.] Also a Mrs Grace Michie who is going out to stay in Somaliland; she says she knows your friend Lord Carmicheal well and Mrs Gourlay. The late Speaker of the House is on board and as dull as dishwater; also a music hall comedienne called Ann Perin who is accompanied by an awful looking man who is her manager. She is very pushy and sets herself at Lord Somer's side wherever possible much to his annoyance. I gather she is covered with bad scent.

There are several Somaliland people on board and they all speak well of the country and the type of people. We get to Aden on Sunday October 5th and Port Said tomorrow.

Hargesia, British Somaliland via Aden, 9 October 1929

I have at last got back to Africa again and am jolly glad to be here. I crossed over from Aden on one of those Indian owned boats; amongst other things we had a deck cargo of petrol. The Captain was dead drunk an hour after we left. The mate was well on the way when I went to bed. We reached Berbera after ten hours which is a typical Arab town with very good houses for the officials and a good rest house. I was met by the DC with numerous boys and cooks to select from and everything was well arranged.

I got orders to go at once up to Hargesia where I am now an Assistant District Commissioner. I travelled up by car, six hours, through the maritime plain thence up about 1,000ft across land exactly the same as the Dawa valley round Mandera. This is a very nice station; a DC and his wife, a doctor and three KAR officers of the Camel Corps. I have a lovely house, well furnished and with a garden. Prices are much less than those of Kenya for servants. Every station has a doctor and a wireless. We can cable all over the world for 7d a word and receive messages. We get a news bulletin daily from England. Most of the government officials have been in Jubaland or the NFD before coming here so there is a sort of band of heroes of the Juba River who always talk Juba much to the annoyance of the other listeners.

I am amused to hear that the promotion exam is being held here next Monday. I am able to assist some of the Camel Corps here who are going in for it.

No sign of my stores from Kenya as yet; of course I hope they come soon as it is most annoying having to buy fresh stuff when you know that you have all in your boxes. It is quite cold here at night but not damp like Meru; my house has a fireplace in it and we wear European clothing at night. I gather that the climate on the whole here is very much better than the NFD with the exception of the maritime plain along the coast which is hot and rather muggy. This station is situated right on the edge of a large river bed and there is none of the barbed wire about as in Kenya; each house being more or less open.

This district touches on the Abyssinian frontier and the same old fun from raids is still going on here.

Please send me at once 1 dozen golf balls,1 dozen tennis balls in tins of six each and a new 13oz tennis racket with tropical gut. I have been playing golf once or twice and also tennis for exercise but I want a lot of practice and my old racket is a bit far through. Also can you get an extract from your Nicholson gardening Encyclopaedia on growing citrus fruits such as oranges, limes et cetera so as to guide me in growing them here.

British Somaliland via Aden, 18 October 1929

The above address with my name is quite sufficient as there are so few Europeans all of whom are government officials.

I am now quite settled in. My chief duties here are those of a 2nd class Magistrate and one spends most of the day hearing cases. There is less red tape than in Kenya. I take cases in my court daily as a second class Magistrate and don't sit as an assessor. I have to give judgements et cetera and only refer matters involving tribal customs to Park, my boss, who is the DC.

In this station we have very little safari work as all is centred round Hargesia town. They bring up the old quarrels one was accustomed to get in Kenya but here you can deal with them better and it is much simpler work as you have what they call political cases as well as criminal cases and in the former it is practically a settlement of a claim while the latter is based on the Indian Penal Code.

The Officials are well done here. I have no less than seven easy chairs in my house and the Government garden provides me with more fresh tomatoes than I can eat as well as two other vegetables a day. We get cauliflower, cabbage, carrots, lettuce and practically all English vegetables while convicts out of the jail provide the labour. It all tends to make living cheap.

One is allowed fourteen days local leave a year and if you are on the coast during the hot season May to September you get an extra fouteen days with Government transport provided, and if in Berbera you are given a free ride out of it; but at Hargesia the climate is excellent, not hot, and we need fires later on.

The Italians are causing a lot of trouble up here by penetrating into Abyssinia and slowly administering it close to their proper frontier. We are now trying to make Abyssinia administer their unruly subjects or else we threaten to take over the district adjacent to our frontier.

I found out today that we have to wear a uniform when the Governor is visiting our station; it consists of a drill tunic with leather buttons; a more appalling outfit I can't possibly conceive but as my boss who has been here about ten years hasn't got an outfit yet one doesn't pay much attention to it.

British Somaliland via Aden, 31 October 1929

Many thanks for your letter. I am now quite settled in but am still without stores which are due up by the end of the week. My wines have arrived.

There is not much of interest going on here now. I spend most of my time as a magistrate from 10.00am to 1.00pm listening to cases in the office and every evening we have either tennis or golf. I am planning to go out about Xmas time shooting; there are fine elephant in the colony and the Government want them shot so rather than get let in for Xmas festivities which are sure to be somewhat alcoholic, I am going to try to get out shooting.

The climate is a bit queer for Africa and is getting colder every day. We have started fires by night and one goes to the office with a woollen pullover on and there is heavy dew every morning but the place is not the least damp.

We have got an Abyssinian Consul coming here next week. I met the man on the Kenya border when I was at Mandera; he of course has to be entertained to dinner on arrival by the DC and his wife and it will be rather difficult as we don't quite know what stage of civilization he has reached. I am supposed to go out and meet him and escort him in. We, however, don't expect that he will last long as the Abyssinian government are usually rather unmindful about small matters like his salary.

The extraordinary thing about the Somalis are their nomadic tendencies. We get letters about them from America, Africa, India, Palestine, Denmark, Berlin, Antwerp, Cardiff and Hull. Every mail they send money back and £500 or so comes in from abroad. Most of them work as firemen in ships but they always come back home again.

I gather that in future the administration of this colony will be recruited almost entirely from the regular officers and they even talk of offering bait to attract them. The housing and conditions of service are really extraordinarily good here there being, of course, no civilians to object to the expenditure. [Somaliland was a Protectorate unlike Kenya which was a colony.] It is only since 1927 that they have ceased to provide you with a de luxe cabin on the boat and even now we are the only Government Officials who travel at Government expense in the train de luxe across France.

An oil company has found oil in the country but no one knows whether it will come to anything or not. They have a staff of men investigating just now.

British Somaliland via Aden, 7 November 1929

I think for Xmas that I would like either a set of the works of Pierre Loti in French; paper cover yellow backs as they are always good reading and easy French. [Lived 1850–1923. Considered to be one of the most original and most perfect French novelists of the nineteenth century. The stories were mainly based on his travels.]

We expect out here some Haggenbeck's representative. [Haggenbeck (1844–1913) was a German collector and dealer in wild animals. The zoo of that name in Germany was known for the naturalistic way the animals were kept.] They transported about fifty Somalis from Hargesia to the Berlin zoo where they have a village. A lot of natives from here who had been in Berlin with Haggenbeck returned last week. They had all grown long bushy hair to look more savage. Haggenbeck's man always brings tinned sausages which are famous out here.

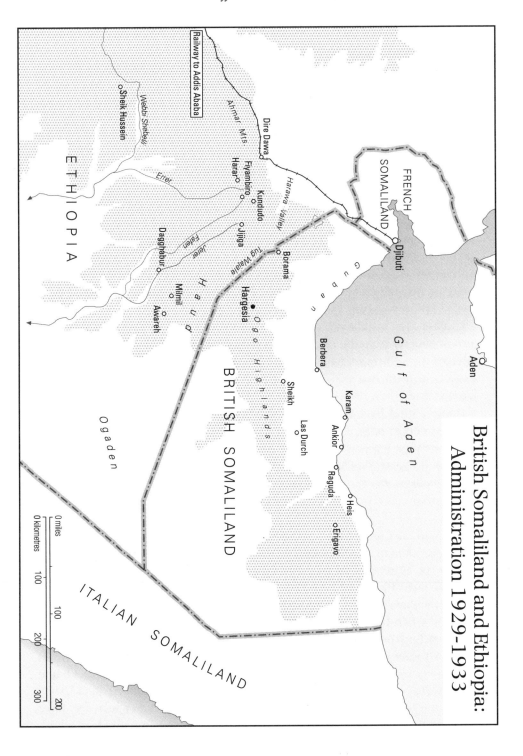

British Somaliland and Ethiopia: Administration 1929-1933

I am getting some things for the museum as I see them about. The utensils here are different to Kenya in many ways.

Don't forget to send on the old Spectators when you have finished with them. I am strafing hard about my kit in Kenya and the rifles. I hope to get them soon but people are so crooked in the Colonies especially any shops that I won't be surprised if I lose my guns.

British Somaliland via Aden, 15 November 1929

I am leading a gentleman's life here; all I have to do is magistrate's work and the cases are more or less of a tribal nature; a stolen camel, compensation for a wound obtained in a fight, blood money claims for men killed, civil suits against natives; all office work and very little outside work. I quite like it and the conditions are so good as to make it worthwhile.

We are planning a great St. Andrew's night dinner; haggis in tins has been ordered from Fortnum and Masons and is due to arrive in time.

Smallpox has broken out which adds to our fun and the appalling droughts of the last few years have killed off such a lot of stock that there is a lot of poverty. In addition locusts have made matters rather worse. We send off parties of destitutes once a week to the camp for them at Buldhar on the coast.

There is a tremendous trade in hides from Abyssinia but we find that their customs export notes are always thirty per cent out ie short in the numbers of bales. What happens is that the Abyssinian Official charges of course full fees for the lot and pockets thirty per cent for himself and only shows about seventy per cent of the cash sum taken.

My companions in the station are a very nice lot. Park, my Boss, started life as a civil engineer and has knocked about in America before the war. He came out here to the Camel Corps at the end of the war and transferred to the Civil. He is a gentleman and his wife is also very nice. The KAR have some excellent fellows. I was at Sandhurst with the present CO. The Subaltern, Collingwood, is a very nice fellow and comes from Coldstream [in the Scottish Borders] and was in the Bays. Being Camel Corps here most of the KAR are Cavalry blokes. There is a fellow Hobbs who I was at Sandhurst with. He comes from the North of England and is connected with shipping. The old Doctor (Charles Gordon Timms) is also a very nice fellow and the Director of Agriculture and Geology is an Australian (Farquharson); he has been away on tour and is just off on leave.

Can you please call in at Douglas and Foyles and order 'Les Oeuvres Libres', the French Monthly Magazine to be sent to me.

British Somaliland via Aden, 22 November 1929

I had quite an amusing time last week; in one day we had a corpse produced in the court: the victim of a murder and an hour later a horrid gory sight rushed in looking like mincemeat; he had been hit up by a highway robber and later in the day a woman tried to stab her husband in the court. Quite an exciting morning. They always produce horrid sights and leave wounds uncared for in the hope that they will get more compensation from the assailant's tribe. We also had a bright man who claimed a hundred camels from the French Company who run the Abyssinian railway in respect of his son who was killed in an accident. We suggested payment in porter's barrows as the railway company won't deal in camels.

We also had to deal with the estate of a man who had been killed in the docks in Marseilles; the bill for his funeral plot and all cost 12 francs; his friends did him cheap but the bill had a long list of other items which one could have as extras: such things as black gloves, crepe for hearses et cetera; the most expensive things in purple ran into thousands of francs.

We had a shower of rain yesterday which did a lot of good but it is getting colder daily. The temperature doesn't rise much above 70° and goes down to 40°.

I am in the Regular Army Reserve of Officers and have to stay there till I am forty.

British Somaliland via Aden, 7 December 1929

Our Abyssinian Consul has arrived at last. He speaks excellent English and is accompanied by a secretary who speaks no English but fluent Italian. We entertained them to lunch and have had little to do with them at the office. He has a wonderful uniform of a super comic opera nature. A black silk cloak with red facings and little gold buttons down the front is worn over a brilliant green and yellow striped shirt with a pair of tight khaki trousers. Bright speckled socks and cheap shoes made of two sorts of leather with straps instead of laces complete the outfit. He presented his credentials one morning. We have not found much for him to do and I expect he is very bored. He lives about 2 miles away from us so he doesn't worry us.

My pony who I paid £11 for is doing well. I hack out on it twice a week or so. The Government provide syce and fodder. The Camel Corps have offered to buy it from me when I want to sell.

I have got some of my kit from Kenya but there is some dirty work going on about my guns. I am going to put the matter in solicitors' hands soon as some £60 is involved.

Where are the old Spectators? Can you ask Jane to post them out to me. The

Times Book Club has been doing badly this tour and sent out so far four of the worst books.

I have instructed Fortnum and Mason to send you some chocolates with hard centres for Xmas.

British Somaliland via Aden, 13 December 1929

The Governor is coming here for New Year and will stay for a fortnight which is rather a jar to us. I gather there is no swank about him and he does pay his weight in entertaining. I am doing my bit early and having them to dine the night they come in [Sir Harold Kittermaster KCMG died a few years later while Governor of Nyasaland].

We had a very slack week; no litigants at all practically and the only news was that locusts are about. You can't imagine anything more annoying than having everything in your garden eaten, which is what happens when the young ones come along in April.

Hyenas are very bad here and often take children so I have been conducting a poisoning campaign against them getting three or four a night.

The Camel Corps Officers are being changed round. I am sorry as they were a topping lot especially Johnny Collingwood who I used to play a lot of golf with; the new officers come after Xmas. Needless to say all the junior postal officials, public works and wireless are all Scotch. I rather gather that Park is being relieved when on leave by a fellow who has Sinn Fein sympathies. Park is furious at having the fellow sent to take over his station and has complained to the Governor about it so I hope his appeal is successful.

I am banking again with the National Bank of India at Aden. A local shop here, an Indian firm, does some banking but they are so unbusiness like and bad that I have closed down my account with them and transferred my credit from Nairobi to Aden.

British Somaliland via Aden, 20 December 1929

I have been able to get you quite an interesting collection of Somali ropes and mats; just samples, a square foot or yard of each with the grass or root it is woven from as well.

I have got a turkey for Xmas which is being fattened up at present in my kitchen yard. Some of the governmental baggage has arrived and we are overjoyed to note a case of champagne in it.

The Abyssinian Consul has to write all his official correspondence to us in Amharic [the language of the ruling ethnic group]. As we have no one who can understand it, it has to go to Harar some 100 miles away in Abyssinia where we have a Consul. He can write perfect English but he must write in Amharic so that his secretary who is sent to watch him can see what he writes. With much difficulty we have compromised with him to write in Amharic, let his secretary translate it into Arabic and our clerks translate it into English. Of course he answers all unofficial letters in English.

I fear that the outward mails are irregular as the coasting steamer company don't bother much about catching the Indian mail home and, if it misses it, our letters get put on a Union Castle or other liner which calls at odd places and so takes about a week longer.

British Somaliland via Aden, 26 December 1929

Many thanks indeed for your Xmas present. The racquet has come and couldn't be better. All my stuff from Nairobi came up and is very welcome as there was the gramophone and all sorts of odds and ends.

We went out some 30 miles in cars to shoot sand grouse on Sunday. We got soaked to the skin as it poured; of course it would choose the one day in three months when we wanted to go out. Some of the party went down with fever before we got back; no birds came to water at all.

My Xmas luncheon went off well; the turkey was excellent and the stuffing very good but there were only three of us to partake. One of our Goanese clerks produced a Xmas card wishing me 'All the Glee of the Season'; they always just miss the boat somehow. We have four days' holiday and nothing to do as I have to remain in the station.

I am very grateful to Jane for the salt cellars, pepper pot and mustard pot; they look topping and are just what I needed to complete my table. I have quite a good cook again if he wouldn't always put up what the boy calls 'Very Old Man Sheeps' but he can get nothing else.

My gramophone has come up from Kenya and I have ordered from Paris my old friend 'Artichauts'. ['La Vie est comme un Artichaut' is a well-known French song.] I may be able to whistle it if I hear it once or twice more.

Can you please do some more shopping for me, there being no shops here; it is a bit difficult. I want one sleeveless pullover with a low neck in grey or other colour such as light blue, no mixtures. Forsyths is the place to get it. I wear them all day here as it is never too hot.

British Somaliland via Aden, 2 January 1930

Many thanks for the citrus book. It is just the thing I wanted and will prove very useful. I have already found two diseases and administered ashes and dried blood to the trees on its recommendation. Can you look up your Nicholson and see what a tree tomato becomes as we have some plants but can't find out what they do. So far mine has reached 5ft but no hint of flowers.

We have had an awful week. The Governor, Sir Harold Kittermaster, and his Lady came back with the Parks on Saturday. He was in the NFP for many years so we have much in common but he is not the colonial type at all. He comes of a schoolmastering family and was one. He has a good opinion of ex-regular officers as DCs which is one good point and is trying to get more of us out. I entertained them to dinner the first night here so as to get the show over. I have had to attend numerous official meals with them where Empire Hock is the staple drink with an alternative of McNeish's Choice Whisky: a couple of fouler drinks can't be imagined. We did get inferior Champagne out of him on Hogmanay but then the demand far exceeded the supply. He is here inspecting for ten days.

I hear my guns are at last on the road for Nairobi and good reports come in of the Jumbos; seven or eight are reported but no big tuskers at all, however three small ones might equal one big one and the licence costs nothing.

British Somaliland via Aden, 11 January 1930

We have had an awful week. The Officer (Captain Fuller Brown) in charge of the Camel Corps here who I knew well was ill with fever at the beginning of the week but developed DT's on Tuesday. We took turns nursing him day and night but he was raving mad, seeing all sorts of people and catching flies that weren't there. We had a fearful time but he calmed down a bit on Wednesday and died on Thursday night. We had to be undertakers and pall bearers and everything and they of course forgot to put the coffin on the lorry coming up so we had to send him through by night to be buried in the European Cemetery at Sheikh where the seat of Government is. Africa certainly offers a variety but I don't want to do night nurse or undertaker to a DT patient again.

The Governor left on Tuesday and we were all heartily thankful when he left and it was a great relief. The DT patient by day and night as well as His Excellency [HE] was too much of a good thing.

I gather I am to be moved to somewhere down on the Italian Border as my French and something of Italian have already been useful in interpreting telegrams they have sent round to me.

British Somaliland via Aden, 18 January 1930

We are settling down again after the events of last week and the Officer who is to administer the bloke's estate has come up to settle things up as it is an expensive business to die of DT's these days. I gather they will have a job to square the bills out here. I bought up some of the stores. They can't get the bungalow where the fellow died right. They have burnt all the bedding and fumigated it but it is still uninhabitable. They are reduced to lime washing with carbolic so that it smells like a cattle truck.

We spent a very busy afternoon on Sunday grafting and budding some Washington navel oranges onto lime stocks in my orchard. If it is successful we shall try with grapefruit. We got the idea from the citrus book and the oranges were in the Director of Agriculture's garden. As he is on leave, the acting Director who is usually the Chief Veterinary Officer was distributing the contents for '*Buono publico*'. We are awaiting the results of our budding and grafting anxiously.

A new Camel Corps Officer has come out, one Skeen in the Berkshire regiment. His family comes from Aberdeenshire. He is a bit young and innocent looking for the colonies and he doesn't look as if he would follow in his predecessor's footsteps and die of drink. [In 1965 he was High Commissioner for Rhodesia in London.] They change even more than the KAR.

Even this Colony is getting about £30,000 out of the Empire Development schemes but they are making a water survey first; another expert I suppose coming out to look round. We already have oil experts prowling round the colony.

I have been pestered with Italian notes to translate for the Government. I have pointed out that I only speak traveller's Italian but it won't stop them. I am however asking for a grant from the colony to study Italian when on leave so that I then know where I am, as at present I told them I won't be responsible for mistakes et cetera, as I treat it as purely unofficial.

I have been pretty busy in the courts; a lot of claims, for camels et cetera coming upon the drought of the last two years, has brought on all the thefts.

I hear that all the ex-soldiers like myself have got very much better terms from the Government than the unfortunates who came here direct; one who has been here nearly two years is always bound to get less pay than we do.

Sambo, the Ethiopian Consul, has gone on holiday; not overwork but sheer boredom I gather.

We can never get anything done as I gather this Lake Tana question is still cropping up and we dare not use threats because we are still after the concession. We have been trying to get it for twenty-two years and meanwhile our subjects get robbed and murdered at will by the Habash and we daren't say anything because of it. [It was a dispute about constructing a barrage on Lake Tana in Abyssinia which would help control the flow of the Nile.] I gather there is a conference on in Paris about it.

British Somaliland via Aden, 30 January 1930

We had a sudden downpour of rain on Friday last and I was across at the Camel Corps, the other side of the river bed, when all of a sudden the river came down and we couldn't get across till eleven at night. We had very little rain but later on it came down in torrents and the next day was very bad, the river running hard. It has rained every day since, excellent for the garden and lime orchard; some of our grafts ought to be coming on. Actually my orchard was a stream, a foot deep, during the torrential rains last week but it did no harm in fact quite a lot of good. We had 3ins in a week.

We are taking advantage of the rain and are planting out a lot of trees in front of my house and all down the road to the DC's bungalow. We have over a hundred; mostly tropical sorts from Australia. Later we hope to plant marshy spots with gum trees as they mop up water like a sponge.

There are no signs of our friend Sambo, the Abyssinan Consul, coming back yet. We hear he is having a row with an official over the border. The Abyssinian Government had a punitive patrol against some people on the northern end of the border; they killed and burnt everything. 111 men, women and children were shot regardless of who or what they were.

I heard from Hughes in Meru last week. The KAR has all been reorganised and cut down and is all cars now, no safari. Those who knew the old days are very bitter about it. Wajir is the only detchment. He says they have had record rains there as well and everything is out of joint as a result. They have wireless now all round so things are not so bad.

British Somaliland via Aden, 8 February 1930

Many thanks for the decanter which I seem to recognise as having held ammonia in the bathroom in times gone by. It is excellent for its purpose.

You seem to have got hold of the wrong end of the stick; I don't touch whisky out here. I drink the wine I got from Uncle Hubert [who was a wine merchant in England]. My friends drink all the whisky but the consumption has fallen off a bit since one died of DT's called in his obituary notice 'Illness contracted on Service'.

I got twenty-five coffee trees for my orchard last week; Government pays of course and over 200 were sold to natives in the town. We got them from Abyssinia.

The Abyssinian Dollar has dropped so silver is now dirt cheap and I have had bowls like finger bowls but larger for flowers made in Abyssinia out of plain silver for under 10s each. They look very well on the table.

Many thanks for your offer of a birthday present. What I would like are two candlesticks for the dining table with shades complete; something to go with my silver and a white tablecloth (wood or painted ones) but you know best and can try on a table and see but it must go with silver. Another choice would be a plated sugar basin of the small Traprain bowl; the size for coffee or lump sugar complete with tongs. [Sandy's father had found this marvellous hoard of roman silver on Traprain Law near Edinburgh, which was and still is on view in the museum in Edinburgh. Sandy's father was presented with silver replicas of some of the items.] I think my stuff is almost complete as regards furnishings.

British Somaliland via Aden, 15 February 1930

Many thanks for your letter. I hope you enjoyed your trip to Paris and got some bargains. [His father was a great collector of objets d'art.]

Locusts are hanging about again but not hoppers only the big ones but they do quite a lot of damage to young shoots on lime. We have piles of grass ready to light and smoke them off when the swarm comes.

Our only news is the wireless press; it is a sort of government propaganda. The last fourteen days we have had nothing but the naval conference and not a bit of other news. [The conference was between Britain, the US, France, Italy and Japan and was aimed at controlling the arms race.]

British Somaliland via Aden, 20 February 1930

Please ask Doig and Wheatley to keep their eyes open for any Snaffles pictures of the Regiment.

Many thanks indeed for the ten Anatole France novels [Anatole France was the pseudonym for Jacques-Anatole Francois Thibault (1844–1924) who was a well-known French writer]; they will be excellent for reading when I am out shooting in the next two weeks. As there are now three of us here I saw no use in staying in so put in for fourteen days' leave to go after elephant. My scouts came back today to report that there are five of them, all very small tuskers, but as the licence costs only £5 no matter what the size, I won't lose money on it. They are about two and a half days out. It will be a nice change at least.

We had a visit from the itinerant Parson from Addis Ababa, Church of England. [Reverend Padre Mathew, still in Addis in the 1960s, aged over eighty]. He comes once every five years or so round here. We had a service in the DC's drawing room, seven of us. The singing was lead by the Postmaster on leave from Berbera, very Glasgow. He said 'One, two, three' and off we went. He broke down in the middle of one hymn, covered his mouth with his hand and said 'Oh pardon me' in a good Glasgow accent. I fear I nearly collapsed.

I hear locusts are reported about again in large numbers. We daily expect a visitation of the hoppers.

No one knows where one will go. Every station has now three people and no one is due to go on leave till April or March.

It is heating up a bit now but nothing much; well under 100° and still almost cold at night.

British Somaliland via Aden, 26 February 1930

I got out on Saturday for my fourteen days shooting. I am at present following up the spoor up a rocky valley; nice country, plenty of good water and very stony. A change from the flat NFD; easier country to hunt in and not so hot and the hills make all the difference. I have been on the track of the jumbos for the last three days and hope to catch up with them tomorrow. Not much game about on the whole; have shot enough for meat and concentrating on the pachyderms. If I get the jumbo I will go after kudu next, then lion. I have got the best guide in the country out with me.

I am lucky to be out of the army these days; pay shows no improvement and in fact it is cut down again while ours is increasing annually.

Mail has just got in having come by runner and I am just scribbling this to send it back with him.

Many thanks for the Spectators; three arrived just now.

British Somaliland via Aden, 21 March 1930

I am sorry you should think I was pulling your leg about my bungalow; it is really the ADC's bungalow Hargesia and the photo is not faked. You would get a surprise if you saw the gardens here; it is not the Africa of fiction at all.

The rains are breaking as I write; a better year hasn't been known for years; rain in November, January, February and March of course usually produces the long rains. We are busy planting out pepper trees for avenues in the town; hundreds of them. [Sandy saw them last in 1956 and they were doing well.] We got most of them in in time. We dig deep holes, 4ft across and 4ft deep and put in manure and ashes and that gives the tree a good start off. We also have to build roads about the Station and engineer culverts to carry off the surface water. I do all the outside works, running the vegetable gardens et cetera. Last week the ADC was down with a septic throat so I was back at the office for part of the day.

The staff of the Abyssinian Consulate here are beginning to desert; no pay I suppose. We are all surprised they stayed so long. We expect the Consul himself will be the next to go.

They are embarking on a great water scheme in the country in September; £15,000 has been voted from the Colonial Development Fund and boring machines et cetera are coming out and the works are to take two years. The wells where people draw water with tins will be replaced with pumps.There is a party oil prospecting now and has been at it for the last two years so they must have found something and it may be a year or two before it is developed. Many thanks for getting the seeds for me; there's nothing like trying these things; we may strike a winner. The soil is very full of lime but the alluvial part near the river is where we would try the azaleas.

Can you look out for a suitable bottle for me to use as a gin decanter; also any wooden candle sticks or small house furniture which can be easily moved about which you may come across.

Please thank Jane for sending the butter making affairs; they are in use and a great success.

British Somaliland via Aden, 28 March 1930

Still no further news about my future but it seems fairly certain that I will go to Jijiga, Abyssinia, as Her Britannic Majesty's Acting Vice Consul while the present fellow is on leave. It is worth about £30 extra pay to me and I have to spend all my time on trek, but I am expected to confine my activities to the district along our border. Harar is about four days off and there is a Consul there and a large trading centre and town. I would be under the Foreign Office for the time being.

The Abyssinian dollar has fallen with a fearful crash and is down to just over a shilling instead of nearly three. A lot of merchants have gone bust.

British Somaliland via Aden, 20 April 1930

Many thanks indeed for the candlesticks; they are a very nice shape indeed and I am very proud of them. They will improve my table no end.

I am still at Hargesia waiting for my appointment as Border Consul to be approved by the Foreign Office and for my passes to come from Addis Ababa. I have also heard that I have a chance of getting it permanently.

A German Doctor came through this week from Addis Ababa en route for Jijiga; he was most amusing on the subject of Abyssinia. He had been three months in Addis and they would give him nothing to do and when he asked for his pay they said there was no money in the treasury. They have quite a number of European Officers, Doctors et cetera simply as eyewash to the League of Nations. They don't use them or pay any attention to them at all. The Hun had been called in to prescribe for an Abyssinian and when the Doctor gave him the medicine he made the Doc take a sample of it just to prove it was not poison. What a time a panel Doctor would have. The Empress sent for a European Doctor before she died and when he had prescribed for her she told him 'Of course I don't propose to follow your advice; my Priest here is better'; so she called the Priest who told her to take a hot bath with charms and herbs in it. The Empress did and died in it.

The long dry season has ended early with record rains. We even had hail last week which smashed windows and went through cabbage leaves like bullets. As a result all the natives are well fed with milk and the usual fight has started. Some Police got blotted out in the neighbouring district but it won't affect us.

We are at present having Easter Holidays; four days with nothing to do. We spend most mornings superintending the vegetable garden.

CHAPTER 6

Consul in Abyssinia, 1930–2

British Somaliland via Aden, 24 April 1930

I go off to Jijiga tomorrow to take over and meet the British Minister from Addis Ababa there, Sir Sidney Barton. I then spend four days there and come back to Hargesia with him where we meet our own Governor and we have some sort of conference with distinguished Abyssinians who come as well. I then return to Jijiga and carry on. I have not got my pass from the Emperor but will get my visa from Sambo, our tame Consul here.

My address is Berbera as my mail is sent up by car or runner to Jijiga. I am under the Minister in Addis Ababa and the Foreign Office lent by Somaliland and paid by Somaliland. My pay is £700 a year and £30 allowance and 6–8s every day I am on trek. I am answering for the proper Consul while he is away on leave. He has reached his maximum salary here and is waiting for the Consul at Harar to get promotion. I, having the experience, was more or less told I would get the job here when he goes. My work will be all frontier and very little consular. I shall have to write all my own dispatches; no clerk and I shall have an Abyssinian interpreter and a Somali one.

Let me know if you want anything for the museum from Abyssinia. Sorry this is so short but I am rather rushed. Future mails will probably be irregular. Keep any stamps from Abyssinian letters.

British Vice Consulate, Jijiga, Abyssinia, 1 May 1930

I motored here last week by lorry. It took five hours to cover the 92 miles. There was a road as far as Tug Wajale and then you just struck out across the plains. On the vast plain you could not fail to find Jijiga. I was only the second person to do it.

The Consulate is at present pitched in tents outside the town. I am comfortably installed and can have all my silver et cetera out. The Vice-Consulate tent is a large European Personnel Indian pattern one with high bamboo supported walls, yellow lining and blue striped *dhurrie* [flat woven cotton rug made in

India] on the floor. This serves as a living and dining room. A 10ft square, double fly Swiss Cottage tent is the bedroom. It has a bathroom at the end. The office is in a square Staff Sergeant's tent with high walls. The servants and Somaliland Police Guard are in small tents.

The Consulate is sited some 500yds from the town which consists of only a conglomeration of single storied stone houses and mud built shacks. Nearby are the pits which hold the grain collected by the government as tax. It is then doled out as part of the pay to government employees.

My job is to look after the interests of the British subjects including British protected Somalis and the tribes who bring their herds over here in order to graze in accordance with the trans-frontier rights granted them under the 1897 Anglo-Ethiopian Treaty. There are a few British Indians trading in the town in cotton goods and general merchandise. The leading one, Messrs Mohamedaly, has branches in the principal towns of Abyssinia. Their managers act as president of the local British Tribunal in each town and settle complaints between British subjects. [Sandy was able to help the manager in 1936 and in 1940 when in both cases he was a refugee from Jijiga].

There is no passport work and the minimum of office routine.There does not seem to be much to do but the present bloke who I am relieving is so pompous that he thinks it is infra dig to go into a shop but otherwise a very nice fellow.

I have paid my various calls on the local Governor [*Fitaurari* Tafassa Hapte Mikael]. He has been selected by Ras Tafari [the Regent] as one of the younger modern minded men who are loyal to him. The idea is that he should improve the administration of the Abyssinia-British Somaliland border. [No doubt the increasingly belligerent attitude of the Italians in the Ogaden needed attention]. There are two Swiss Officers who are training the soldiers and then the German Doctor.

I have been initiated into the slow working of Abyssinian Justice; you see the debtor and creditor chained together till they settle their case.

The whole show is very primitive and rather amusing. As I have to spend most of my time dealing with Abyssinian Officials I should imagine they will try my temper a bit. They are a far more sophisticated lot than on the Kenya frontier.

The Minister from Addis Ababa arrives tomorrow and is to be met with great ceremony. We all dine in the evening with the *Fitaurari* [the Governor]; I shall imagine a fearful banquet. The next night we entertain the *Fitaurari* and my silver will come in most useful. On Monday we all go back to Hargesia and I stay a day or so there for a conference and then come back here. I am trying to get this job permanently as there is a house being built and it will be an excellent station.

British Vice Consulate, Jijiga, Abyssinia, 18 May 1930

The *Fitaurari* left for Addis last week for a week but that means a month at least. The whole town turned out to see him off and the French Consul gave him a lift so far in his Citroen caterpillar. The bloke who is answering for him at once started tricks and never answered one of my letters so I wrote and told him I was sorry I didn't realize he couldn't write so could he come up and saw me; this drew him well and he replied that he hadn't heard that I was officially here and couldn't correspond with me so I told him it was useless for me to stay here as I could do nothing so was off to Aw Boba; the last place they want me in. [Aw Boba was in the Ogaden region of Abyssinia where the tribespeople were predominately Somali and notoriously unruly. The Amharas were never happy about foreigners travelling there, nor did they like going there themselves – it was just so different from their own highland country]. The *Fitaurari* continues to correspond with me by wire from places on his journey.

The Swiss Officers are still here; they are not going out. The Captain is a Professor of psychology at Lausanne in civil life and the Adjutant an electrician. [The Professor once told Sandy that after studying him he noticed that the British had an in-built natural command of men which the Swiss did not have. Perhaps it was Sandy's military training. The electrician had previously been employed putting electric lights into houses of ill-repute in Paris.] The Abyssinian Government has issued the Captain with a British Trooper's Cavalry Sword while the Adjutant (an NCO) has a French Officer's. They have had no pay since February. [They were the first foreign military advisers selected by Ras Tafari to instruct the feudal soldiers to handle frontier incidents and to form the nucleus of a standing army.] The local soldiers, sent for training, have a fine assortment of arms; eight different sorts including a hammer American rifle. The unfortunate Swiss who are instructing cannot carry on with musketry when such an assortment of ammunition is needed.

Oscar, the German Doctor, is a most amusing card; he is a typical Hun and a keen sportsman. He makes a wonderful figure in a pair of atrocious dark green breeches stalking a pigeon. His ceremonial kit is a morning coat which does not fit in the least; I should think pre-war. He has got the Iron Cross, 2nd class.

A French Count de Roquefeuil arrived last week; a typical seedy adventurer who has been all over the world. He was lost for a time and we had to look for him but he turned up all right. He has a mica mine near here and he is the real wrong un. The Count's dual purpose Lady Secretary arrived in an aeroplane to look for him. His Secretary's son by a former marriage acts as a resident engineer in the mica mine and is a music hall artist and cabaret singer. [The Count de Roquefeuil and his secretary were found to be Italian Agents and were deported from Ethiopia in 1934.] He is wonderful as an after dinner performer. There is also an alcoholic looking Swiss waiting for a pass to shoot elephants; a real bad one I think and a renegade poacher.

There is a Roman Catholic Mission here where the majority of the priests and nuns come from Malta. The head of the mission is the brother of the Prime Minister of Malta. He shows distinct leanings to fascism. [In 1934 he was caught red-handed sending information to the Italian Consul and was deported by the Abyssinians].

Our village Post Office rivals Drumsheugh easily [his father's local post office in Edinburgh]; they only occasionally sell stamps when they remember to get them. For three months they never changed the date on the stamp, from March to June it was the same. The Harar mail got put in the wrong bag and went to Port Said and the Port Said mail was put in the Addis Ababa bag; what a land. The man in charge is always drunk and asks you why you didn't send an answer to a wire you had on Tuesday for example and your boy will probably be able to tell you about a wire which has come for you before you get it. The mails are so unreliable that we register all letters.

We have two Greek wine shops in the town which specialise in 'Kanick', a type of wine which would interest Uncle Hubert.

It is really a most amusing job but having to type all your own dispatches is a bit of a trial. My Abyssinian interpreter writes my letters to Abyssinian officials. One certainly deserves to be well paid as they are trying people to deal with.

While one walks down the town, people bow low at you and almost touch the ground with their hats; it seems a poor reply to such a gesture to merely touch your hat as we do.

Most of the trouble here is caused by Somali renegades who stir up trouble against the British tribes. The Abyssinians listen to them and pay attention to what they say while we disown them.

I have got Oscar, the Hun Doctor, and one of the *deux petit Suisses* coming to dinner tonight.

The climate is excellent here; about the nicest I have struck in Africa. It is a little windy in a tent.

British Vice Consulate, Jijiga, Abyssinia, 6 June 1930

I got back at the beginning of the week having had a very interesting trip. I just got down to Aw Boba in time to stop a war. Aw Boba is on the frontier and some of our tribes have hit up the Abyssinians. [The forthcoming coronation of Ras Tafari had resulted in a wave of enthusiastic tax collecting on the part of his subordinates. Two Abyssinian soldiers who were collecting taxes were killed by local tribesmen.] I also had a look round the old ruined city there which was most interesting. [The ruined town was one of a group of thirteen each side of the Abyssinia-British Somaliland border. Later on Sandy had the opportunity to do a more thorough investigation]. There were no roads and we followed camel tracks. After leaving Jijiga one crosses flat plains with occasional rocky hills; on these hills are little villages with round huts surrounded by walls. They grow millet, maize, barley and wheat. After 20 miles of this we got into the hills; very rough and rocky indeed and very cold, down to 40° in the early morning. I did one march with the local Ethiopian headman, a *Balambaras*; he is a soldier of sorts; a local Lieutenant I should think and we progressed surrounded by his blackguardly soldiers running with us armed with an assortment of firearms. We were mounted but they had to keep up on foot. They live by looting on the land. [Sandy crossed over to Borama in British Somaliland to discuss the situation with the DC and warn him of the possibility of Abyssinian tax gatherers crossing into British territory. Calm was restored on both sides of the border.]

There was no game at all up the direction I was last time but I hear that there is plenty down the Ogaden where I am going this time.

The French Count with his outfit has cleared out and everyone is pleased to have seen the last of him. The local natives threatened to kill him so he cleared off. Oscar, the Hun Doctor, and the Swiss Officers are still here.

I must pack up and get ready to be going out. I am glad I have no longer to sit in a court; for the time being I only have to hold one with the Abyssinian *Fitaurari* once a month.

I have put in for the Consulate at Mega on the Kenya border which is vacant. I don't expect to get it at all but they can but say no. I have put in through the British Minister in Addis; also through the Governor of Somaliland. It is worth £900 a year.

I have started a garden in front of my tent. I have got some seed boxes going as well with some of the seeds you sent; for which many thanks. I am getting some plants from Hargesia.

I am getting out a wireless listening-in set and hope to hear Nairobi; have got expert advice on it from the Berbera wireless expert.

I have sent three rolls of film off to you. Can you please get them developed; two copies of each and three of any with any groups.

You won't hear from me for about three weeks.

British Vice Consulate, Jijiga, Abyssinia, 1 July 1930

I have found three letters awaiting me. Many congratulations on the CVO. I hope it will next be a K. I think there is a Courtier's suit in the attic; little Lord Fontleroy; you might get it dyed for the investiture. I am sorry I am not at home for the rejoicings. [This would have been in recognition of his work as Director of the Royal Scottish Museum.]

As soon as I got back from my last trip I found that the Ogaden people had raided our British Protected tribes who were grazing their flocks in Abyssinia so I had to rush off down there; Milmil and Dagghabur on the maps. I had to try and goad the local authorities into action. They always say that of course the trouble was in the next district; so I produce pen and paper and ask them to put it in writing. They will never give a decision if they can avoid it.

I left here on 8 June with camels. It was a six day camel march. Owing to my staff being ill with fever, I had to delay a day. I went down the west side of the Jerer River. The first day out it poured and the mud was awful but we passed through 10 miles of maize and millet fields. Next day it was a dull journey through thick bush; mosquitoes all day long. At about 8.00 pm as I was getting into bed the interpreter rushed up in a frantic state and said we were surrounded and about to be attacked. I told him not to be an ass but he was right. Some Ogaden Somalis had surrounded us but the sentry had spotted them and at the commotion in the camp they cleared off only to appear at odd intervals during the night but did nothing. We saw their tracks in the morning. They mistook me for a trader I think and meant to loot only. The next trouble was that half my men went down with fever and I ran out of quinine. I as usual escaped.

On the road I met the *Balambaras* in charge of the town of Dagghabur. Having heard I was coming he had cleared off away from the place; that made me suspicious at once. I duly arrived there at Dagghabur. I was given sheep and grass for my ponies. There are only about twelve Abyssinians there and they are afraid to venture outside the town. I made inquiries and found that the recent raid against our tribes had started with eighty men from the town itself; they had gone 60 miles and looted 1,500 camels, killed 2 men and wounded 4 and yet the Abyssinian Officials told me they had heard nothing about it at all.

I then went to Gagab and on to Awareh. On the way I was subjected to a close inspection by all the women and children as the country there is unadministered and no Europeans ever go there. They came to my camp to look at the European. My shaving was a source of much inquisitive interest. At Awareh we found a large lake with Egyptian geese on it. The British tribes came in to see me and water their stock. I spent four days there and returned to Dagghabur via Dusle Milmil and Sheik Hussein.

I was met on my way back by an escort of soldiery; they run all round and are a beastly nuisance. They get $7 a month here and some 100lbs of grain; the dollar is now worth about 1s; of course they live on the land and hence are more trouble than they are worth. I have two police of my own who escort me out; the officials were afraid that I would get shot up and they would be responsible.

As soon as I got back yesterday, the *Balambaras*, who had been sent down from Jijiga to inquire about the raid, came to see me and told me that the night before he left Dagghabur he had handed over as prisoner the man whose name I had given him. He was given to the town official to guard and when he sent for him in the morning to be brought here he had escaped; and as he remarked, he had escaped from eight soldiers and he was chained and locked up. Of course the Dagghabur town officials had let him go fearing further disclosures. What a Country it is. I wrote to the man in charge here asking for the arrest of the Dagghabur Official; my interpreter chased all over the town only to come back with the letter to say that the acting Governor had that morning taken medicine for his tapeworm and had hidden himself for two days. What a comic opera country it all is. It has to be lived in to believe it.

With the Swiss Officers and the German Doctor we have a very cheery party here in Jijiga. As they are employed by the Abyssinians, they envy me here being able to say what I like to them.

I may have to go up to Addis which will be an interesting trip about this raid but I don't know yet. I will probably go to Harar in the middle of the month to visit the Consul there.

British Vice Consulate, Jijiga, Abyssinia, 8 July 1930

I am still in Jijiga but am off tomorrow for a week's trip. The Governor is still away and the Acting Governor has twice in the last week been unable to do any business for two days as he has again been taking his worm powder; it is a truly priceless country to work in. They are getting nervous when I go out now as each time I have found things wrong so when I told them I was going out this time they said I would have to wait but I told the Governor I wasn't asking leave I was telling him I was going out; it is the only way to treat them.

On 1 August the Swiss Officers are having a dinner for their national fete and we have arranged to have all the eminent Abyssinians and are solemnly going to drink the health of King Oscar 7th of Switzerland coupled with that of the future Emperor Haile Selassie 1st, the Swiss Army and Navy.

Trade is going ahead here; two Arabian ones added themselves to my flock of subjects last week.

I have been having tea parties for all the leading Abyssinians; the Chief of Customs who is covered in foul scent and wears button boots and the Provost, who has an all black suit and suffers from being a little educated but not enough.

My garden is going on well. I have tried some of the seeds but they are not a success. I can't supervise them properly when I am out.

British Vice Consulate, Jijiga, Abyssinia, 17 July 1930

I have just got back from a short trip to the Harawa Valley, 30 miles due north from here. The Acting Governor who is a clerk at $35 a month refused to let me go but I told him I never asked his leave and just went. He didn't know what to do. He also refused to allow all Europeans to go out of the town but he forgot the Swiss in Abyssinian Government Service; they could not go to parade for two days but they didn't mind. In the end they sent and told the Acting Governor that they were packing up their kits and going to Europe; he came and bowed and apologized to them and said it was all a mistake.

The *Fitaurari* came back from Addis this week. He has hopes to install a school of aviation on the plain, 200yds from my tent. A French pilot [N. Videl] is to train three young Abyssinians to fly before the coronation on 2 November; an excellent idea but rather too near my tent to be comfortable. I am sorry for the Frenchmen; my only hope is that they will bring only one plane and it will crash before long. Any native is bad with a pram far less an aeroplane. We are anxious to see what the French pilot will be like and his mechanic as we have a very happy society. [The actual idea for the school came from the Regent, Ras Tafari, who foresaw the future for aviation. The vast plains round Jijiga provided a natural landing ground. This was the start of the Ethiopian Air Force.]

The *Fitaurari* is recruiting 500 soldiers who are being trained by the Swiss; they are to follow him in the coronation procession on 2 November. He obviously thinks this following will increase his prestige in the feudal hierarchy. He wants to have the Swiss leading his troops but they have refused point blank to go.

I am off at the end of this week with the *Fitaurari* to Borama for a Conference; then I return and go to Harar to stay with the Consul there and hope to go to the Ogaden Country from there.

We have been promised all sorts of things as a result of my revelations at Dagghabur; 300 soldiers with 4 machine guns, roads and telephones but you don't pay any attention till you see the goods delivered so to speak.

I may have told you I sent over a dozen different sorts of seeds to the Botanical Gardens some time ago; I hope some of them come up.

British Vice Consulate, Jijiga, Abyssinia, 24 July 1930

Many thanks for your letter; the photos came alright and I have given copies to the victims.

I have been trying to get out for the last week with the *Fitaurari* to the Borama area; he promised the Minister to visit the area but needless to say he has found a 101 excuses and when I had finally arranged a day he sent up a message to say that as his wife expected to be confined shortly he had to stay at home. When I said surely your Excellency has some idea of the approximate date he replied that she had forgotten how to count. Really these Abyssinians are impossible to deal with.

Our aerodrome started by the arrival on Saturday of a plane, a Fiat Moth; a French commercial pilot brought it; not a very nice type; he has been in Addis Ababa two months and thinks he knows all about the land. He has gone to bring another plane from Dire Dawa and then he commences his instruction. One of his pupils is a pure bred Abyssinian, the other a half-caste, Russian-Abyssinian [Micha Babichef who became a fighter pilot in the French Air Force in 1940]; his father was one of the notorious Russian renegrades under Melileter.

I had tea with one of the Judges in his mud house the other day. He produced Dubonnet and biscuits but the mural decoration consisted of two finished Singer Sewing machine calendars 1927 and a BDV cigarette advert. Bugs are the danger when calling. I have got some 'Keatings' which I cover myself with first as a deterrent.

The dollar has fallen to under 1s so things are cheap here; a horse costs about £2 so I bought a couple of horses last week to mount my staff on; £2 a pair at present exchange.

Very cold here now; in the town they get as much as forty days with frost a year according to the mission records.

Borama, British Somaliland, 1 August 1930

I got a letter last Saturday from the Governor asking me to go down to Hargesia to see him and discuss matters; so I got in a car the next day and went through. My investigations at Dagghabur have bucked things up and we are claiming a lump sum compensation from the Habash. I then came through here with him as we had to discuss matters. At both places the Chiefs asked me to stay on as Consul as they said the proper fellow never did anything; don't know what will happen about it.

The Dollar has fallen to nearly 9p from 3s and as all the stuff for the Coronation has to be imported and three Princes are coming, it is quite on the cards that the country will go bust and civil war break out again.

I am due home in October about 23rd or 26th and have three months but I may be kept back to do ADC to the Governor if the Duke of Gloucester comes here after the Ethiopian Coronation [the coronation of Emperor Haile Selassie on 2 November].

Borama, British Somaliland, 10 September 1930

Many thanks for your letters from Norway. I got two this week.

We have had a most annoying time going on with another frontier incident. The DC Borama followed up a tax gathering party of Abyssinians who had strayed well into what was recognised as British Somaliland and shot at them. The boundary is not demarcated and it is hopeless to say who was where. We had no casualties at all but three Abyssinians are known to have been killed and four were taken prisoner. In addition one was wounded and another is missing and was probably killed, but they claim also that fifteen Somalis were killed; however we have proved their list to be false since one man was alive in our camp and eight others were known to have been buried in the last year. When we visited the scene of the fight they pointed out to us nineteen places where there were blood marks and they claimed that each of those places was the death scene of a man; some of course were traces of wounded horses et cetera but they stoutly maintained that each place was where a man was killed. They said seriously that since there were no casualties on our side, their men were well disciplined! Soldiers had stood calmly still awaiting orders to fire but not doing so while they were murdered like cattle for a sacrifice by the DC, all for the sake of a few pieces of cloth.

I spent yesterday riding for eleven hours with the Abyssinian Consul round the villages, tax gathering and looting. [It was the Abyssinian Consul who was doing the looting.] We covered 26 miles and I came on here this morning. I will get back to Jijiga in time to hand over to the proper Consul a real good collection of troubles.

I gather I am to be bothered at home about this fight and the Boundary Commission Affairs as I know all the ground. I have been out thirty days on end; as it is worth 5s a day I don't mind. I pay my bills out of my allowances.

I don't know when I will arrive home; I expect to spend some time on the way but still sail on 15 October from Aden. I was asked up to Addis Ababa for the coronation to stay with the Consul, Andrew Chapman-Andrews, but I will be at home at the time.

Later

Just a line to let you know I am alive and set sail with Lady Kittermaster, Governor's wife, in tow on Monday from Berbera so this will get to you after I have landed at Marseilles. I had been asked to go on the same P and O as her as she had had a miscarriage in Somaliland.

Sandy felt that after his life at Jijiga, it was going from the sublime to the ridiculous escorting the Governor's wife back to Britain.

Whereas he had been continually on safari around his district and had stirred the Abyssinians into action, his predecessor had not ventured out so far. Sandy's investigative trips were greatly appreciated by the British Protected Persons who were grazing their flocks in Abyssinia. It gave them a sense of being looked after and gave him a unique knowledge of the Ogaden which was to prove most useful in future years.

But Sandy had greatly enjoyed his time at Jijiga and he had made the most of it. He felt that he had been incredibly lucky as a 'Junior Administrative Officer on Probation' to get such a job. He thrived in the close-knit community represented by British, French, German and Swiss to which he returned after his safaris, the experience standing him in good stead in later years when dealing with foreigners and Ethiopians. It was a far cry from the Edinburgh of his youth.

There is a gap in the letters from the end of 1930 until June 1932. During that time Sandy was employed as Assistant District Officer (ADO) at Burao and Hargesia. It was dull routine work and none of the letters have survived. In the meantime he had married Frances.

In 1932, Sandy was acting Consul in Harar. In the interval the new Emperor Haile Selassie had been crowned in November 1930, from which point Abyssinia started to be more universally known as Ethiopia by the outside world. Ethiopia had indeed always been its proper name.

British Consulate, Harar, Ethiopia, 24 May 1932

I had a very comfortable voyage out with various friends who were in the regiment on board; got to Aden and found the coasting steamer commanded by an old friend who comes from Inverness and was also Captain of the *Cetrina*, the one that sank off Kismayu in 1923. I got orders at Berbera that I was for Harar till December and I had to go up via Hargesia and Jijiga. I gather the pay is £800 and allowances which are quite good and all my stores and things are duty free. I got Gin my old dog back at Berbera.

I spent a week at Hargesia and stayed at the rest house. I collected my staff and hired some thirty baggage camels which I sent off with my kit to Jijiga. I travelled by lorry to Jijiga where I found my camels waiting for me and my tent was up. I had to call on the local potentate and drink sweet champagne and then he called on me in return. I am relieved to find that under the Foreign Office, champagne is debited to the Government; it is such foul stuff that no one would drink it of their own free will. It is referred to in the Consular Budget under the heading 'Presents to Chiefs'. From Jijiga I rode my pony in company with the camels through rotten country. The road lies through Fiyambiro and gradually enters hilly and mountainous country with small coffee plantations and terraced hillsides like Italy. The road is awfully like the bed of a burn, across the face of cliffs and down precipices. It is almost incredible how beasts manage to get along. The high plateau of Mount Kundudo is allegedly the haunt of wild horses. It rained the last day and some of my wooden camel boxes from the Army and Navy stores were 6ins deep in the water. My Cargilfield brown school trunk which I have used ever since is still watertight. I really have never seen such a test for these boxes but they had all stood up to it. I of course had breakages through falls and lost seven bottles of stuff and an early morning tea set which I will claim insurance for.

Harar is an ancient walled town with narrow streets. All the rubbish is emptied outside the walls round which we have to pass. [Probably founded in the twelfth century by Arabs from across the water, its present walls date from the sixteenth century. It is a major centre for Muslims in Ethiopia. As Evelyn Waugh wrote: 'Even in 1935 after a generation of Abyssinian misrule and Indian and Levantine immigration, it retained something of the gracious fragrances of Fez or Meknes.'] The five town gates are closed at night and guarded by part time soldierly who sit by a lighted fire in the gateway. There is a tree close to one of the gates where condemned murderers are suspended from a branch while seated on a mule. The mule is whacked on its buttocks whereupon it moves forwards and the condemned man is left hanging. The body has to remain for a certain number of hours to serve as a visual deterrent to others before the relative can take it for burial.

Our altitude is 6,400ft, quite high enough, and the climate is excellent; never very hot. The Consulate is well above the town. It has a topping garden with wonderful roses and other flowers. We have real turf and a mower. There are hedges with wild roses, lilies and all sorts of English flowers growing in them and rivers really run amid rocks; a topping country after the plains. The actual house is the reputed birthplace of the Emperor. It is a three storied building with an outside staircase. The Consulate has a sign outside the gate like a public house but we don't get many visitors, only a few sent on with letters from the Minister. I am sure Frances will love it.

Harar Consulate is a very different situation to Jijiga. It is outside the Somali area. There is far more coming and going. The British subjects and the British Protected persons consist of British Indians and Somali traders in the main with one small Bible Mission with two or three subjects in Chercher which is an outlying area. I have all the passport stuff here to do; give visas, issue passports and deal with bankruptcies but it is not as interesting as Jijiga. We get the black lists of prohibited aliens which make quite amusing reading. I have to give a reception on the King's birthday to all British subjects; tea and coffee is all they get. It is a great thing getting the experience here and I hope in time I may get the job. Harar has just been opened up to the outside world by the opening of a motor road to Dire Dawa. A British Somali living in Harar does a hire car service when the Consul wants to go to Dire Dawa. In the old walled town there is one good Greek grocer. The market is particularly colourful and picturesque. The various traders tend to have their booths together such as the silversmiths specializing in filigree work and the cloth merchants who deal in Bombay and Manchester piece goods. They sit in the open or inside shops peddling away at Singer sewing machines making up garments. There is one Armenian run hotel which is called 'Lion d'Or' which can only be described aptly in French as '*Infect*'.

There is a telephone network with lines from Addis Ababa to Harar and Jijiga. This consists of an Erksen handle-operated set deriving power from a Leclanche cell, which has to be topped up with rain water, standing on the verandah. You turn the handle and in theory you ask the operator for whoever you wish to speak with; more often than not the lines are crossed. Elephants and giraffe often break the lines and hunters steal sections to make snares. Nevertheless it does just work which is surprising considering that the line runs on short poles with almost no insulators.

The local Galla around here are an industrious lot. Bananas, sugar cane, maize, millet, red peppers and of course coffee are grown. Harar coffee is in demand by London coffee merchants for blending. Chat which is a mild narcotic is also widely grown.

I am having a very gay time with visits to my Italian and French colleagues and dinner parties at their houses. The Italian Consul and his wife here are really very nice people indeed so there will be some company. We have no Doctor here now except the leper one but there are plenty at Dire Dawa, two hours away by car. I have to call officially on all the local Ethiopians who are a better lot than the Jijiga crowd. This area used to belong to the Emperor himself before he was promoted. The town is the seat of the Provincial Government and the Governor General, Dejazmatch Gabre Mariam has his residence here [Senior Court Official or Governor].

All official calls are made on horseback. You ride down to official dinners at the *Ghebbi* [Palace]. Ladies keep an old frock for the purpose which they call their '*Ghebbi* Gown' as some of the guests are apt to chuck the bones from the banquet over their shoulders. The Consulate employs six locals as armed retainers who act as guards. It is the custom for the retainers to accompany the Consul when he goes to town or out on official business. They run in clearing the way through the crowd. At night we carry a Dietz hurricane lamp on our way out to dine.

As in Jijiga, Sandy thrived in the cosmopolitan world. It must have helped that he spoke French and Italian. Several interesting characters called by. Amongst the more colourful personages living around Harar was the adventurer, gun runner, journalist, drug smuggler and author, Henri de Monfried, who, having retired to France after his African sojourn, wrote around seventy books. His very popular novels made the Red Sea famous. Sandy was once invited round to his house. The value of de Monfried's books lay, Sandy felt, in his unrivalled knowledge of Ethiopians and their way of life. Numerous stories told by the locals were committed to paper. He subsequently bought a dozen of de Monfried's books in French. It was later that the Ethiopians became suspicious of de Monfried and impounded a small bag of white powder which was a hard drug. Two years later the Anti-Drug Chief in Egypt complained of drugs being smuggled in by de Monfried. Alas no mention is made of the poet Rimbaud who lived in Harar on and off from 1880 to 1891. The doyen of the European Harar community was the Bishop of Harar, Monseigneur Jarrouseau, who had been there since 1884 and would have known Rimbaud well.

In six weeks time I have to go down to Hargesia for a Commission on frontier raids. The object is to endeavour to settle claims between the Ethiopians and our tribes in British Somaliland regarding raids across the border. I don't mind as I get an extra 10s a day for allowances. I will go by Jibuti and meet Frances at Aden and then up to Hargesia.

British Consulate, Harar, Ethiopia, 1 June 1932

Got no letter from you last week; expect it went to Berbera.

I have spent most of the past week in bed with a chill. I got soaked camping and the local missionary who was called in said it was not malaria which was something.

On Monday night we had to go to the local *Dejazmach's* [senior court official or general] house to attend a dinner in honour of the Crown Prince's wedding. We had a grand mixture; the Italian Consul, Long (who I am relieving), a half caste Italian who is secretary to the consul, the leading Greek grocer and the Governor's private pianist. The Governor's wife dressed in a black cloak like her husband presided and never said a word. We had nine courses; six of them meat in various forms; however it was a better show than those Jijiga banquets were.

I have put all our stuff out as we have a great big drawing room to furnish and it just manages to make it seem covered.

British Consulate, Harar, Ethiopia, 7 June 1932

Had hard work this last week getting used to things. The Minister comes to stay next week. I go to Dire Dawa on Saturday and meet him there on Sunday; here on Monday and he then hears two appeal cases. He will bring his wig which will shake the court and is sure to get fleas in it as they abound here if he doesn't get a bug. I have met the Minister, Sir Sidney Barton at Jijiga.

I have been having a grand clean up here and getting shipshape for the Minister.

I had a successful King's birthday reception: Indians, Arabs, Cypriots et cetera. We drank tea and made rotten speeches and I have to send a wire off to the King through the Minister assuring him of our loyalty.

My accounts are appalling affairs; I use rupee stamps for passports et cetera. I take in money in Ethiopian Maria Theresa dollars which weigh exactly one ounce of silver. [Maria Theresa dollars, introduced in the eighteenth century, were still very much in circulation in the country areas even though the Emperor Menelik and the new Emperor Haile Selassie had introduced their own currencies.] The exchange rate to the pound varies with the international silver market. You can imagine the fun we have when variations occur.

There is no doubt things are improving here; much has been done in the last two years and the appalling obstructers who existed in high places are now replaced by sensible men who get things done.

My Ethiopian interpreter has disappeared for the day; they are an unreliable race. I shall probably find he has only taken his tapeworm medicine or some such futile excuse.

Dire Dawa, Ethiopia, 20 June 1932

We have had an awful week. Last Sunday I met the Minister, Sir Sidney Barton, at Dire Dawa which is a foul hole, fearfully hot. I came in a day before and had to attend receptions of all the British subjects: Arabs, Hindus et cetera and go into their troubles. I have a large Indian Community at Dire Dawa who are an awful nuisance; the Ghandarites won't agree with the Muslims in any case and they cause a lot of work. It was an opportunity to visit my French colleagues. There was a bad affair here when a Frenchman had his house broken into, his wife and family beaten and he was dragged by his hair through the streets. The Railway went on strike and the Abyssinian Mayor was removed.

Then Lij Yasu, who had been one of the rivals for the throne and one of the big Rasses [Ras Haylu], revolted and were out for about fourteen days. They were caught about a week ago and yesterday they brought them to near Harar as prisoners. Our proper Governor is looking after them. There was no excitement and no soldiery went from here. The Emperor's position is now secure; they will probably poison Lij Yasu soon.

The Minister stayed with me at Harar and we had a really nice time but very rushed. Anyway he said it was absurd having no clerk and ordered me to send off at once for one to Aden which will make things lighter. We had to call on all sorts of people and they called on us including the French Bishop and the *Fitaurari,* the acting Governor, who was rude to the Minister.

The Minister is a charming man. He advised me to take a course of Amharic and Economics at the London University as he said there was no one in Ethiopia or no British Official who could speak Amharic and there were openings.

British Consulate, Harar, Ethiopia, 2 July 1932

Many thanks for your letters. I have had a fearful week of work, being the end of the quarter and I am about to start off for Hargesia and Berbera.

I got back from Dire Dawa in time for our consular meeting and then found that Baron Scarramacca, the Italian Charge d'Affaires, had come down so had to do the necessary dinner. The mixed Court was on Monday and I had to spend the morning at it. The acting Governor is a terrible fellow; he at first tried the usual well known games on me such as waiting till I had arrived before he put it off and then calmly telling me to come back tomorrow. However he was the mug and I let him have it full when I got him in the court. I don't think he will try any more tricks next time; they are all like that unless you keep them up to every promise.

I dine out with the Italian Consul and his wife; they are great friends. The Consul periodically has a bust up with the Ethiopians and they don't correspond for weeks but it usually calms down. At present he is convinced that the *Fitaurari* is mad and he has not spoken or written to him for a week.

I don't know how long I will be at Hargesia; it depends on the meeting. I go to Berbera on Sunday to meet Frances and up again to Hargesia on Tuesday. I don't expect to be away for more than two months. I may go down to Italian Somaliland by car after the meeting, with Frances of course. The Minister wanted me to try.

I have a lot of bulbs for Sir Stick-in-the-mud in the Botanics. I have spent the early mornings cutting back over 40yds of rose arches but get no time off in the evenings.

A topping climate here; if I ever get permanently here I am sure you would love a trip here. It is like England every day.

Hargesia, British Somaliland, 16 July 1932

I came down in three nights along the awful road; spent two nights at Jijiga and found British subjects galore in jail. Called on the Governor, a nice helpful old man who actually did something and then came by car to Hargesia and so to Berbera which is very, very hot.

I met Frances who had had an awful crossing but was very much better and really well again; better than she had been for years. We had a bad trip up.

The Conference I am on opened today with each side standing the other sweet champagne. Mine was 'Methode Champagne'; pretty foul. We got down to business on Monday and discussed the claims between the Ethiopian Ogaden Somalis and British protected Ishaak Somalis. Very busy as I still have to do all my consular work after hours.

Hargesia, British Somaliland, 23 July 1932

Frances is much better and looking forward to getting up to Harar to a house. At present we are lodged in the rest house here; quite good shelter from the elements but lack of furniture or comforts.

We are still anchored here for this Conference and look like being here for another six weeks. The Ethiopian's lists of persons whom they had claims against was so incomplete that we have to spend our time trying to unravel the names and we won't start on the claims for another week.

My old horse died today; very sad; he was a good brute. Horse sickness caught at Harar killed him. We had to bury him 6ft down and burn him. Now my other horse is down with horse sickness but this morning they have brought better news that its temperature has dropped to normal so I hope it may get over it. The Pony Company of the Camel Corps are losing horses at the rate of one every ten days and no one knows how to cure it.

Today is the birthday of the Emperor of Ethiopia; so we have to go and drink more sweet champagne I suppose.

The Air Survey squadron of the Boundary Commission is here now. They have found the frontier to be a mile or two out on the map in favour of Ethiopia which is bad luck.

Hargesia, British Somaliland, 5 August 1932

We are still at Hargesia and look like being here for some time. The Conference still goes on; we start hearing the claims next week. The Ethiopians submitted their lists last week and they contain some fatuous claims dating back to the Mad Mullah times [end of the nineteenth century]. It is very trying work but we usually finish by 1.00pm. I have the least to do as I have no district in Somaliland like the others.

They have condemned to death all the ring leaders in the recent revolution in Ethiopia and cut off one arm and one leg but for foreign consumption have informed everyone that they flogged them instead which is untrue. The Principal leader Ras Haylu has been condemned to rigorous confinement for life and all his goods and property confiscated including a hundred watches. I will send you next week two papers with the trial of the revolutionaries in them. They will perhaps interest you and Uncle Jim

When I am finished here we go down in a truck to the Ogaden to inspect the new roads the Ethiopians have been making; a pioneer trip: Dagghabur, down the Fafen river and then to the Webbe Shebelli and Italian Somaliland.

Very interested in your excavations and hope the Stone Age levels yield some good relics.

Hargesia, British Somaliland, 9 September 1932

Many thanks for your letter and for the Sunday Times which I was glad to get. We are still stuck at Hargesia at this conference every day. We have decided 285 claims and given judgement for sums involving $131,808; another 458 cases remain to be heard. A dismal outlook and I feel we won't have long at Harar when it's over. It is most provoking to think of the lovely garden there with a comfortable house while we are stuck in tents in Hargesia for weeks. I of course get Consul's pay here and all the duty-free privileges.

We moved into tents on Sunday; we got fed up with the Rest House and being charged rent for it when we had to share it with odd travellers. We never seem to get a house to live in at all.

I hear now that Long, the Consul, is coming back to Harar so I return to Somaliland in November; don't know where we go yet. Our ranks have all been changed to DOs and ADOs; I suppose District Commissioner might have been mistaken for H.M. Commissioner.

I am pestered by people wishing to expand their overseas trade; in whisky last week, footballs this week and, as I have to do that sort of correspondence in the afternoons, one gets fed up with it. Another bright fellow, an Ethiopian, wanted to be a British subject and buy a passport. They all need answering.

Hargesia British, Somaliland, 23 September 1932

We are still at Hargesia, but our Conference is going along better now. We did over 100 cases last week. One of the claimants surprised us by coming in dressed in a black tunic with 'Motor Inspector' on the collar. He had the usual cloth round his waist and he looked absurd. We all burst out laughing.

We got thanked by the Commissioner for our work in the Conference the other day.

We have had a dozen or so mangoes sent up from Harar as a present; they are jolly good. One of the planes here went over to Aden for a day and came back with some fresh bacon for us; a nice change.

I have not had an evening off this week and am getting a bit fed up with the work. I hope to get a clerk in a week or so; they suggested I should again wait till Long came back in December but I refused to be put off and asked for one at once.

British Consulate, Harar, Ethiopia, 8 November 1932

We have had rather a rush this last few weeks. We went down to Berbera for three days fishing which we enjoyed no end. We spent every afternoon out in the boat. I caught nothing; Frances lost one as it was being landed in the boat.

We stayed with the Sheppards; he is a police officer. We came up to Hargesia and next day pushed off by car to Jijiga where I promptly fell ill with a chill or some such ailment and was laid up for two days only to find that the tent was not sunproof so I got a touch of sun as well.

They have now started a motor road to Jijiga which will connect up with Berbera and they even seem to be pushing it along quickly so we may go down by car in December.

We got to Harar on 1st November and had to attend a Coronation Celebration; a ridiculous affair at the palace, drinking sweet champagne and the doyen of our Consular Corps made a speech. On the way to the show, my Ethiopian Interpreter was arrested which somewhat cramped my style.

We have to go down to Dire Dawa tomorrow on our monthly visit along a so-called road in a car.

I think I told you we have got $53,000 out of the Ethiopians to be paid in nine months time as a result of our conference. I won't have the fun of collecting it anyway which is the great thing. There is another conference in April in Ethiopia but with any luck I will be out of it and have nothing to do with it.

There is a Swedish Mission at Harar. Frances went to call on them the other day. We are going there for a tea do on Monday.

British Consulate, Harar, Ethiopia, 25 November 1932

Many thanks for your letter. I am still at Harar and won't be leaving till about Xmas time as Long does not arrive till then. We will be sorry to leave as it is really delightful here.

I have engaged a Clerk for a couple of weeks and been able to get down to more serious things. As usual the *Fitaurari* found some excuse and put off the mixed Court; since I got $1,540 out of him he is afraid of being stung for more.

I have found that there are no forms available here to carry out the Marriage Ceremony. No one ever expected a marriage here. I turned everything upside down and can only find two forms, so I have had to write to Addis to borrow some. I find we can register Births and Deaths easily many times over.

Things are fairly quiet now and our relations with the Ethiops are not too bad. We don't manage to get much done but still we keep worrying them.

My new horse, the one I got cheap at Jijiga, is turning out well and in the evenings we try our hand at polo on it in the large park which belongs to the Consulate.

We are having our pond dug out and the mud put on the roses; it certainly smells very fruity. I transplanted the wisteria from the rose trellis to under the house and it is certainly growing very well.

The Italians are having trouble on the Somaliland-Ethiopia border and were very worried in case we had concluded some agreement with the Ethiopians at Hargesia.

Sandy recalled that the Italian influence was then building up very strongly. The Italian Consul, who had come up on the wave of fascism, constantly interpreted every complaint to show up the impossibility of getting justice in Ethiopia. On one particular occasion in his search for 'Dirt' against the Ethiopian authorities, he forced his way into the prison in which conditions were pretty awful and took photos. The pictures duly appeared in 'The Memorandum of the Italian Government on the Situation in Ethiopia', annexed to Volume II, and were amongst documents presented to the League of Nations in 1935.

The Italian Consul was a nuisance to everybody but he was flamboyant and great fun.

Sandy also remembered that the Italians invited local Somali chiefs to go down to Mogadishu (the capital of Italian Somaliland) for holidays, showed them the town and gave them European suits. They came back with venereal diseases. They were extending their influence that way. The British Administration just looked on and took it for granted.

British Consulate, Harar, Ethiopia, 22 December 1932

We have had our usual trip to Dire Dawa and there met Zaphiro, the Oriental Secretary to the Legation, staying on his way back to Addis Ababa.

We have had the German Ambassador and his wife for lunch.

The Longs came back just in time to marry the Plowman's late Governess to the Cypriot Bank Manager [Plowman was the previous Consul]. Frances and Mrs Long put up an excellent lunch and the Italian Consul and Frances acted as witnesses.

The Boundary Commission on the Ethiopian side has reached a deadlock I fear. They look like being years at the job and the Commissioner, Major Lawrence, has been recalled from leave a month before his time, we gather, to try to settle the affair on the border.

We have been busy handing over everything and laying in a stock of stores for trek and start down for Jijiga on 24 December. By trekking it saves us money and we get an allowance for it. We shall follow the line of the newly cleared track for the motor road to Jijiga. Apparently it is awful for cars but excellent for camels. They are making roads everywhere, but as the Emperor retains the monopoly and won't allow competitive traffic, they don't do much good to the country and you still see all the coffee going on donkeys.

I got a very nice letter from the Minister thanking me for all I had done while I was at Harar.

I have got a sack of over 100lbs of coffee being sent to you from us both. I am afraid you will have to pay some duty on it and get it roasted but you will find it delicious. It is Harar coffee. I fear it will last a year or so and do for distribution to relatives.

Sandy was very struck, at the end of his second tour as a Consul in Ethiopia, how the Emperor Haile Selassie was gradually making his presence felt throughout the land. Feudalism was slowly being done away with and dealing with government officials was noticeably much easier than it had been in 1930.

CHAPTER 7

Survey of the Gum Arabic Areas of British Somaliland, 1933

Berbera, British Somaliland, 26 January 1933

I have now been posted to Erigavo, which lies in the hilly country on the Italian Somaliland Border; a nice change from Harar and a new part of the country. I am posted to map the Gum Arabic areas there; not the usual District work, thank goodness.

Sandy had never imagined that he would end up doing this job – his only knowledge of topography was what he had learnt at Sandhurst. Undaunted he set off with a plane table from the Public Works Department and his own prismatic compass. He, his wife, cook, cook's chokra (cook's boy) and a Midgan, a member of an outcast tribe who acted as sweeper and dog-boy, went by lorry to Erigavo. Two dogs and a capuchin monkey completed the party. At Erigavo he was very lucky to be briefed by the DC, Reginald Hopkins Smith, who was a fluent Somali speaker and had produced a genealogical tree of the tribes. Gum arabic, which in the Bible is known as frankincense and myrrh, exudes from the trunks of various varieties of acacia trees. The coast of British Somaliland along the Gulf of Aden where Sandy was to travel was known to antiquity as the 'Aromatica' coast. Classical and mediaeval writers referred to it as 'The Land of Punt'. Gum arabic is mostly used in the food and drink industry. Rowntree's Clear Gums had bought some gum arabic which had been shipped from Aden and had been traced back to British Somaliland. This was reported in the press when some gold dust was found in it. The Governor was obviously spurred into action to make some investigations before awkward questions were asked as nobody knew quite where the gum arabic came from. Once the government had more knowledge of the extent of the acacia trees, they could embark on a scheme to improve the collection and marketing of the gum and conservation of the trees. Sandy was therefore engaged to do this extraordinary job, walking along the

'My excellent Platoon Sergeant, Brunton. A Lanarkshire miner from Blantyre and a regular soldier. 1919.'

'The Company officers "B" Company in their cattle truck. Dunkirk to Cologne which took three days. 1919.'

'HM The King's Guard, Balmoral. Lieutenant A.T. Curle in the centre. 1921.'

'Gobwen, Jubaland. I have moved into my new house. 1923'

'Gobwen. The Guardroom and
Magazine with the barbed-wire
fence surrounding the *boma*.'

'Gobwen. Fixing
up five targets.'

'Gobwen. My native officer is an excellent fellow, Yusbashi Sheffi Ahmed Effendi.'

'I embarked at Kismayu in the time-honoured fashion. 1925.'

'Mandera. My house, which I at last reached after trekking hard for six weeks. 1926.'

'Mandera. The Quarter Guard with Guardroom behind. 1926.'

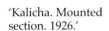

'Kalicha. Mounted section. 1926.'

'Kalicha. Lewis gun mounted on a mule. 1926.'

'Mandera. The first motor car ever to reach Mandera. 11 March 1927.'

'Safari to Moyale. I stopped for a couple of days to rest the camels and had a saddle inspection. 1927.'

Sandy with tusks from an elephant shot on the Lorian swamp. 120lb and 110lb. 1928.

'British Vice-Consulate, Jijiga. The Consulate is at present pitched in tents outside the town. 1929.'

'Our Abyssinian Consul has arrived at last. We entertained them to lunch.' Sandy centre back. 1929.

'Our aerodrome started by the arrival of a plane on Saturday. Fitaurari Tafassa, Monsieur Videl and Adjutant Widmer (Swiss). 1930.'

'I did one march with a *Balambaras*. We progressed surrounded by blackguardy looking soldiers. 1930.'

'Somaliland Camel Corps escort make the track passable to Dagghabur.' Walwal, 1934.

'Truck in the Ogaden bush.' Walwal, 1934.

'Johnnie Collingwood and the MT both refuel.' Walwal, 1934.

'In the sand at Dagghabur.' Walwal, 1934.

'Making a *zareba*. A camel herd with his axe. 1936.'

'A married woman with her hair done up in a black calico cloth. 1936.'

'Breakfast at Wada Gumared. I always travelled with china, table cloths et cetera and had fitted boxes for them. 1936.'

'The Koran teacher with his pupils. 1936.'

'The Somaliland Camel Corps on patrol. 1936.'

'I am off tomorrow to the Esa country for a final run round and to hand over to Shirley. 3 November 1936.'

Bantu door which Sandy found near Sumbawanga, Tanganyika. He arranged for it to go to King George V Memorial Museum in Dar es Salaam. 1938.

Local enjoying a smoke at Kipili on Lake Tanganyika. 1938.

'Kasulu. Our house is a square fort, built by the Germans, very highly decorated with pinnacles everywhere and masses of pointed Gothic windows with brass fittings. 1938.'

Picture by Major Kametz of Sandy at the head of a foot safari with his wife being carried in a *michaela* or hammock. The cook, at the head of the porters, was always an important personage and carries an umbrella.

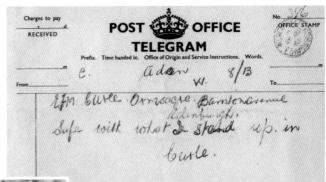

Telegram received by Sandy's father after the evacuation of British Somaliland. 21 August 1940.

'Ethiopian Feudal Soldier. The type from whom most of the men of the 2nd Irregulars were recruited. 1940.'

Picture of Sandy and Kametz with soldiers of the 2nd Irregulars (the uniform is accurately portrayed). Painted by an Ethiopian artist, Yohannes Tessema who signed it in Amharic. Found in a 'Tedj Beit' (local bar) in Addis Ababa in 1949.

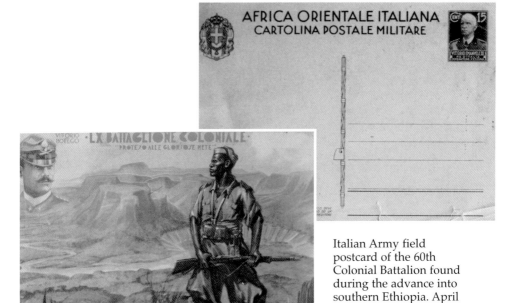

Italian Army field postcard of the 60th Colonial Battalion found during the advance into southern Ethiopia. April 1941.

'I find a place in Ethiopian mythology midst a distinguished company.' Painting by an Ethiopian artist, Yohannes Tessema. Sandy depicted as a giraffe due to his height, the three Ethiopian Princes, Emperor Haile Selassie, Churchill, Stalin and Roosevelt. Note the Emperor, though short, is painted as being above all.

Sandy, as Captain of the 2nd Irregulars, with the distinguishing slouch hat with a bunch of black ostrich feathers.

coast and the hills, which he found was very interesting but not exactly very productive.

I am jolly glad we are going on this mapping business. I will do my best to keep out of the magisterial net and specialize in as many lines as possible outside it.

We start off for the Gum areas on the 30 January and will be out till we sail home in May. We are going down to the cost at Heis, then trekking along to Karam where we turn inland to Las Durch where our headquarters is to be. I intend to try to fix prominent points by triangulation and then do a detailed plane table survey of the intervening areas where the Gum plantations are.

We go as far as Heis in company with the government auditor, one Seed, a very nice fellow who has never been on trek before and he will be good company. He has had no experience of trekking with camels so will be delighted to be able to join up with us. Seed is to inspect the books of two rather nebulous customs posts.

We are taking our fishing gear down to the coast as we may get a chance to fish.

Near Ankior on the sea, British Somaliland, 10 February 1933

We have now been out nearly eleven days having left Erigavo on 30th and took five days to Heis. We had to come down the escarpment 3,000 feet in 6 miles by an awful track; the scenery was magnificent but somewhat arid looking with hills rising over 7,500ft. We arrived at Heis at 7.00 pm and found a gale blowing and it was impossible to get the tent up so we had to shelter for the night in the custom's shed, 18ft by 36ft, with a huge stack of hay one end; Seed was one end and ourselves the other, also the monkey and the dogs. It was quite apparent that the customs recorded almost no business so Seed was able to go back to Erigavo with some of the camels.

Next morning I went off to look for a camping place and the wind had dropped and I got a good site a mile along the coast.

I went out to look at the site of Mossylum which is mentioned by Pliny but only saw a number of cairns. I could not get to them as I got on the top of a hill and could not get down near them. [This must have been the site at Salwayn which was discovered by Revoil in 1882. Some of these finds are in the Musée de l'Homme in Paris and appear to date from the first century BC to the first century AD. They are of Graeco-Roman origin. It was Revoil who suggested that this site could be Mossylum. Revoil mentions gum arabic in his book, *La Vallée du Darror*].

We camp for the night just back from the high tide mark. We put up our surveying umbrella in front of the tent so that our camp resembles a beach tea garden. When there is a full moon it is an unforgettable experience which makes up for the other discomforts. Never a sail is seen. No ship hoves into sight. There is however the inevitable jetsam from the steamers round Aden. Turtles come up from the sea at night to lay their eggs in the sand. Jackals range along the beach looking for clutches of eggs.

Sharks are very bad indeed. We have seen big brutes half out of the water; 6ft from the shore cruising along. Today on reaching camp we went down to bathe and were horrified to see a couple of 3ft sharks just where we selected to go in. I usually fire a couple of shots into the sea before bathing as a precaution.

From Heis we have followed the coast towards Berbera; the first part was dry stony desert but since Raguda it has been better with trees and some grass appearing. This morning I got a Pelzahn gazelle.

We have hired a fisherman to come with us and so far he has kept us supplied with excellent fish. We got in today to find an excellent fish about 4lbs waiting for lunch. Sharks always keep taking the bait but haven't yet got the fisherman. Our Somali Interpreter was employed at one point in the kitchens of a hotel in Johannesburg under the fish chef. We have been able to call on his expertise.

It has been impossible to get any information about the coast as very few Europeans have ever visited this region. None apart from Revoil have recorded their experiences. We were prepared for an 8 mile march today but to our horror found 24 miles. Poor Frances was very tired as we didn't get in till 12.00 pm having left at 6.00 am. She got burnt by the sun as well but has now recovered again and going strong.

I start mapping when we get to Karam going up a river bed to Las Durch which is our base.

Gin the dog has pulled up a lot since Harar and is now putting on flesh and his bones are no longer visible. The Monkey one day ventured down to the sea when it was calm; took a drink of salt water and ran back to the tent like a scalded cat. We keep him loose except at meal times when he is apt to be a bother when an ashet is put down; there is nothing safe from him.

We are very hard put to it here for supplies and cut off from all eggs or vegetables. We can occasionally buy a sheep but the fish and sea bathing compensate us. Our fisherman has come in with five good fish and an eel which attacked his hand and bit him. We do get a regular supply of fresh citrus fruit which comes from Berbera with the mail camel. Tins and dried foods are our staples but in a month or two we will feel the lack of vegetables and milk. Soon we will get some shooting. I hope for spur fowl and guinea fowl.

British Somaliland, 18 February 1933

Many thanks for your Birthday letter and £10.

We are mapping a pretty stiff piece of country. The track into the hills was very rough but as the camels from Erigavo were already used to hills there was no trouble. Imagine the Cairngorms without a blade of grass and take the stunted birches growing up the small streams as the acacia bushes and you have our country. The Somali pickers would at times resort to rolling boulders down the rocky slopes to knock down the bushes. Groups of natives join together and arrange for a Somali dhow to take the produce over to Aden where Indian or Arab traders barter for it. This survey is not concerning itself with the marketing side.

Very hot midday but I rather like the job. We are well inland now and expect the McCallums to join us; he was going to do the main areas while I did the outlying ones but now we have to work together it will be quicker since he is good at plotting where I am weakest but he knows nothing about plane table work.

An infernal wind blows all my papers about; Frances has already been chasing most of her mail up the river bed. She wears trousers now or rather my old khaki ones with the legs shortened; we are both the same size round the waist.

Frances rides on ahead surrounded by dogs like the advance agent of a cinema, chooses a site for us and has everything ready when I come in including my glass of white vermouth and soda; she makes things so comfortable for me. We have two large tents and send one always in advance so that it is ready for us to go into on arrival.

On Tour, British Somaliland, 27 February 1933

Our mails are a bit irregular I fear now. We have made good progress in the surveying and have got about 90 miles done; all awful country without a blade of grass and fearfully hot and lots of water which tastes of Epsom salts but we don't have to drink it. I go up hills daily and take bearings onto points ahead. I have a level which I use, like you had some years ago for the Ancient Monuments Commission.

Mange has broken out in the family; Gin and Loyal have it but not the monkey yet.

Frances has a touch of fever and is not feeling too fit at the moment. She has just taken 10 grams of quinine with a few drops from Mary's Xmas present which arrived on 27 February and was very welcome.

We haven't seen a vegetable now for a month and only a few eggs but we manage wonderfully; the horses suffer most from lack of grazing and are getting thin.

The Italians on this border are being an awful nuisance with their armed 'Banda' always raiding over and adopting a policy of aggression.

The compass traverses which Sandy had worked out were vetted by the Survey Section of the British Somaliland-Ethiopian Boundary Commission and the results forwarded to the Geographical Section General Staff for inclusion in future maps. Sandy felt rather proud that he had at least left a small mark on Africa. His sheets were left in the Erigavo office. In 1942 he happened to meet the British officer who had been the first into Erigavo after the liberation of British Somaliland. His maps were blowing about in the wind outside the District Office.

Sandy's efforts were wasted as regards the gum arabic – Italian aggression was building up and the development of such minor colonial products ceased to be of interest as greater issues were at stake.

Gum arabic was one of the most important exports of the Somaliland Protectorate but now it does not feature in Somalia's exports. There appears, however, to be a buoyant trade in gum arabic from other countries and it is an important export product for some areas in tropical Africa. The trade is dominated by the Sudan. Indeed it has been rumoured that Osama bin Laden's terrorist activities were partly funded through investment in the production of gum arabic in that country.

There is now a gap in the letters from March 1933 to September 1933 when Sandy and his wife must have been home on leave.

CHAPTER 8

Boundaries and Walwal: The Run-up to the Second World War, 1933–5

S andy was now Political Officer and Assistant British Commissioner on the British Somaliland-Ethiopia Boundary Commission.

> British Somaliland-Ethiopia Boundary Commission,
> c/o Postmaster, Berbera via Aden, 17 October 1933

We left Borama on the 12 October and trekked over a bad track for three days with our ponies. Colonel Clifford, the Senior Commissioner, who is with us is not an experienced trekker and goes very slowly. We used to nip along ahead and get in an hour or so before him. We had three trucks and a touring car waiting for us at Damal which is 62 miles from Zeila. We came in along a fearful road and it was pouring with rain for the last few miles.

Zeila is a small town with a few buildings almost surrounded by water and dismal salt flats which stretch miles all round. The sea is very shallow in front at low tide but there is a bathing pool which has been dug out which is a great thing.

The resthouse is three storied with wide verandahs built many years ago and all the furniture is of teak. It is right on the beach to the south of the town. [Sandy actually stayed in it in 1957, twenty-four years later]. Loyal, the dog, is in great form but is suffering from boils. He loves the sea and bathes with us always.

The day after we got in Colonel Clifford and I had to go out in a car to the French Boundary to have a look round and try to identify the line in accordance with the various treaties. It is 17 miles out from Zeila, all across low lying salt flats with thousands of salt pans scraped by natives. On the 19th we move again in cars out there and on the 20th we meet the French representatives. When we have finished the work on the coast we go up to Jalelo to try to decide the tri-junction point with the French and Ethiopians and from there we go along the Ethiopian frontier back to Borama.

It is grand here; we get dressed crab and no end of fish and our new cook although aged about eighty is turning out a success. He has been in only six jobs in thirty years but he is too old for walking and fell off a camel but once dug in anywhere he is grand.

We are hiring a fisherman to come along with us to the frontier to maintain our fish supply.

Jalelo, British Somaliland-Ethiopia Boundary Commission,
c/o Postmaster, Berbera via Aden, 31 October 1933

Just back from a most delightful trip to the island of Saad Din which is where the former town of Zeila stood. It is an amazing place; ruins all over of houses about 100yds away from the next with walls dividing off the plots; a sort of ruined garden city. There is the tomb of a Sheikh which was decorated with various odd cloths et cetera including a yellow flag with a white centre which is used in the army to denote a European Latrine; strangely out of place. There are no pots or relics about. I think the whole place must have gone under in a tidal wave several hundred years ago. I have got the RAF to take an air photo of the island of Saad Din with the ruins on it and am anxiously awaiting the result. [The original town of Zeila and the ruins on the island of Saad Din were part of a group of ruined towns in Somaliland which flourished in the fifteenth to sixteenth centuries. Sandy thought that some of the ruins might have been slave pens.]

On Saturday we went out to the *Tuna*, the steamer we usually cross from Aden in and had lunch on board with three Officers. She comes into Zeila every second week on the way from Djibuti to Aden thence Berbera. [The *Tuna*, with her Captain W.R. Malling, was the last boat to leave Berbera when the British evacuated it in August 1940.]

On Sunday I spent the day at sea fishing; caught nothing but lost two. Was nearly seasick and took two hours to get back against the wind. I saw a dugout canoe anchored at low tide on the mud with a stone with a hole in it exactly the shape of one you found in Shetland. [It would have been the anchor.]

On Monday we came out to Manda by car as usual and then collected our camels, some sixty, and came on to Jalelo where we are now camped; no grass at all, all volcanic rock and stones, black and red. It is worse than the gum areas. The Ethiopians are on one side of a low hill and the French the other and ourselves on the third side. We crossed the last 10 miles of the plain last night by moon; very cool indeed and it would have been hell in the day time.

Things here are a bit vague as in 1888 we chose a line with the French and made a Treaty. They then chose a line with Ethiopia taking as their point a place off our line with them.

British Somaliland-Ethiopia Boundary Commission,
c/o Postmaster, Berbera via Aden, 15 November 1933

We are still camped in the desolate wastes but have moved to a place called Abbaswein about 8 miles from Jalelo, a little less dreary. Here we have to fix the point with the French for the line of our boundary with them. [Sandy remembered that where the French Somaliland and British Somaliland frontiers met they had been very fortunate in finding a very old Somali Inspector of Police on the British side and a very old Somali on the French side, both of whom had been present in 1888 when the frontier had been first decided. These two remembered that there had been a palm tree which had been taken as the start of the boundary line. On digging in the sand the actual stump of the palm tree was found. Forty-four years had elapsed.] We duly put the mark at that point when all of a sudden the Ethiopians objected that it ought to be in the road; 4yds difference. We argued for two hours over it and they still maintained their futile attitude. However we have paid no attention to them and are going on without them, letting them put their objection in the Process Verbal. We have to do the Process Verbal in French which is the key copy, then an Amharic and English version.

British Somaliland-Ethiopia Boundary Commission,
c/o Postmaster, Berbera via Aden, 28 November 1933

Here we are still stuck at Jalelo trying to fix the tri-junction point; the French have sent out a harbour engineer as their Commissioner who has made a most awful mess; poor man he apparently didn't realize that we weighed up every sentence he wrote and of course he has contradicted himself on paper in a most blatant way. We have wired home to get some pressure brought to bear on the French. Luckily we agree with the Ethiopians for once and they are delighted to get us to help them against the French so to speak. We look like being here till Xmas unless things look up a bit.

You can't imagine a more desolate place than this with a permanent gale blowing and not a blade of grass; nothing but rocks and small stones. Our tent got caught in a dust devil which ripped up the outer fly so that we had to have it down and sewn up. It took a whole day to do.

The busy time is just coming on for me. I have to do a monthly report on the political side and as we have had nine meetings so far it looks like being a sort of book this month. Copies go home as well as to Addis Ababa and it takes me half the month to punctuate it.

Frances is not liking the life at all; these high winds and the general discomfort of camp life in such a vile spot are getting her down I fear but she will be happier when we move out of this area. It is hard and we have had such a lot of it really and never had a home.

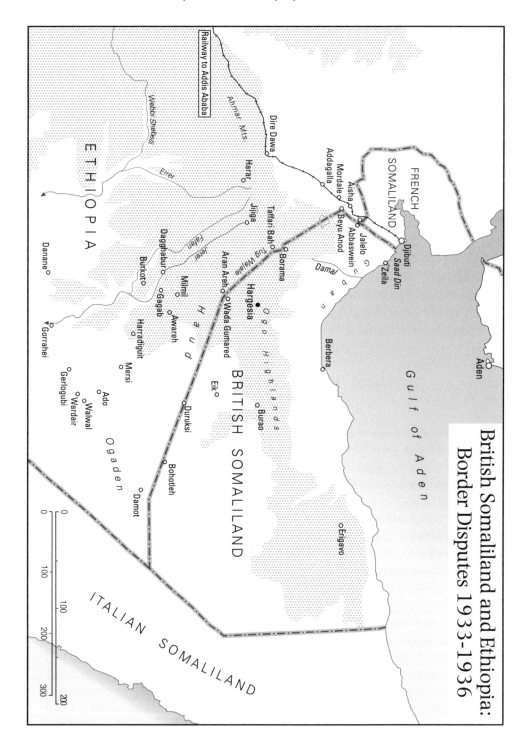

British Somaliland and Ethiopia:
Border Disputes 1933-1936

British Somaliland-Ethiopia Boundary Commission,
c/o Postmaster, Berbera via Aden, 10 January 1934

Here we are still at Jalelo. We are slowly getting down to bedrock in our arguments; each meeting now becomes a sort of attack in words on the French representative who has committed himself so badly by his ignorance of history et cetera that he simply sits dumb and nearly weeps. You can hardly credit it that the representatives of France could put up such rotten suggestions. Another really good effort of theirs was to demand that their frontier should be lengthened in distance from an alleged loss. I hope we shall soon get them to stick to the Treaties and then we shall make progress. The Ethiopians are a gift from heaven to deal with compared to the French.

Our mail last week got involved in a fracas although it got here all right; four of the party have disappeared into thin air. I presume they tried to demand something from a caravan and had their bluff called.

Frances is a little better this week but she is going down to Berbera as soon as I can get off to take her up to the road where a car will meet her. I hope the change to the sea will do her good after Jalelo.

Rahale, British Somaliland-Ethiopia Boundary Commission,
c/o Postmaster, Berbera via Aden 7 February 1934

We are still in these regions which are better than Jalelo and we have had a week of English rain; everything soaking wet with light rain and eight days on end and now grass is coming up and everything looks green.

We had great excitement last week as thirty French native troops and six Europeans had the infernal cheek to walk right through the middle of our camp; no sooner had they gone than two French aeroplanes arrived and circled overhead. A very ill-timed demonstration at a place under discussion by a Boundary Commission.

We got another excitement too; we got a telegram from London saying that the French Government had given full latitude to their representative to agree to the tri-junction point at the place we suggested. We waited a couple of days and pushed the French a bit till they said they had no new powers. We then produced the telegram and they admitted that their instructions were almost the reverse of the meaning of the telegram; so another wait. It is obvious that the Governor of French Somaliland is trying to do the dirty over the business.

The Colonel and I have had some good shooting at Rahale; spur fowl and with plenty of coolies as beaters they have risen well.

Godfrey-Faussett has I gather to take his wife home as she has been very ill. He is leaving the Commission [Major B.T. Godfrey-Fausett was an officer on the Boundary Commission]. She has been five weeks on her back. Some miles of road was made in order to get a car sent to her.

It has been decided that Frances will return home. It will be the best thing as it is no life for a woman out on these shows and our next outing is down into Ethiopia where she could not come. I shall be much happier to feel she is safely at home instead of having to live in tents et cetera alone. [Frances was presumably heading for a nervous breakdown. Life in these remote places was certainly demanding. Some women thrived on it, notably Alys Reece, wife of Sir Gerald Reece who ended his career as Governor of Somaliland, and Beatrice Turnbull, wife of Sir Richard Turnbull who was latterly Governor of Tanganyika.]

British Somaliland-Ethiopia Boundary Commission,
c/o Postmaster, Berbera, via Aden, 14 February 1934

We are still carrying on with our negotiations. The Governor of French Somaliland will interfere and refuses to give any latitude of discussion to his unfortunate representatives. Luckily for us he is so careless and does not apparently bother to read the minutes of the meetings that we have found he can always tie himself up into a mess if we give enough rope.

It is wonderful propaganda against the French in Ethiopia as we have done our frontier without anything like this bother they have made. I had no idea that representatives of a power like France could make such an awful mess of things; practically all due to the fact that they will not trust any official and make them refer everything. The trouble appeared to lie in the fact that in spite of instructions from Paris, the French Governor did not seem to be very good at delegating to the actual Commissioner working on the Boundary.

British Somaliland-Ethiopia Boundary Commission,
c/o Postmaster, Berbera via Aden, 19 February 1934

We are still at Rahale but I have occupied my time with a collection for the British Museum and the Botanical Gardens and have quite a good exhibit. [Sandy sent back forty-five samples of woodwork, tools and ropes from the Esa tribe of Somalis and was very often able to provide the local name for the object. In addition he sent details of how the Esa made poison for arrows from the roots of the Wabi tree (*Acokanthera Schimperi*) and included samples of the poison in various stages of its cooking. When he sent Yeeb nuts to the Botanical Gardens in Edinburgh, the director was delighted as he had not previously had the opportunity of growing them. A box of bulbs and plants was also despatched which the Director was delighted to receive as he had few opportunities of obtaining plants from that area.]

The French still continue to annoy; they deliberately violated Ethiopian territory by flying miles over it and round about. Very bad form to say the least of it.

It has been decided that I am to remain with the Commission till the end which I don't mind. We are at a place where Marchand and his band came through years ago. [He was a French explorer and soldier (1863–1934), famous for the Fachoda incident in 1898 when he challenged the British occupation of Egypt, nearly leading to war between Britain and France.]

British Somaliland-Ethiopia Boundary Commission via Aden,
25 February 1934

Here we are no further forward; the French commissioner has been laid up all week and nearly passed out; at least he thought so. He had a poisoned foot and fever and lost all nerve and was fully prepared to die. However he is to be carted away to hospital in Jibuti and he shows signs of life accordingly. Poor man had lived in an office all his days and the discomfort of camp life and a little mild exercise had finished him.

We have just waited all week and got our files in order, but I hope we shall resume discussions when a man has been appointed, perhaps this week.

Got some excellent Italian sausage from Djibuti and my Greek white wine is due to arrive soon.

Can you ask Douglas and Foyles to send me out a second-hand copy of 'I was a Spy' [by Martha Mckenna with a forward by Churchill] and some five or six other exciting discarded library books; something light and exciting or a novel or travel book? Also can you ask them for two copies of 'The Abyssinian at home' by Walker, 7/6d. I get no time for reading seriously; only after my dinner at night as a relaxation so something fairly light is essential. Put them down to my account there please.

Frances sails this week but as mail is late in, I don't know how she is.

Near Aisha Railway Station, British Somaliland via Aden, 4 March 1934

Well I thought Jalelo was a bad bit of country but this is worse; all black stones with a howling gale and dust.

We had an exciting weekend; the French came to say that 150 Esa Somalis had collected near their camp and were extremely truculent. We didn't pay much attention but went for our usual walk; during it we heard chaps blowing horns et cetera but it didn't worry us. However it was clear when we got back that something was up and the tribesmen were increasing in numbers round the French tent. I took the business in hand and got our camp with our three Police concentrated in a square. Then I went with the German who is the Ethiopian adviser to see the French who had wound up proper as the whole show was against them. Since all the demonstrators claimed French protection, we asked them (ie. the French Commission) if they could give us a guarantee that we would be able to carry on our work in peace without the unwelcome attentions of the mob. This they could not do so we said all right we are not a patrol we will move to Ethiopia where we can work in peace. The wretched French passed a sleepless night and in the morning apparently gave the mob who were still round their tents two sacks of rice and a sheep. No one came near us at all although we were only 400yds away and our runners et cetera passed by without interference.

It is the usual show apparently in French Somaliland, which they administer for the Esa, for the locals to collect and say, 'what are you doing here?' Pay us something and they always pay so each time they get more and more out of control. The Esa knew it was hopeless to try us as we plainly showed them we will have no nonsense and they have a healthy respect for the British Government. We impounded stray stock in our camp and put a thief in jail for six months and that showed them. It was a terrible showing up for the French as the whole business was against them only, not against the Christian or the white man or the Commission.

The best show of the lot was when we eventually left the valley of Rahale, the French Commissioner having been ill and lost his nerve. He left mounted on a donkey and as he couldn't ride he was supported on each side by two natives while a third attendant walked behind holding a parasol over him. Beside this outfit walked six coolies carrying his bed and deck chair. He had about 10 miles to do to reach the railway; he thought he would never reach Jibuti.

The French show no signs of returning yet so we are profiting by the delay in getting down to our records all the translations which have to be checked et cetera

The French have appointed a new Commissioner, a soldier, Captain Fargues, Legion d'Honneur. The Doctor said at least this one will be able to ride a horse not a donkey.

Mordale, British Somaliland via Aden, 11 March 1934

Things go from bad to worse here and a terrible tragedy overtook us yesterday. Beitz, the German, who was adviser to the Ethiopian Section, went out in a truck without an escort to supervise road work; at a point about 12 miles from Rahale, he was ambushed and the car was stopped and he was hauled out and speared to death and robbed. The driver of the car got away with bruises. The body was brought back to the railway station buffet which now assumes the role of a mortuary. The Ethiopians are terribly cut up about it as they liked him and he had their confidence. They wept in their sorrow.

The whole business is due to the French weakness and refusal to control their natives; the people were the same lot as the demonstrators a fortnight ago. The Ethiopians are fearfully bitter and blame the whole thing on the Jibuti Government [in French Somaliland] for failure to administer and for inciting the people.

Now all is quiet and I have ordered a Camel Corps Patrol to patrol our frontier.

The Colonel and I had to go into Dire Dawa (Ethiopia) for the funeral and then returned here. On arrival at Dire Dawa, we found the Deputy Governor of Harar Province with hundreds of soldiers drawn up on the platform. We all walked in a procession to the Greek Church where the coffin was put for the night. The next day the Minister of Public Works came from Addis by air for the funeral. He arrived in his Ethiopian clothes with an opera hat. They awarded Beitz posthumously the Order of the Trinity and placed it on the coffin. A Greek priest took the service and we all walked in procession to the cemetery.

British Somaliland via Aden, 2 April 1934

We have had a visit from the Minister, Sir Sidney Barton, who came down on Friday for a week so as to try to make the Ethiopians get a move on and do something about catching the criminals in the murder business. The Deputy Governor of Harar also came with 250 old pattern soldiers; the real old tough sort with swords and the like. He brought his own Greek doctor and numerous dirty looking slaves. He has camped with his tent in the middle of a square of soldiers.

The same day as the Minister arrived Major Bennet, 2nd in command of the Camel Corps, and Plowman who used to be Political Officer, came through from Somaliland to discuss the question of joint action. Somaliland seems to have the wind up over the business.

We went out by car to see the place where the ambush was and where Beitz was killed. It was very cleverly laid indeed; they had blocked the main road on a hairpin bend. We also saw some gruesome traces of poor Beitz's blood. We had numerous exchanges of visits with the Deputy Governor. Eventually the Minister succumbed to a bilious attack and has been 'Hors de Combat' all day.

We heard last night that the ring leader of the murderers was passing along a track near the frontier making for Ethiopia with his stock; so we sent out fifteen men of our escort in a truck for 20 miles and they ambushed the road catching the wanted man. He fired when caught but our Police replied shooting him through the heart. His knife which had cut off Beitz's ear was hit by a bullet which had also severed one of his fingers; he was drawing his knife at the time. We got all his sheep, goats and possessions and found a tin of petrol he had looted from the Ethiopian car the day of the murder. The Police brought the body back and the Ethiopians asked for it to be displayed for twenty-four hours in the town '*Pour encourager les autres*' but we refused. Forty-one men are still wanted.

A new Ethiopian called Lorenzo Taezaz has come as Assistant Commissioner. He was seven years in France studying law and is quite a good fellow. [Lorenzo Taezaz was later a close advisor to the Emperor and Minister of Foreign Affairs]. We are now trying to urge the Ethiopians into action. We have suggested a scheme to them and are sort of pushing them on; once they start they sweep up and shoot up men, women and children and loot wholesale. It certainly teaches the Esa a lesson but they are the limit to get under way. Their Easter is coming off next Sunday so they will be unwilling to move.

I have to collect all the Intelligence in connection with these operations and generally try to buck up the Ethiopians so am pretty busy.

Mordale, British Somaliland via Aden, 11 April 1934

We had a week of official meals given in the station buffet; we all ask each other so we had three dos. The fellow really put up a very good show and considering everything did us well. We had to ask the Greek Doctor who accompanies the Deputy Governor of Harar so as to avoid thirteen. The French did their do at night; got fish up from Jibuti in rich sauces.

The Esa hunt is going on well; three more caught and hundreds of head of stock bear witness to the gallantry of the Ethiopian soldiery. The Esa are being chased all over the place. I hope the Camel Corps get on to them.

The Governor of French Somaliland has been kicked out so they are starting to co-operate and try to catch some of the people who have fled there; sudden change in their view.

We hope to be on the move next week again as we shall probably fix the tri-junction point at last this week.

The Minister and Plowman have gone back but Major Bennett remains running the war. We are in close touch here with all the news by wireless. The Ethiopians give us information so we can send out to arrest wanted men.

Up to my eyes in work over this business as I have to do liaison Officer as well as my ordinary duties.

British Somaliland via Aden, 20 April 1934

We have at last fixed things up and signed the Agreement with the French and Ethiopians regarding the Junction point of the Frontiers.

We move tomorrow to near Beyu Anod at the corner of the frontier and from there go down the caravan track to Jalelo again with the Ethiopians as, according to the treaty, it forms the frontier. We have to decide on it and then on the return trip we decide where the new line is to run. It ought to take us about a fortnight I think; then we go back to Borama for a month or two before starting work on the areas where the tribes graze on both sides of the border.

We are all thankful to be out of Mordale; these places are all right for a week or so but after that they become wearisome.

It is very hot in the afternoons here and the flies are terrible. The Ethiopians and French have no sanitary services or cleansing department; they just consign papers and rubbish to the wind and as we are downwind a little to one side we get some of the flies.

The Post Office here is grand; they have no weighing machine and you bargain to send off a registered letter or any letter. You then see it departing by train in the hand of the guard.

British Somaliland via Aden, 26 April 1934

Would be glad of some more books like the last selection, please. They were magnificent reading for this job.

We shall miss our visits to the railway buffet at Aisha; they were the one change we had. I think the buffet keeper was sorry to see us go as we were good customers.

We started out on Tuesday; got soaked on the way. We were due to meet the Ethiopians the next morning but late at night they sent a note saying they were delayed and would we wait twenty-four hours. We refused as we had met their camels which they had not ordered till four days before on the way in. We did our first march down the caravan road which forms the present boundary without them. They joined us late at night.

We had a fearful hurricane of dust yesterday and it blew down some tents before the deluge came. I was flooded out properly but managed to keep my stuff dry.

We have a big party this time; the Colonel, myself, the Doctor, Taylor who does the survey part and one of the NCOs, Corporal Griffiths. We have a big escort. I believe we are getting an Officer to run it; one Dunlop in the Argylls. I have to run the camp. Hard at work getting a trench dug to avoid a repetition of yesterday's flood.

British Somaliland via Aden, 3 May 1934

Here we are on the move again. We have had a good week's exercise; did 20 miles before lunch on Monday, out to Rahale, and back to sign up a final stretch with the French.

I did quite a lot of shooting last week and got four gazelles. My saluki, Nukie, brought down two I wounded in fine style. Myself and Taylor had to run 2 miles after the dogs and found they had brought the beast down by the throat; so you see I am pretty fit these days, running about.

The Ethiopians are being foolish again; they are lost without a European adviser and have no idea of siting the frontier; we may be weeks arguing with them here.

The Soldiers of the Deputy Governor of Harar apparently ran amok amongst the Esa on Saturday at Addagalla on the railway. They killed forty-five and had only four wounded. It must have been a proper massacre; but it will teach them it doesn't pay to kill Europeans. They have still to foot a bill of £10,000 for Mrs Beitz's pension; it will take many thousand camels before they pay that off.

We shall not be finished now till October or December I fear.

Envy you in Shetland; I could do with a bathe in that cold water. We have had it 100° occasionally last week in the tents.

British Somaliland via Aden, 8 May 1934

At last we have been able to get things settled up on this last bit of line. For two days the Ethiopians stuck their toes in and refused to listen to reason; then at last thanks to Lorenzo Taezaz, their Political Officer, they became reasonable and we have been able to secure the bit we wanted and run the boundary along the top of a rocky plateau. We work from the basis of the Treaty of 1897 we have with them and then make the necessary modifications so as to ensure a good frontier line which will avoid scrapping over our wells. We then had to go all over our proposed line; climbing up on to a plateau strewn with black lava, stones all over and fearful walking and as hot as the nether regions. We are out from 6.00 am to 12.00 pm.

After one of the stiffest climbs Taylor and I found a deep pool in a river bed so we just took off our shirts and stockings and shoes and had a good bathe. Our clothes soon dried on us after. Yesterday evening we had another bathe in a pool and had a bottle of beer waiting for us on the bank with chairs.

After a long day yesterday we got into camp at 2.00 pm having stopped to refresh ourselves at the Ethiopian camp on the way in. We drank Crème de Menthe and soda; it is extraordinarily refreshing and we all agreed that it was better drunk like that than as a liqueur.

The Motor road is through from Aisha to Zeila at last and, as it goes close to the frontier most of the way till it crosses at Jalelo into our territory, we have been able to get mails out by it. Last week's mail had an adventure being washed away. The 6cwt truck was caught in the river and the escort and mails got away. The truck was turned on its side and washed down for 8yds. It was soon put right again and on the road in three days. The mail was taken on by the Camel Corps truck.

We expect to be sometime in camp out here finishing off lists of names et cetera; at least the Colonel and I. All names have to be spelt according to a system adapted by the Royal Geographical Society. Sheets are made out while we get the name said over to us and write it down. In addition to that they have to be done in French and Amharic.

Shall be glad when we have done with this bit of country; it is getting hotter daily and the rain makes little difference as there is no grass to grow; only the bushes become green. We shall have had six months of it and all under canvas.

Illustrated London News and Truth are much appreciated. Many thanks for them. Our papers go the round of the various messes and end up at the Ethiopian camp months after.

Beyo Anod, British Somaliland via Aden, 16 May 1934

We have been having a rest during the past week, at least as far as climbing hills is concerned.

Bennett, the 2nd in Command of the Camel Corps who is in charge of the operations against the Esa, has his Rolls Royce here and we had lunch at Aisha Railway Station on Sunday.

We had a great 'Do' from our Ethiopian Comrades on Friday; they were so pleased over the selection of the boundary that, after we had had a Crème de Menthe and water, they produced two bottles of Champagne, quite good dry stuff at 10.00 am which had to be duly consumed.

The Ethiopian who is head of their mission got a helmet out from England, cash on delivery, with our mail. He had to cut his hair to make the hat fit; we tackled him on it and he admitted it.

I have been busy all week getting the various copies of the minutes, agreements and reports sent off to Addis Ababa and London.

We got four more of the murderers last week including the Lieutenant of the gang. They have been living in the hills for months and chased about all over the place and finally they surrendered; between the three Governments we have got most of them.

The French have packed up and are not pulling their weight.

Start back along the frontier to Borama next week; it has been demarcated and we are doing the final inspection.

Borama, British Somaliland via Aden, 6 July 1934

We had a fearful storm yesterday just after dark; a hurricane with gusts of rain coming parallel to the ground; everything soaked and water running through the tents but no damage as every box is always put on stones to keep the white ants off so the water just flows under them. The tents were ripped up. They have been in use for two and a half years so most of them are about done by now.

One of the Ethiopians is sick in Addis with congestion of the lungs; he will delay us a bit I fear. We are finishing off the routine stuff for the end of the quarter at present and get back to final documents in a day or so. Our Surveyors will be in next week with the Doctor and we shall all be together for the rest of the time.

The horses are very fit. After all the rain there is good grazing; they deserve it as they did not get much in the Esa country.

Borama, British Somaliland via Aden, 22 September 1934

I was down at Hargesia last week for a conference; spent the night there. I go off to Harar with Taylor on Tuesday. We shall do a bit of mapping on the way in and put the road in. I have also to get some things from the Consul. Taylor also hopes to collect snakes on the banks of the Jerer River so my next letter will be from Ethiopia. I shall stamp it liberally if I get the opportunity. [Out of gratitude to Sandy, Taylor called a new lizard which he found 'Hamadactylus Curlei'.]

We had another successful excavation last week. We got the usual Celadon ware fragments, Chinese pottery and a coin in perfect condition; goodness knows what it is; small with queer squiggles on it. I have three now in the course of our Sunday trips. I shall bring them all home when I come. It is extraordinary the way we come across fresh towns no one knows of. We greatly enjoy our Sunday trips. [Members of the team were greatly encouraged to pursue their various hobbies. Sandy, assisted by Taylor, investigated fourteen sites within reach of Borama. In 1937 he had an article on 'The Ruined Towns of Somaliland' and another on 'Carved Stones' published in *Antiquity*. It is still one of the few references on the subject and is referred to by Neville Chittick in his article on 'An Archaeological Reconnaissance in the Horn: The British-Somali Expedition, 1975' in *Azania*, the journal of the British Institute in Eastern Africa, vol. 1, and in I.M. Lewis's book *A Modern History of the Somali*, 1965. Several thousand items were sent to the British Museum. Some coins were identified as coming from the reign of a Sultan of Egypt from 1467 to 1497. In addition, Sandy donated seventy-six items to the National Museum in Edinburgh. This was following in the family tradition as his father had donated 876 items].

Borama, British Somaliland via Aden, 2 October 1934

Just got back from Harar in Ethiopia; we had a most successful mission. We actually accomplished something. I hope I have been instrumental in securing the release of some sixty-three prisoners in jail for no reason.

We had an official dinner given in our honour but the Greek hotel keeper who usually caters on these occasions refused to play as the Governor owed him $4,000. His substitute believed in quantity not quality; result twelve courses; most of them loathsome messes all capped with a bottle of sweet champagne badly corked. Our hosts did not of course worry about that trifling fact; '*Quelque chose a boire*' was all that really mattered.

There are five Belgian Officers at Harar [under Major Dothe, later Major General] training the Ethiop to fight the Italians; very nice fellows indeed. We had dinner with them in their mess. I was also taken on a private tour of the new wireless station there; modern and up to date but how long they will work it for I don't know.

One of the local Officials has some peculiar bundle for me. I was asking about wild gladioli and he said he had one he would send me. It may be a turnip but I shall send it home when it comes. I have arranged about wild delphinium seed in a few months from Addis.

Off for a few days holiday excavations tomorrow.

On 18 January 1934, Sandy had written to the Minister, Sir Sidney Barton, at the British Legation in Addis Ababa suggesting that the Commission should visit the Ogaden region of Ethiopia where Walwal was. This, as Sandy wrote years later, 'was the letter that started it all'. Walwal, in the arid Ogaden, was of strategic importance as there were so many wells.

Dear Sir Sidney,

I have been working up the 'Grazing Area' problem so as to have the points at my finger tips ready to tackle the question once the tri-junction point is fixed.

According to our instructions we are given a free hand and only have to submit the report. I have been talking over the matter with Colonel Clifford and the following points have occurred to me which I should like to bring to your notice.

It appears we ought to visit the limits of the areas (which include Walwal and Wardair) and fix the principal features on the limits and the wells by astronomical observations, especially as in some cases the name on the map indicates a group of wells covering a large area, each well having a different name; this will help towards avoiding ambiguity such as has been encountered all along the 1897 Treaty frontier.

We realize it may be difficult to get the Ethiopian Section to agree to visit the areas and of course no marks et cetera would be set up as not only would they arouse suspicion and be certain to be destroyed by the Somali. They are unnecessary since the problem is not one of boundary limitation, but tabulating clearly the limiting areas to which we claim access for our tribes, in such a way that, should subsequent developments call for the use of these limits for other purposes, we should have left a sufficiently unequivocal description to ensure the avoidance of misunderstandings.

The second point is what should be our attitude if we find Italian *'banda'* or *'dubad'* in occupation at Walwal and any other points? The point being the possibility of undesirable repercussions in connection with The Zeila Corridor, or other political contingencies of which we have no knowledge.

Alex T Curle

The Commission was told to go ahead with the plans to visit the grazing areas and that the Italian Foreign Office and legation would be told in due course when all had been arranged

It was only after reading Sandy's personal memoirs written in the 1970s that the contribution of the Boundary Commission to the Zeila Corridor came to light. Sandy recalled that the survey staff, in addition to their routine work of deciding on and demarcating the boundary, had been engaged in a top secret operation. This had involved surveying three possible narrow corridors of varying width in British Somaliland which would give Ethiopia access to the sea via the port of Zeila in British Somaliland. Zeila was a small, rapidly decaying port. The proposal was that Britain would cede Zeila and the Zeila Corridor to Ethiopia in return for a part of the Ogaden region in Ethiopia where the British protected tribes exercised their right of trans-frontier seasonal grazing afforded by the 1897 Anglo-Ethiopian Treaty. The officers had all jokingly remarked that the only place any secret document could be read was in the lavatory tent. However Sandy then heard from Sir Sidney Barton that the Foreign Office had told him that 'His French colleague knew all.' It appeared that the son of the French Minister in Addis, who acted as wireless operator and handled the codes, had bust the Foreign Office one. Absolute secrecy had been essential as the French would be very angry as the plan would allow Djibuti, the port in French Somaliland, to be bypassed and they would lose their monopoly of transporting goods to Ethiopia on the Franco-Ethiopian railway. The Emperor was sympathetic towards the exchange of territory as he dearly wanted a port for Ethiopia and to be free from the stranglehold of Djibuti for his imports. The Ethiopians had never cared for the Ogaden which was very different to their heartland and populated by Somalis, so that was considered to be no great loss.

In June 1935, the proposal was actually submitted to the Italians by Anthony Eden who was then a junior minister. According to A.J.P. Taylor in his book *The Origins of the Second World War*, 'The professionals at the Italian foreign ministry wished to accept the offer.' Mussolini refused with the result that Eden became very anti Italian.

Borama, British Somaliland via Aden, 6 November 1934

We are at last getting packed up to start for our trip down the Ogaden. The Ethiopians of course, as we almost expected, have found some further excuse for delay, and we have told them in plain language that we shall start on 8th November whether they are with us or not. They are as usual trying to do the impossible and crowd sixty soldiers into two small lorries. We expect to reach Walwal and Wardair where the Italians are in full force about 17 November; our Ethiopians will be following on I expect. [The area around Walwal was clearly in Ethiopia but the Italians claimed it and had built a fort there in 1930. They had their irregular tribal retainers there.] Collingwood is with us as Escort Officer [he was Adjutant of the Somaliland Camel Corps who were escorting the Boundary Commission]. We have eleven vehicles in the convoy. How many will break down I don't know but, as we shall be pushing, not following a road, for most of the way, we are sure to have a smash or two into trees. It is an awful job arranging all the water, rations, seats et cetera for all our convoy with two months' stores. I shall be thankful when it is all underway. Goodness knows when we shall reach home but once we are started our Ethiopians will not waste time; that is certain as they are in a blue funk now.

We have to make out fearful reports on all we see and find. I feel like taking a false moustache and beard to do a little spy work which is what they expect us to do.

I shall send letters off as we get the chance; Italian Somaliland or Ethiopian mails.

Sent some roots in a small packet recently; quite pretty red flowers.

Dagghabur, Ethiopia, 10 November 1934

Many thanks for the Scotsmans.

We reached Dagghabur this morning after two nights on the road. We came by camel caravan track; bush pushing as we call it and landed at a place called Milmil on the maps where we struck an Ethiopian road which took us on in. We have however to send back for some more stuff before we push on to Walwal which will be about the 18th.

I was here when I was at Jijiga about four years ago and the place has grown since then. We were met by the Officer in charge of the town who had been six years in the 3rd KAR at Nairobi and in the war till 1915. He was a Lance Corporal but gained promotion in the Ethiopian Service; a nice chap who when the guard turned out for him gave a British salute and then turned smartly in the military fashion and stepped into a bush which rather spoilt his style. He bought us two chickens and thirty eggs as a present.

I believe our Ethiopians arrive tomorrow. I thought they would start once we got under way and adhered to our programme.

It now remains to be seen what the Italians will say when we suddenly appear in their midst and fly the Union Jack; their wires to Rome will be red hot. They have built forts at Wardair et cetera. They will be so excited; it will be very funny really.

Found a lot of flints round our camp here.

This goes back with our ration convoy.

Dagghabur, Ethiopia, 12 November 1934

Just a hasty line by the Ethiopian mail which I trust will reach you. Our 'Comperes' have not yet turned up but a second relay in the form of one of them appeared today. Apparently they have arranged to move by stages as they have just found that you can't get sixty men onto two trucks with water and rations.

The local officials here have a fight so can get nothing done. One writes letters to another who refuses to obey them so the whole system is out of joint!

We shall adhere to our plans and move on by a round about route on Friday. We leave Dagghabur thence Milmil, Awareh, Harradiguit, Mersi, Walwal and Wardair; at the last place the Italians are firmly dug in, wireless, tanks et cetera so our arrival with a large Union Jack will be great fun.

Went out to a local ruin today and found similar relics to those found round Borama.

Ado (10 miles or so West of Walwal), Ethiopia, 21 November 1934

We are having a halt for a day so I am taking the chance to write. We left Dagghabur on Saturday and as we were leaving the Ethiopians stopped us and told us we were going on the wrong road; they said they had made a mistake and the way was through Awareh to Harradiguit; we said we were prepared to risk it and went. At first we found a good road and went through a country packed with game but featureless. I shot a gazelle for meat.

Our convoy consisted of nine trucks and of course our pace is that of the slowest; if one has a puncture we all stop. It is an awful business travelling in convoy; my truck is third and I get all the dust et cetera and the thorn bushes scratch me. We sleep in the open at night, getting up at 5.30 am, breakfast and are off by 7.00 am. We halt for an hour for lunch otherwise go continuously. My truck carries all my kit, water, petrol (48 gallons at the start) and three boys and an interpreter.

After reaching Awareh we followed a camel track; pushing aside the bushes to Harradiguit which is a large area with a number of rain ponds, some of which were full. We met the Ethiopian section there and arranged that we should wait at this place a day for them and push on to Walwal together. They told us there was a road on to Mersi and Walwal. We camped the night and got off as usual the next day. I have never seen such thick bush in my life; the cars pushed through it and we got torn to ribbons, windscreens broken, no road whatever existed. One Ethiopian car passed us and we heard that an Official had drawn money to pay for the road and done nothing but pocketed it for himself. The Ethiopian car was crowded on top with soldiery who were torn to ribbons by thorns. Our first car picked up five hats and odd pieces of clothing festooned on the bushes.

There is a huge camp of 400 Ethiopian troops and Somali levies under an ex-Interpreter [Ato Ali Nur] who was with the British Consulate at Maji in Southern Ethiopia and when the Consul died there he made off with the cash and rifles. The 2nd in command is an Italian Somali renegade who killed an Italian and cleared out here, while the bugler who blows British calls was dismissed from the Camel Corps for stealing; goodness knows how many others of the same type they have.

The country while flat is very thick bush; not thorn but all types of deciduous trees and obviously has a far greater rainfall than anywhere in Somaliland.

Today a great commotion occurred and a *Fitaurari,* Governor of the Province, came in from Gerlogubi; it was a fine sight, the old type of soldiers with a rifle and sword, some mounted on mules with a herd of donkeys carrying their goods behind. No rations or anything of that sort of course as they live off the country. The bugler blew the general salute ten times to impress the *Fitaurari.*

The Italians at Wardair send patrols to Walwal daily so I expect they have heard of our arrival by now and will be getting very excited.

The Ethiopian caught one of the Italian spies with a list of questions written in Arabic on Italian Government notepaper so they have supplied the answers and sent the man back. I don't think we shall have any trouble on the whole.

It is much warmer here and we are quite enjoying it after the cold of Borama. We don't need coats in the evening. Goodness knows when we shall be home, certainly not till January now. This letter will go back to Dagghabur by our ration convoy and thence on to Jijiga when opportunity offers so may take weeks to reach you.

22 November 1934

The Great Army marched out by night last night for Walwal; no rations or anything with them. The Italian irregular troops are there so it will be interesting to see what happens; we follow tomorrow.

Had a duck shoot last night on the local ponds and got a fan tailed duck of sorts and a snipe while this morning I got a gazelle for meat.

23 November 1934

Reached Walwal at noon to be confronted with Italian levies. Our Ethiopians chased them off in great style without firing a shot but situation is very, very strained. We are only 300yds from an Italian fort with their flag flying and according to the map miles in Ethiopia. I don't think they will attack but the fun will start if someone fires a shot. We have the Union Jack flying over our camp at the request of the Ethiopians.

Tomorrow we go to visit the fort and see if they are going to obstruct the work of the Commission. It is really vastly amusing seeing the Ethiopians in action so to speak; yells and whistles and no sort of order and no one knows what to do. Collingwood walked into the middle and took a cinema picture of it all. We stand on the tops of the cars and watch the fun.

Must close now. Should have some exciting news by next letter.

Ado Ethiopia, 25 November 1934

A quick line to let you know I am still alive. The Italian Officers duly arrived at Walwal and visited us and tried to come to an arrangement with the Ethiopians to withdraw troops from the front lines; while we were talking two Italian aeroplanes arrived and flew very low just over our heads and circled round our camp which was flying the Union Jack. The observer in one of the planes was aiming with his machine gun at the Commission on the ground. This was about the last straw and, as it was plain that the Italians were asking for trouble, we decided to withdraw the British section so that we should not be involved in any incident. The troops took up their positions again and started digging in. And when we left this morning they were waist deep in holes in the ground. The Ethiopians did twelve-hour stints in the front line, while the Italians did about the same. I expect they will have a proper fight once we have gone. It would not take much to start them.

[The Ethiopian Commission withdrew along with the British but left their escort behind.]

Extraordinary show; two nations who have just expressed their friendship for each other! The Italians' attitude was impossible and even before the aeroplanes came there was little hope of reaching a settlement before an answer came to our formal protestation. They simply say it is Italian Territory and there is the end. London and Rome and Addis will be hard at it talking as they expected something of the sort would happen. [On 2 August 1928, Italy and Ethiopia had signed a twenty-year Treaty of Friendship, and on 29 September 1930 they had released a joint statement denying any aggression between each other.]

In a tape which was recorded for the Imperial War Museum, Sandy states that the Italians had taken exception to their arrival. From the very start extremely rude letters had been received from the Italians asking them what they were doing. An interview had taken place with the Italian Officer, Captain Cimmaruta, who had been barely polite.

Ado, Ethiopia, 30 November 1934

Our Walwal war continues; both sides are dug in. The Ethiopians are getting short of rations and deserting in small batches. The Italians are trying to justify the arrival of the aeroplanes by saying that they didn't know we were there and that we ought to have known from native sources they were in control there. They say we ought to have warned them. Our reply is simple; we told them that since they had never informed either our or the Ethiopian Government of their new acquisition we had no official knowledge and therefore presumed and still do that the country was Ethiopia where we have a perfect right to circulate. I expect they will be having some fun at home as they were expecting this to happen and have everything ready accordingly to shoot at Rome.

Our only excitement here was an alarm one night when all the Ethiopian camp let off their rifles, some in our direction, one round going just over Collingwood and I who were having a glass of beer. They apologized profusely next day.

We are back to the no vegetable life again; meat is hard to get as every man runs miles from an Ethiopian army. We live in an atmosphere of spies; the Ethiopians love catching one with letters on one, usually harmless, and everyone is a spy.

I don't know when our next move will be, probably Gerlogubi. We shall be glad to get a mail soon. Sending this via Burao so it ought to reach you for Xmas for which feast I send all good wishes. Provided we are not shot by the Ethiopians or Italians we might get home in February but one can never tell. I shall be mighty glad to get home.

7 December 1934

The Ethiopians and the Italians have had a fight at last at Walwal. About 3.30pm on 5 December someone fired a shot and that started the fight. The Italians brought up at once two tanks and three aeroplanes which dropped bombs and fired with machine guns. The Ethiopians were massacred of course being armed with various weapons firing lumps of lead dated 1870 and swords; they didn't stand a chance and 300 were killed. One aeroplane crashed behind the Italian lines. Under cover of darkness the Ethiopians retired 20 miles to Ado leaving the wounded, 150 mules, rations, tents et cetera behind but taking the dead bodies of five officers killed to bury in holy ground. They then of course threw up the sponge and retired to Harradiguit having started 70 miles from Ado with no water on the way. Any officers of course went in a car; wounded et cetera all on the road in the sun with a bottle of water, no food or anything – just a rabble. We of course had to evacuate to Harradiguit leaving Collingwood to secure the road back in case the Italians became aggressive. He took command of all the Ethiopian troops left at their request. [Years later Johnny Collingwood had a great story to tell of the incident which was recounted to a friend of mine. In the middle of the fighting the Ethiopian Major General summoned him and told him that he had to go off to his tribal area to bury his grandfather (or some such family matter) and would Johnny take over the division. Johnny led the Ethiopian division away, thus preventing even more slaughter. On the hazardous journey back to Somaliland with his comrades he was clasped and kissed on both cheeks by a ferocious-looking Ethiopian who turned out to be the Battalion Commander who had heard of and greatly appreciated his actions in extracting his soldiers and saving their lives.]

We found the unfortunate rabble on the road; they had already done 20 miles since midnight. They were offering us cartridges, swords, rifles, anything for a lift in a truck. One chap kissed and grovelled at my feet to get a lift. We gave them water and dates and had to leave them. Our Doctor who has been in five campaigns since the war was quite at home and has a field hospital under a tree. He has medicines and drugs in plenty but no stretchers or blankets. The wounded were just lying on the grass in blood-soaked torn clothing covered with sacks, not even a table for operating. Real Napoleonic war touch. Two of our cars have gone out this morning with dates and water to bring the wretches in. They of course have no organisation, no hospital or anything. The seriously wounded were sent on with the bodies for burial in holy ground; some 250 miles on an unmade road in open lorries with the sun full on them. I should imagine the whole lot were dead on arrival.

Appears the Ethiopian soldiers put up a magnificent fight but their officers ran.

We are now at Harradiguit awaiting the arrival of more wounded and the retreating force.

We shall get on with our job in a day or so again.

Typically aggressive show on the part of the Italians who were of course miles in Ethiopia and obviously had everything ready and there was really no need to massacre the unfortunates. I expect the Governments at home will have something to say about it all.

Several times afterwards, even as late as 1962, Sandy was approached by Italian journalists wanting to know about Walwal. He obviously recounted it as in this chapter, but they were not interested in his version.

An official report of the incident was compiled by Clifford, Sandy, Collingwood, Taylor and Godding and sent to the Under Secretary of State at the Colonial Office. According to Sandy the Government refused to make the report public. In due course the reply came back from Sir Samuel Hoare at Downing Street.

The reader should be aware that these are the most significant letters that Sandy ever wrote, and bear witness to the fact that, as many historians consider, Walwal was the beginning of the Second World War, or as Sandy would have said, the run-up to the Second World War.

Harradiguit, Ethiopia, 12 December 1934

The 'War' seems over for the moment. Collingwood and our escort narrowly missed being bombed by three hours when they left Ado. An Ethiopian brought one of the dud bombs into us having sat on it for 70 miles in a lorry! We buried it very quickly. All the retreating force has passed on; they sent them off from Ado to Harradiguit, 70 miles without food or water and if we had not been here all the officers would have beat it straight for home. We sent out cars with food and water to them and brought them in the last few miles. Our car load of wounded was evacuated and I found at the last minute that they had made no arrangements for food or water; it was an open lorry and 200 miles to do!

They are very grateful to us for all we have done for them. The Amhara soldiers look upon us now as sort of universal providers and I have had rifles with cartridge cases stuck in to mend. In addition men wanting tins, bottles and our old engine oil for lubricating their rifles; all come and ask me. The official casualties are 107 killed or missing and 45 wounded. The force was not a regular one, only old soldiers called up under their district chiefs for a month's service. They had hundreds of servants and slaves with them which complicated matters. The Italians must have massacred them. We have evidence from deserters that the whole thing was a put-up show and the aeroplanes and tanks were all arranged for.

I shall send you a copy of the documents later; some of them being in Italian will serve as an exercise. The Emperor is putting the whole business to the

46011/35.

62

D R A F T.

LIEUTENANT COLONEL
E.H.M. CLIFFORD, D.S.O.,
M.C.

DOWNING STREET.

March, 1935.

CONFIDENTIAL.

Sir,

I am etc. to inform you

that His Majesty's Government have

given careful consideration to the

joint reports, dated the 30th November

1934 and the 10th December 1934, which

you submitted, in conjunction with your

Ethiopian colleagues on the British

Somaliland – Ethiopian Boundary

Commission, in regard to the attitude

adopted by the local Italian

authorities on the Commission's arrival

at Walwal on the 23rd November last.

Consideration has also been given to

your reports on the events which took

place after the Commission had

withdrawn from Walwal to Ado.

2.

2.   You are aware that, as a result of the encounter which took place on the 5th December between Italian and Ethiopian forces at Walwal, a state of acute tension began between Italy and Ethiopia; a position of affairs which has caused issues of the greatest political importance to be raised, bearing not only on the relations of Italy and Ethiopia but on the general European political situation. Having regard to the more momentous events which followed at a date subsequent to the refusal of the Italian authorities to allow the Commission access to Walwal, and to the very important issues thereby involved, His Majesty's Government have come to the conclusion that no useful purpose would be served by taking any action vis-à-vis the Italian Government in regard to the protest submitted by the Joint Commission.

3.   At the same time, the difficult position in which you were placed as a result

League of Nations. [On 3 January 1935 the Emperor appealed to the League of Nations.*]

We are getting on with our usual job now. Sending this via Somaliland.

On 28 November 1949, Sandy organized a party on the fifteenth anniversary of Walwal at his house in the Embassy in Addis Ababa.

'Our small cocktail party went off very well. We had mostly Ethiopians including some who were on the Boundary Commission.'

Dagghabur, Ethiopia, 28 December 1934

Many thanks for your letters and sweets; they are always welcome. The last lot of books are much appreciated.

We have had a busy week getting on with our grazing discussions. We worked all Xmas day up till dark. Things are going all right but it is an awful business trying to argue with a fool who knows nothing of the Somali and cares still less; that is what we are reduced to as my opposite number has succumbed to nervous exhaustion and been sent to Addis Ababa.

The Italians raided Gerlogubi and took away a car; they had bombed the place a few days before and all the Ethiopian garrison fled leaving it deserted but the Ethiopians got back the car.

I enclose a copy of the interrogation of a deserter from the Italians; he deserted before the fight; the Italian is his. Please keep it for me; it is a confidential document I suppose but gives you a good idea of the Italian methods.

We did not, as you know, return to British Somaliland in spite of the Colonial Office panicking. We have stayed and are getting on with our job. Our next move is to Jijiga and then back to Borama; up to Addis in February and home soon after.

Sir George Hill [the Director of the British Museum] has very kindly arranged with the Professor of Anthropology at London School of Economics to admit me to his lectures whenever I want free of charge. I shall of course take advantage of it. He has also offered me or rather allowed me to do voluntary work in the British Museum, Ethnographical Department while I am on leave. What with the relics from the old towns and the collections I have sent home I shall be busy there anyway I think. Some of our finds are quite new, such as the worked soapstone plate-like affair and the soapstone beads. I imagine they are a new line for Arabian or East African medieval towns.

A further outbreak of rabies at Hargesia in which two officers and an officer's wife are involved. Thank goodness our Doctor is really efficient and took active measures here or else we should have had the outbreak far worse.

* The National Archives, Ref: FO 371/19105 (see pages 140–1).

The Doctor [Major Godding] has been in four shows since the Great War and in spite of that he is very up to date, an exception in the Royal Army Medical Corps (RAMC).

The Sunday Times account of the fight was very good; the bit about the Somaliland Official is rubbish of course.

Borama, British Somaliland via Aden, 18 January 1935

We got back to our base camp last week. I promptly caught a cold; I suppose the increased size of my living tent was too much for me after the small one. Anyway it does not freeze here at night.

I had some shooting during the last two days, just for meat; got five gazelles.

We are getting on well with our discussion and I hope to be in Addis by my birthday. I have started burning all my old office files and clearing out rubbish.

The Ethiopian who left us on Xmas day with a nervous breakdown was met by Collingwood twelve days later running all the arrangements for the reception of the Crown Prince of Sweden at Dire Dawa. They just loathe the Somali country and develop an acute inferiority complex once they are in it.

The Walwal incident still goes on I fancy. We have got an Official Italian map 1934 which marks only Ogaden tribes round Walwal; exact opposite from the claims in the press. I fancy most of the blatant lies have been exposed now and they have been rather badly shown up. We are out of touch with things now.

I start my Sunday excavations again with Taylor this week. According to reports there are two new towns to be visited.

British Somaliland via Aden, 31 January 1935

We are still hard at work finishing up our Final Agreement and Grazing Area Report. I shall be thankful when it is done. We are making good progress now.

There is a very good if somewhat journalistic account of the first incident at Walwal in the Daily Herald of January 12th. They have got it I suppose by bribing the Ethiopian Minister at Rome. It is Mr Proce's verbal they quote. I have asked Douglas and Foyles to send you five copies. As we thought, the Italian bombast died down once some of the documents were produced and we have no news of late.

I think we shall be up to time and I contemplate being able to get away from Addis about middle of March. We leave here February or thereabouts but have to undergo festivities en route. One of these fearful banquets is already foreshadowed at both Harar and Dire Dawa as guests of the Ethiopian authorities. Other dinners with foreign Consuls are also on the programme; if I don't have a liver at the end of it I ought to. We have to give a huge dinner at Dire Dawa for twenty-nine guests. I am arranging the whole affair now; as it is official, the order of precedence and all that is most important especially as the French will be there. The Consul from Harar is coming through here tomorrow and we hope to discuss with him our proposals for the dinner and our visits to Harar and Dire Dawa.

I was unable to go out digging last week but I have been able to hear of another four towns and I send two coolies out to them to report on the size and bring back surface finds. I hope to be able to visit them perhaps next tour if I do not get a transfer at once. Hope to get some digging done this week.

British Legation Addis Ababa, Ethiopia, 5 March 1935

We arrived up here last night after a good journey. I came through to Harar and Dire Dawa in the car of two Americans, a very nice couple who were shooting in Somaliland. It was very comfortable after the trucks. They came up to Addis with us.

We are in luxury here; Taylor and I are in the guest house but feed with Sir Sidney and Lady Barton. The Legation is outside the town on a hill surrounded by blue gum trees and lovely gardens. The town is about the foulest place you could imagine. I was given a lift from the station in the Consul's car; we knocked a chap down on the way which caused a little bother.

We came up in the same railway carriage as the new Italian Military Attaché and we were tackled by the Correspondent of the Correra Della Sierra. Things are pretty bad and it looks rather as if there will be a war; both parties being members of the League of Nations makes the repercussions rather serious as Ethiopia is bound to appeal to the other members of the League and if Italy resigns it does not make things any better. It looks like having repercussions in Europe.

The country round here is all cultivated and very fertile. We spent the night at Awash in the hotel there attached to the railway and one stops at various places for lunch. First day it was at Afdem, second day at Modjo. The buffets are run by Greeks and really quite well done. We ran into a camel or rather the engine did and I suppose killed it or at least knocked it off the line and we saw it lying at the side.

We have been interviewed by the Daily Telegraph, Daily Express and Times correspondents. There is a rumour of more to follow by Achille Benedotti of Correra Della Sierra who as I told you we met in the train.

I hope to goodness I shall be able to get away without delays and reach home end of month or early in April. However I have been warned I must be prepared to return to Somaliland at once after we have finished here. I presume they have some special job for me or else they would let me go on leave.

THE SCOTTISH DAILY EXPRESS   MARCH 6, 1935

THREE BRITONS KEEP ABYSSINIAN SECRET

SAW TROUBLE THAT RAISED WAR THREAT

Britain's "Biscuit Tin" Territory Watched
During Dangerous Clash At
Ual Ual

By HAROLD PEMBERTON,
"Daily Express" Special Correspondent.

ADDIS ABABA (Abyssinia), Tuesday.

THREE men who know the truth about the Ual Ual incident (which gave rise to the present tension between Italy and Abyssinia) have arrived in Addis Ababa.

They are Colonel Clifford, of the Royal Engineers; Mr. A. T. Curle, British Political Officer; and Captain R. H. R. Tayler, of the Royal Artillery.

They are the British members of the combined British Abyssinian Commission which has been drawing up the boundary between Abyssinia and British Somaliland.

Ual Ual is on the border of Abyssinia and Italian Somaliland.

Their arrival caused a buzz of excitement in the foreign legations here, for these three sunburned, travel-stained Britons who have spent a month in the desert hold a secret of international importance.

They will preserve their secret.

Britain does not want to be mixed up in the Ual Ual affair, though if the matter ultimately goes to the League of Nations for arbitration these officers might be asked to give their views.

Their presence here, however, has nothing to do with the crisis. They have come to Addis Ababa from the interior to fix up a final border agreement between Britain and Abyssinia.

All these negotiations have been carried out amicably.

The commission had completed their border inquiry on the spot and were travelling round settling matters concerning the grazing rights of nomad tribes when, unfortunately, they bumped into an Italian post occupying Ual Ual.

EMBARRASSING POSITION

Presumably the British commission thought it was Abyssinian territory. Possibly they were led into this belief by their Abyssinian escort.

Anyhow, the position was embarrassing. The British, with their escort, immediately retired about twenty miles from the Ual Ual "volcano."

They stuck the British flag in a biscuit tin to mark the British camp.

To stick the flag in the ground would mean, according to Abyssinian custom, "We are claiming this territory."

An Abyssinian garrison had squatted down opposite the Italian post at Ual Ual.

No doubt the two opposing forces hurled insults at each other.

SHOTS FIRED

Shots were fired, and there occurred the incident that has led to the present crisis.

The British Commission kept out of it except that a doctor attended the wounded.

Colonel Clifford was anxious in no way to discuss the rights and wrongs of the affair when the Commission received me this afternoon at the British Legation. The political situation is too delicate for that.

British Legation Ethiopia, Addis Ababa, 7 March 1935

Find the bag does not close till Friday now so am adding a second letter. Yesterday we went round to call on the Minister of Foreign Affairs, a funny little Ethiopian with a son who was at Brasenose, Oxford and plays cricket [Heruy Walda Sellase, Ethiopian Foreign Minister and his son Siraq]. The poor youth had to interpret for his father. Then in the afternoon we had to go and call on the Emperor where we were received by him sitting at a table; very small man not the least impressive. He had two King Charles Spaniels who played about which was the nicest thing. He is having a bad time as the old school want to fight the Italians at once before more reinforcements arrive. They say they beat them at Adowa and can do so again but of course do not appreciate the modern weapons. [Italy was defeated by Ethiopia at the Battle of Adowa in 1896.]

The Minister, Sir Sidney Barton, was many years in China but has not very much fine stuff in the jade or snuff bottle line. [Sandy's father had a very good collection of Chinese snuff bottles.]

It is nice living in a house with good food well served, silver tea set et cetera. We shall be nearly three weeks here.

British Legation Addis Ababa, Ethiopia, 13 March 1935

Here we are still stuck at Addis. Had a round of calls on missionaries, the local British lawyer and the Germans who were with the Ethiopian section.

Taylor and I walked down to the town on Sunday and on the way passed one dead donkey, one dead horse and a dead sheep all lying in the streets. Some of the landmarks are two traction engine wheels, one on each side of the road; they are half buried by now but must have lain there for years [they were still there in 1941]. It is an incredible place.

We went round the Church of St. George yesterday. The English Padre [Padre Mathews] who had visited us in Somaliland showed us round; curious place. The inside is a mass of crude biblical scenes painted on the walls. We were shown round the vestry, a sort of jumble house with the priest's trousers hanging up and the books bound with leather on vellum, holy drums, censors, bells, gold embroidered trappings for mules for Palm Sunday, vestments, umbrellas and modern bedroom toilet set.

We get little or no news about the 'War'. The rains, due in ten days, will probably delay matters.

The Italians have had the irrigation pumps for a dam on the Webbi Shebelli ready in Mogadishu for the past six months. Their orders for petrol and oil are perfectly colossal, I believe, as they have 200 aeroplanes at Mogadishu [in Italian Somaliland]. If they do fight, they will make for the upper waters of the Juba and the Webbi Shebelli and the Bale province but their troops will die like flies from fever.

British Legation Addis Ababa, Ethiopia, 18 March 1935

Things still look pretty grim here and no one knows what is happening.

We all went to a race meeting on Saturday; not up to much but we got a good lunch after. I sat opposite the Italian Minister who was very lavish with his champagne.

We all dined with the Kametz family in the evening. He was on the Commission with the Ethiopian section. We had a Hungarian meal; very good and fresh strawberries as good as home grown.

I have now received orders to return to Somaliland and proceed at once to Dagghabur to act as British Delegate at a claims conference; all home leave has been stopped for the time being. Dagghabur is one of the foulest spots on this earth. I have been there already and we spent Xmas and New Year there. It is only 180 miles from Walwal so if the fun starts we shall get it from the air. It is a nuisance and would appear unnecessary. I have done nearly nineteen months out here. The Minister and the Colonel are both doing all they can to help me to go home at once. I hope I shall succeed. Meantime I do not propose to hurry and shall just take my time to return to Somaliland. I have to go alone. I have disposed of all my stores and shall have to lay in a fresh lot. However I cannot land at Berbera for another three weeks, ie 8 April, so it will be some time before I reach Dagghabur. Things may have changed by then as I am wanted at home to finish off some of the work of the Commission. I am afraid I shall not be home till May.

They are making tremendous progress with their roads here; you can motor to Kenya in three days now from Addis Ababa.

We were shown round the new parliament house on Monday. Ferro cement building with highly coloured frescos round the walls, some amazingly good – The Queen of Sheba three times life-size visiting the Court of Solomon. The laying of the foundation stone of the building is a triumph – the architect is depicted in a very ill-fitting tail coat – life size. The native artist is defeated by the boots of Europeans and can't make them look right. Anyhow it is an attempt to do something with all local artists.

I am putting in my application for transfer to another colony. I have had quite enough of this; the prospect of two months or so at Dagghabur is more than I want at the end of nineteen months in the country.

We are threatened with an official reception at the palace next week.

I see they have refused to publish the report we wrote on the battle of Walwal in spite of the official requests and also to publish the documents which Ethiopia laid on the table of the League of Nations – the interrogation of the Italian '*Banda*' – threatening letters et cetera.

The various members of the Italian Legation who we have met at parties have tried to pump us in turn on the question of what we thought of Captain Cimmaruta – hinting that he had been too long in the colonies; they want it would seem to put the blame on him for his tactless handling of the situation when we first met him at Walwal. [In the official report to the Colonial Office, Colonel Clifford mentions that members of the Italian Legation said, 'Of course we do not know him here, but he seems to have been too long in the colonies and to be rather severe.' It would appear from this that his behaviour at Walwal had met with official disapproval.]*

Cimmaruta had a book published titled *Ual Ual* which Sandy felt was distorted and inaccurate.

The press cuttings are very interesting. Did you see the one about Mussolini's speech to the departing Fascists 'It is better to live for one day like a lion than a hundred days like a sheep'. An Ethiop is reported to have replied 'It is better to be a live dog than a dead lion'. The lies in the Italian press are appalling. It was Ethiopia who suggested the neutral zone not Italy. It was Italy who held the business up because they said they had no instructions.

Am feeling pretty fed up with life; it is too hard really on Frances my leave having to be put off and off like this but it does mean I get longer anyway which is a small compensation.

Djibuti, French Somaliland, 4 April 1935

This letter will probably get home the same time as I do; that is I expect on Easter Saturday. They have at last given me leave and I got a telegram saying so two days ago.

We had the usual rush at the end of our time in Addis.

We went to dine with the Emperor one night; only our Legation and the Royal Family. The knives, forks and spoons and even the pincers for serving the inevitable asparagus were solid gold. The plates were encircled with gold. The dinner was not bad. On entering the dining room I saw a big bug on my napkin; it fell to the floor as I opened it out and must have climbed up my leg as I was beautifully decorated round the waist with half a dozen appalling bites. The Emperor is a pleasant and intelligent little man. They all wear their own dress with silk capes. The European Lady-in-waiting who accompanies the Empress and the Princesses came out to the country some years ago as a midwife. We all wore tailcoats and white waistcoats.

* The National Archives, CO535/11116.

On Thursday we signed up all our documents at the Ministry of Foreign Affairs and duly had photographs taken of the ceremony. After we adjourned to the Legation where we presented presents from the British Government; silver cigarette boxes, field glasses and so forth. They were all very touched.

On Friday morning we left. At the station the *Fitaurari* presented the Colonel and I each with an Ethiopian '*Shama*' or shawl; a thing which they all wear and worth about 3s. I shall give mine to the British Museum if they have not got one.

We had the usual journey down in the train; uncomfortable. I was in a carriage with an Armenian American, a merchant in a big way in Jibuti, quite a nice fellow. We spent the night at Dire Dawa and I met lots of people I knew. Left next morning and lunched at the buffet at Aicha station where we were rescued by the Greek proprietor, Mr Kara Nicholas, who we knew well as we had spent three months there when Beitz was murdered.

We reached Djibuti about 4.45pm. It is a town with a harbour and large stone buildings; hotels run by Greeks, bars and shops; the latter are quite good. Our friends, the Pretceilles, met us and we stayed at the same hotel. They were very pleased to see us and made all arrangements for us which was a great blessing and we fed at the same table. Clifford left the next day on a French boat and I remained on. The British Vice Consul, a trader here and quite a decent fellow, did what he could to entertain us.

I have called on the Ethiopian Consulate and the Governor and met lots of people I knew from Harar and in fact have made the best of a bad job. Dined out once or twice. It is pretty hot but that does not worry me.

The Ethiopian Consul threatens to come and see me off on the Indian steamer when I go on Saturday to Aden. The Captain of the boat is the fellow who was Captain of the *Cetriana* when I made my first voyage to Kismayu twelve years ago and which sank the next trip.

I went over to Zeila, took some bearings and did some plane table work. I also went out to the island. I walked inland 50yds and found a pocket full of Celadon ware. I have a big box full of finds for the British Museum, all the stuff we got round Borama.

There is a rush of arms sellers now. The Belgians got in first. The Mission they sent to announce the accession of Leopold 4th was headed by a merchant who paid all his own expenses and then swapped rifles for coffee. Over 300 tons have just arrived here, all ammunition. Various Danes, Czechs, Germans and English are all out to sell different weapons. The Ethiop has already nine different sorts of machine guns! 22mm and AA guns of the latest pattern from Switzerland have also just arrived but they always forget the spares and cleaning materials.

We get well looked after in this hotel. We get special dishes, lobster and oysters whenever possible at no extra charge.

The Emperor wishes to give us an order and they have written home to ask if the Colonel and I can have permission to accept it; Order of the Trinity – Star of Ethiopia or what not.

I have five great boxes of maps and documents to take home with me to deliver to the War Office. I have got a free pass through the customs at Marseilles for the stuff.

I have no stores or clothes and am feeling very Bolshevistic. I shall be heartily glad to get out of Somaliland.

CHAPTER **9**

On the Border of War: British Somaliland and Fascist Italy, 1935–6

Whilst home on leave Sandy's marriage was breaking up. On 2 October 1935, Italy finally invaded Ethiopia from Eritrea in the north, while another Italian army invaded from Italian Somaliland.

Sandy now returned to British Somaliland as Political Officer attached to the Somaliland Camel Corps.

Burao, British Somaliland via Aden, 3 October 1935

Very little news indeed; Aden has issued notices about bombing from the air and what to do with gas, as it appears that if we impose sanctions, Italy will adopt offensive measures against us to get Berbera and Djibuti as parts of their territories, provided they have by that time conquered the Ogaden. But we shall not impose sanctions till we are ready.

The French have already landed more troops at Djibuti. There is another ambulance coming out via Berbera to help the Ethiop, run by an influential committee in London under Lord Lugard [former distinguished Governor General of Nigeria]. Colonel Jack Llewellyn, who commanded the 3rd KAR when I was in it, is leading it and has already gone to Kenya to enlist dressers and transport officers; I should imagine they would get some stiffs.

Had a very busy weekend; the fortnightly intelligence report, eighteen pages, I gave them for a start. My agent on the Indian coasting steamer produced an amazingly interesting report. These fellows, in this case the usual Scot, are looked down on in Aden but if you ask them to help in a job of that sort, they are only too delighted.

At present a sort of game of chess is going on in the Red Sea with the fleets. We are pushing ships in while the Italians are sending submarines I gather.

We hear the balloon has gone up at last but we have had no orders yet. I expect I shall be moving out to Eik at once. I have a very nice fellow to work with, a Captain Hill, a Gunner. We have discussed all the questions together.

Have all my stores packed up ready so that I can get out at once. Telegraphs are open till midnight in case of urgent orders and I have a runner sleeping in my bungalow ready if a wire comes.

I believe our torpedo and munition factories at home are working as they have never worked since 1918. We are taking no risks.

Eik, British Somaliland via Aden, 16 October 1935

At last we have got out; orders came on Thursday and we started off the same afternoon.

I am under the Military now and have to report direct to the Camel Corps. I am attached as Political Officer to a section of the frontier. It is the very long straight bit on the map, 250 miles or so. My section of the boundary, Bohotleh to Aran Areh will get most of the people but will not be so interesting as the next section towards Borama, which has the road traffic. It is patrolled by cars with machine guns mounted on them. One troop of four cars does each half every other day.

I live at Eik at the HQ with the reserve which is 30 odd miles from the boundary. I am ensconced in the middle of the town; get bits of celadon and Arab pottery from under the rugs on the tent floor. The ruined town covers about half a square mile on the fringe of the new settlement. The houses are about 10ft high but scattered anyhow; rubbish heaps all over the place. We have a European Doctor here; true he is a lunatic but appears very keen on his job. There is also an aerodrome as there is an air patrol of the boundary daily and the plane lands here for messages. The bed of an old lake forms the runway. We have each got a T made in cloth, 6ft long, and we place circles at various prearranged points which have a numerical significance. We then have a code against the numerical combinations and so can signal to the plane if we want him to land. I shall do so to get him to take this mail in to Burao. All our water has to come from Burao so baths are difficult.

I have an interpreter and ten armed locals. I have them posted out on the main caravan tracks coming from the Ethiopian side and they collect the news from passers-by and inform the car patrols as they pass. In addition we have agents over the other side who bring us back direct information.

I went out the first day down the boundary to Aran Areh at the west end of our section and collected all the information about the tribes. Spent the night in the camp of the Camel patrol of the neighbouring section. Went with a Camel Corps truck, just boy, cook and bedding; slept under the stars. The boundary cut has been widened and makes an excellent road. We passed several villages who all asked for news of the war.

Collingwood has taken over the intelligence job. Last we heard was that the Italians have eight submarines in Massawa. We had fourteen vessels, all destroyers and battleships in Aden last week and we are awaiting more submarines. The Italians will feel the oil and coal question first; they will be very hard hit. An agent estimated 600 cars an hour use the Massawa–Mogadishu road; that combined with aeroplanes, armoured cars, refrigeration plants, water distilling plants et cetera must use a lot. [Sanctions on oil were expected to be applied but in fact never were.]

The Italians will come a terrible cropper when their organization at home goes west; they will never be able to evacuate all the soldiery out here or feed them and the result will be appalling.

Gas masks and everything are ready for us in Egypt in the event of military sanctions being imposed.

This open air life and really interesting work in ideal surroundings is making me feel ever so much better.

What is the Aunts' address now? They are very wise to get out of Italy. I wonder the cook and the butler let them go.

Eik, British Somaliland via Aden, 22 October 1935

We are in touch with the outside world but in such a way that we get no real news. Two aeroplanes a day come over us and one usually lands to take up letters but they only stay a few minutes and are off again. At places where there is a patrol but no aerodrome, they have a message picking-up arrangement. This involves a small bag tied with a long loop which is put between two forks; the plane dives on it with a rod with a hook on the end lowered from the plane and this catches the loop and the message is hauled up through a small door in the bottom of the plane.

Was up on the boundary one day last week and got one deserter from the Ethiopian forces. Gerlogubi in Ethiopia fell some time ago. The Italians attacked it with aircraft; seven tanks and native infantry and the garrison fled whereupon the aeroplanes flew low machine-gunning them; 40 survivors got away to Gorrahei out of 150. Twelve Somalis deserted with their arms et cetera. Gorrahei is being attacked from the air. Forty-seven per cent of the Somalis deserted with their arms and are now forming an armed band just across the border. They mostly belong to our tribes and are a disturbing element. Hear that since Gorrahei has fallen, the Italians are reported being 17 miles beyond it. They dropped propaganda leaflets on it saying they would be in Addis in three weeks and that then they would punish the Muslims who had sided with the Christian Ethiopians.

The Italians are apparently expecting us to occupy the areas our tribes graze on in Ethiopia up to the Fafen and Harradiguit line; and as it is our sphere of influence, it is just possible that they will respect that area. So far they have not looted our tribes at all.

Various mystery aeroplanes have been flying across the Protectorate. It is a quick means of communication of course from Assab to Mogadishu without asking permission.

An American woman journalist from Ethiopia reached Berbera and chartered a car and disappeared, eventually being traced and found at Bohotleh in our section; they have sent out to arrest her. She was trying to get to Walwal or Gorrahei. It was a desperate attempt. She had spent four years in Russia. She never came our way.

I hear there are now in Aden one Fighter Squadron, one Light Bombing Squadron, one Flying boat Squadron while a hundred planes are at Port Sudan in case.

British Somaliland via Aden, 30 October 1935

An Italian plane was trespassing over Khartoum and was forced down by our planes. They found it had a camera and when developed the plates were all of Khartoum defences.

I have been out for three days this week along to the east of our section to Bohotleh and beyond. Met Tony Phillimore who regaled me with paté and champagne.

It is a tiring game along that frontier, mile after mile. The active operations have virtually ceased opposite us. Gorrahei still holds out. They played a ruse on the Italian aeroplanes by putting paper and clothes in the bush and hiding some way off. They bombed the paper in great style.

It is quite true that an Esa shot down an Italian aeroplane west of Jijiga; it came low and a fellow fired a shot at random which killed the pilot. The machine came down and the fellow fired his second and last round at the observer and they knifed the mechanic in the usual brutal fashion. [Sandy recalled later that it had been sheer luck as the weapon would have been a lump of verdigrissed lead.]

The Italians gave out to their troops that the French were too old and tired to fight, like the Fusil Gras rifles.

Italy is apparently more united than ever at home but the climate out here will tell in the first place with the poor food. Their small posts on the border are left without food now. While I was opposite one, they let off volleys of shots at game and apparently do this daily to live. They only get a very little olive oil and flour neither of which the native likes.

Our chief bother at the moment is deserters, Somalis with arms and ammunition from both sides.

It is very hot and dusty here now but baths are better as we are able to create a reserve of water in the empty petrol tins.

Our air patrols still continue but don't seem to see much.

We have got our wireless back; not that it is up to much or any use but it is a means of communication.

British Somaliland via Aden, 6 November 1935

I have lots to read in the Daily Times and with being out so much 'Boosting' along all day in a truck I don't have any time for reading but should love some books later – spy stories – something really light and 'Tripish' are best.

Delighted at the thought of a Fortnum and Mason parcel; many thanks, it will be very welcome as I have cut out all purely luxury stores from my lot this time, but have the sound, solid essentials. Vegetables come out by air once a week, cabbages and French beans.

Was out last weekend down at the west end of our beat and off tomorrow up to the east end. I had some shooting last time out; gazelle of sorts and saw a leopard. Have kept myself in fresh meat for three weeks. Do a bit of poaching on the Ethiopian side of the border as of course no Habash is ever there within hundreds of miles.

Rain has come on late and appears to be falling well in the Ogaden around Walwal. We have ordered all our tribes who had crossed the border following the rain to come back into British Territory for the meantime.

The rain will upset the Italians who were supposed to be starting to attack Gorrahei this week. They are very short of food for the native troops and a looting party ran amok last week and got several thousand camels and killed a man and a woman with a child on her back, all British Protected victims. That will cause a stir at home.

The Italians are very anxious to keep on our right side. We can see from telegrams from Graziani [the General commanding the Italian forces in Italian Somaliland] that he has changed his tone from Walwal days. Even admits now that our tribes graze at Walwal.

Baldwin's speech at Bournemouth was excellent and I am surprised to see such an anti Italian feeling at home. [Adowa in Ethiopia had just been bombed by Mussolini. In his recent book, *At War with Waugh: The Real Story of Scoop*, Bill Deedes mentions Baldwin as saying then 'that it was useless for Britain to accept obligations under the covenant of the League of Nations unless the country had at its command adequate forces to carry them out'. Sandy must have been agreeing with this statement.]*

Glad I got my supplies of white vermouth here in good time with Italian exports closing down.

* Deedes, W.F.R., *At War with Waugh*, Macmillan, 2003, p. 65.

Sir Perceval Phillips is out in Berbera looking for news. He might find some from us up here if he came. [He was special correspondent for the Daily Telegraph.]

Many thanks for the Illustrated London News and Sunday Times; both most welcome. I pass them round and then on to the Political Officer, Church, in the next section, who sends me the Listener in exchange.

British Somaliland via Aden, 21 November 1935

We have moved up 30 miles to a new camp on the boundary. We are now in touch with our patrols and the tribes. It is incidentally a much better site for a camp. No ruins but an open space which we are already converting into an aerodrome landing ground. Meantime the planes do the picking-up business in front of an assembled audience of coolies and troops.

The Italian native irregulars continue to spread civilization; there was a very brutal rout sometime ago for stock. A party of irregulars simply shot up the villages of British Protected natives across the border. The casualties were one man killed who was riddled with bullets, his wife and two month old child, three women wounded and three men and a 1,000 head of stock carried off. They gave the troops unlimited ammunition and I have lots of the cases and clips as evidence. Since then another has been reported under similar circumstances.

Reports all indicate things are not going too easily for the Italians. The troops are not keen to fight all day in a tropical sun and in the Ogaden it gets hotter every day now. Even the Times thinks they are getting fed up in Eritrea.

Gorrahei is reported to have fallen at last but not till the European troops lost large numbers. They wear a pack and full equipment and so they must be suffering hell; it is bad enough with only the minimum of clothes on.

Hill, who commands the Section and who I work with, is going on leave on medical grounds. I shall be very sorry when he goes as he was very nice to work with and we used to help each other. We get on splendidly. I do the aerodrome and he combines a visit to his patrols with collating information for me. He is one of the best fellows I have ever had to work with.

I have had my eyes on an Ethiopian deserter who has been living with some of our tribes. I hope to get him in soon. If the Italian irregulars hear of him they will shoot up the tribes.

When I was going along the boundary the other day in a truck, a village, newly arrived, was camped beside the track and all the children ran screaming, so we asked what they were doing. They asked us if we were Italians. When we told them we were English, they stopped and said they heard the Italians looted everything so they were running away. The Somalis would much sooner have the Ethiopian; he does not oppress them quite the same.

The ration and food question will get the Italians; sanctions of course stop Kenya or us from selling camels et cetera. [On 18 November, the League of Nations had imposed sanctions against Italy but that did not include oil which if included would have stopped the war.] We are in touch with a post of Italian '*Banda*' at the end of our Section opposite one of our posts. They beg us for rations – tea and sugar et cetera. They have unlimited S.A.A. so shoot everything.

Once the Italians reach Jijiga it will not be long before they reach the railway. There is open country for 30 miles west and then there is a road down the escarpment which overlooks a vast plain to the railway. South of Jijiga is hilly of course.

Looking forward to the Xmas parcel. Never will it have been more welcome than this year when luxuries are luxuries and we are living really a very hard life.

British Somaliland via Aden, 10 December 1935

Many thanks for the letter and papers, also for the Fortnum and Mason parcel. I have started on the cherries in brandy and they are excellent. The box will give me the greatest pleasure; what with caviar and paté and turtle soup it is grand. Again many thanks.

Heard this morning that the Air Mail line is starting from Berbera, a branch of the Ala Littoria, the Italian service to Mogadishu and that we can send letters home at 9d for half an ounce so I sent a short one to Jane to try it out. It seems a bit high priced to start with; six and a half days home.

We have had an outbreak of smallpox amongst the coolies; it has given our Medico something to do.

The state of affairs in Eritrea is curious. The supply arrangements are appalling; if a car breaks down it is just capsized on the edge of the road and its load put on to another. Animal transport is terrible; soldiers overload the beasts, then put their equipment on and then themselves. There is no discipline on the march or veterinary service. The European troops never come into the front line and never shoot but do everything else; the good units are the blackshirts apparently. Sanctions have begun to hit them. Their lack of essential organizing and maintenance capacity leads to terrible waste. The price of meat in Italian Somaliland is fantastic.

The accounts of the Italian reverse in the Ogaden are interesting; a motor column walked into an ambush; they had no advance guard out and underrated their opponents; six officers were killed, two wounded, two taken prisoner and some 600 natives killed and 72 wounded. They had seventy trucks of which fifteen carried Whippet tanks on them. Their tanks got down as soon as the fight started but the anti tank guns knocked four out at once and the others retired. The importance of the show is that it has exploded the invulnerability of the tank which the Italians had so impressed on the native. Now their two great assets, the tank and the aeroplane have lost their moral effect to a great extent.

We have had two letters from the Ogaden; one from two big men asking the British Government to come and take over the country and command it as soon as possible; others wanting to become British subjects with their tribes. We of course refuse to interfere.

British Somaliland via Aden, 19 December 1935

Things seem to be going pretty badly for the Italians now all round; they are content with sitting quiet opposite us but they are uneasy not only about the Ethiopians but about the food question as well and there is talk of requisitioning stock from the tribes. [Shortly before this letter was written on 8 December 1935 the famous Hoare-Laval plan was taken to Paris. Mussolini, thinking that the war was going badly, was all set to acquiesce. This new plan was more generous to Italy but still included for Ethiopia a corridor to the coast through the Danakil, this time to Assab in Eritrea. Uproar ensued when the plan was leaked to the press. The Corridor was referred to by *The Times* as a 'Corridor for Camels'. Sir Samuel Hoare resigned and the plan was rejected.]

The Italians are consolidating their administration of the Ogaden and starting disarming the tribes which means they send their rifles on to our tribes. We shall of course be compelled to disarm ours in due course.

British Somaliland via Aden, 28 December 1935

I celebrated Xmas day by staying in bed till 8.00am.

Our landing ground is now complete and has been passed suitable which means that our mail arrived in a more orthodox manner than before.

I got a letter asking me if I was prepared to accept an MBE (Civil Division) in the New Year's honours. I replied in the affirmative; it is not up to much; something to be thankful for. [Colonel Clifford had written to Sandy's father telling him that he hoped that Sandy would get an honour appropriate to his performance with the Commission. He had been trying to influence folk to give him an OBE, though MBE would have been normal considering his lack of seniority.]

The Italians have started clashing with our tribes in a mild way round Damot; an aeroplane shot at some water camels for no apparent reason and their irregular troops assaulted a native. They have not moved at all since the last reverse and their confident note is changed to one of boastful desperation;

at least the officers, who our Camel Corps see up the far end, have conveyed that. They are still terribly pro Mussolini. We have an Italian speaking Officer up there and they keep in close touch with the Italians opposite.

We hope to listen to the King's speech tonight if the operator can get it; he is rather nutter fisted with the tuning in.

'Truth' is interesting on the 'War'. Their 'Old War Correspondent' is quite good. Shortage of food is their trouble opposite us. You cannot make roads to take very heavy traffic unless you have the proper stone and no matter how hard you try; that is what is defeating them opposite us. Only earth is no good.

Must betake myself to the Camel Corps tent to have a bottle of beer and some caviar to celebrate Christmas.

British Somaliland via Aden, 31 December 1935

Italians are getting very windy now and their aeroplanes bomb and shoot anything. Rumours again that Gorrahei has been retaken and an Italian retreat but unconfirmed. There have been three air attacks on British tribes in the last few days who were mistaken for Ethiopians.

I have been on my usual round, 200 odd miles every week collecting information and they have trebled my irregular native scouts which will help us no end and improve our results.

A tramp steamer has arrived at Berbera with 2 million rounds of SAA from England with papers in order but a large number of anti tank guns from Estonia have no papers so can't be unloaded. The Ethiopians sent down 6 trucks to bring the stuff up; it will take 300 at least. Meantime the steamer lies in Berbera. Luckily the Italian submarines did not get it. In addition the following have also come through Berbera:

14,000 rifles (German and Belgium)
1,020 machine guns (German)
44 cannons (German)
37,200 shells for above (German)
13,000 grenades (German)
430 swords (English)

Indications are that the Italians will be making an offensive soon. Accounts from the Northern Front seem pretty bad. When they admit that twenty-seven Europeans have been killed it is bad. All is quiet opposite us except bombing of the wells all over the place.

The tribes are co-operating splendidly and I got no less than five letters in Arabic last week from them and they send in men who saw bombing et cetera which is a great help. I have a good lot of helpers. I give them things like rice which is cheaper than money and more appreciated. Give them a cup of tea or rather the interpreter does and they are happy.

Two native Italian soldiers of eight years standing have just deserted to us, one a corporal and the other a private, on account of hunger. Their tale of hunger is pretty grim but of course they put it on a bit.

Out suddenly on New Year's day to investigate tribal movement. No rest for the wicked.

British Somaliland via Aden, 8 January 1936

Actually had a fairly quiet week. I had to come back from my trip down the border early to meet Air Vice Marshal Gossage who is OC Aden. He is a very nice fellow indeed; he landed for breakfast and we took him up to the boundary. We had an extra patrol along the boundary on Sunday to see if the movement across the border was still on. When the plane got back it was one mass of oil and it just got in, the big end having gone; so they had to bring out another engine and we had a spate of air activity. We put up the fellows; they were a Sergeant Pilot and a leading Aircraft man, both very nice fellows; very good class and better than their officers. Other NCOs came out and we were immensely struck by the very fine class of fellow they had. They took three days to patch it up and left this morning.

The Italians have been having a black week; a plane came down near Dagghabur and the locals shot two of the fellows who staggered out half dazed and a third took two bottles of water and walked away unharmed; however he was followed and found dead. Second-hand information says they beheaded him and ate the others but I refuse to believe it till I get an eye witness account. It must have been about fourth hand by the time the Italians got the news, therefore very unreliable.

I have been given charge of the political work of two sections now; the one from Aran Areh to Banka Wajale has been added on. My organization for getting news has been so successful that we were getting all the news from the next section as well at half the cost and while they could produce nothing we produced the goods. It is a fearful lot but I shall be able to compete all right.

I get given anything I want now; air patrols, extra men, extra money so there is really some inducement to work and get a good show going. I have an Arabic clerk now to do my Arabic letters to people. I have been getting quite a number in with news. Off again down to my new section.

British Somaliland via Aden, 16 January 1936

I had a trip last week along our new section and went into Burao and spent two nights with the Colonel of the Camel Corps. The change and living in a house out of the eternal glare and sun and being in a very cheery mess did me a world of good and I felt ever so much better when I left; not that I was ever ill. I sent my boy in by air to get my dinner jacket out of store. It was grand to have a bath covering one's tummy and to change into a silk vest, silk socks and a dinner jacket and have another bath in the morning.

Things are moving now and the Italians are advancing along the road from Ado to Harradiguit [both in Ethiopia]. They are sending out aeroplanes to protect their flanks and patrols to loot. [In December Mussolini had replaced General de Bono with Marshal Bodoglio who he hoped would finish off the war more quickly before damaging oil sanctions were introduced.]

The Italians did a week's strike against the Ogaden in retaliation for the beheading of the two Italian airmen. They bombed native villages and shot them up with machine guns, killing or wounding calves, camels, young sheep and goats; also a few men and women. Typical 'Civilization' show.

The millions of munitions for Ethiopia are still held up in Berbera I believe. We have had various Italian spies round and I gather they have bombed the railway as a result I suppose.

British Somaliland via Aden, 23 January 1936

I have had a very hard week, up and down the boundary keeping pace with the Italian advance. They are looting all our villages now and I have to take statements from the survivors.

I am very lucky in my Company Commander in the Section; he is a grand fellow and backs me to the hilt.

With things humming like this I am doing seven days a week of twelve hours each and don't get much time off. I am fearfully busy now and have piles of letters to answer from kind friends who have written to me on the MBE. Many thanks indeed for your congratulations.

British Somaliland via Aden, 31 January 1936

The Italians have had another reverse, this time on the Webbi Shebelli and a number of Europeans are said to have been killed, cars and tanks captured and 2 wireless cars, 671 rifles and 2 guns and 10 boxes of ammunition. It was about three weeks ago. Two more Italian planes are also reported to have been shot down or fallen down; in one case the occupants were saved and cut up and beheaded.

The chief feature of the week's news has been the dead set against British Protected Tribes grazing near the Walwal-Harradiguit track along which a column advanced. They seized all stock and as many people as they could and shot up several men and women for no apparent reason. It is a way of getting meat stock for rations and denuding the country of possible hostile elements; they have spy mania and lock up all and sundry which means we merely get better information as natives rush back to us with news and get a reward. We employ no spies but simply rely on natives bringing the news in.

There is a lot of discontent in Italian Somaliland as they have virtually conscripted the male native population, even the Mullahs, and although they pay them well, the rations are bad; flour and olive oil. The European soldiery are in a bad way and even beg rations from the native troops.

The Ethiopian is just waiting for the rains to attack when the Italian in boots is immobile and his rations can't get up for the mud. Life in the rains in Ethiopia when it pours every afternoon and a single fly tent leaks like a sieve and you have to go to sleep wet is no joke and I should imagine would about finish the Italians off.

I have a collection of the propaganda warring leaflets, the ones they dropped saying 'You will get what you deserve'. They are printed on pink, green and white sheets and are dropped in showers apparently from the planes, the Italian colours adding insult to injury. I have sent one of the pamphlets to the Illustrated London News. I have got several.

They waste £3,000 a time in bombing Dagghabur, an average of 4 times a week; the results are nil. I had a letter from Taylor, my friend who is Assistant Military Attaché in Addis Ababa who said they dropped 300 bombs and killed a chicken. He saw the bombing at the Red Cross at Dagghabur or rather the results the same evening; 20 bombs fell within 100yds of the centre of the camp which is 1 mile from the town, incendiary and explosive. There are no doubts whatever it was a deliberate show.

I have a series of branch and grass huts at various points on my beat and I can always time it so that I can lunch or sleep in one of them. The Tug Wajale is very cold and full of fleas and bush rats. I have a tent there at the far end of my beat.

Many thanks for the pamphlet on Ethiopia. I have written to the Editors for more. They amuse me the blatant lies they tell. The number of *Dubats* [Italian-Somali irregulars with Italian officers] killed recently published as 40 is of course absurd, nearer 4,000. They cart any wounded away to Mogadishu at once and no one is allowed to talk to them. The native troops are not allowed to mix freely with people but we hear enough of their state from the frontier posts they have along at the East of the boundary.

British Somaliland via Aden, 14 February 1936

The authorities at home are getting more and more apprehensive of trouble here from the Italians. I presume they are afraid that if the Italians get Jijiga they will try to push to Berbera. Last week one Battalion of the Royal West African Frontier Force and one Battalion of KAR from Nyasaland were actually ordered here but then it was cancelled. A full Colonel, one Hornby, who has just completed command of the 16th Lancers, a mechanized cavalry Regiment, is coming out here on the 24th to take over command. He was out here in 1918. We may expect reinforcements soon. It will mean that I come completely under the military without constant interference from the Governor and the forces will be under direct control of the War Office. The present CO remains; it is all very hush hush and secret.

They have invalided home in the last four months no less than five officials, none of the administration but two Camel Corps, one Police, one Public Works and one Treasury Fellow. As a result they have restarted normal leave conditions again and people are going home every boat.

Always being on the move means one has to open tins frequently as the cook hasn't time to always have a meal ready. As a result I have had to send home for some of the more solid necessities of life such as soup squares and oatmeal. I have just been having a plate of porridge for my breakfast owing to the egg shortage.

British Somaliland via Aden, 20 February 1936

I have just had a real snorter of a trip. I had to wait till Monday to see the Colonel at Duruksi and left about 9.00 am that morning only to have a series of punctures and get caught in the rain, most unexpected at this season. I had no tent only a ground sheet 6ft by 7ft which I tie between two trees. The second day we did 12 miles when a tyre burst and then it rained cats and dogs. I could only sit in the front of the truck and read. Everything gets damp and clammy. The third day we got in to Tug Wajale after a very slow trip ploughing through sticky mud and frequently having to dig the truck out. The aeroplane passed me and dropped my mail and the packet hit a tree and burst all over the place. I trust it was all picked up.

The Ethiopians launched an attack at Harradiguit at dawn and captured the Italian fort, killing 2 officers and over 200 natives. They came by car by cover of night to about 10 miles away and attacked from the rear. There were no prisoners or wounded. Quantities of stores were taken. This is the first time fighting has actually come within our recognized grazing areas. It is some 79 miles from the Boundary.

I am trying to arrange for a small tent for the rains as I don't relish a daily soaking. The war will continue in front of us; the Ethiopians we gather propose to fight them.

The Italians have got 150 miles from Harar up a branch of the Webbe Shebelli; they are showing great activity there.

British Somaliland via Aden, 27 February 1936

I have been held up at Tug Wajale for a whole week by the rain and at last it shows signs of abating and cars are able to move about again. There were thirty stuck on the main road from Berbera to Hargesia for two days. How far the rain has gone I don't know but gather the Italians have got it too.

The French railway refuses to carry munitions from Djibuti to Addis Ababa so we have got the trade via Berbera, not that it amounts to much now.

Things are in the air and there is a lot of activity on the coast; a survey ship in Berbera is sounding the harbour. In addition six moorings for flying boats have been laid down and the new OC Troops has arrived. I have to go into Hargesia to see him on Friday. Fighter aircraft and flying boats are continually crossing from Aden.

It is extraordinary how air minded we are getting here; the new OC Troops and even lesser fry wire for a plane to take them round the boundary et cetera and it saves them days.

My garden does well; potatoes, beans, spinach, lettuce and then mushrooms abound here in the rains.

The Ethiop is pouring troops into the Ogaden with a view to advancing. They send a small party of natives to fire a few shots at some Italian posts during the night just to bait them. The Italians and the native troops in the post lose their heads and fire off every gun they have got while the natives are well under cover. When that has died down they repeat the game and so on till dawn when they have withdrawn. Last week one day they dropped nine bombs on Dagghabur and killed a chicken and a dog. The air activity is increasing again, bombing direct.

400 Italian native troops deserted last week to the Ethiopians after a meeting in which 4 of them were shot by the Italians.

They are advertising refrigerators delivered in Berbera for £30; 2 cubic feet capacity. Life in the tropics will soon be as comfortable as at home what with wireless and refrigerators.

The fellow who got typhus at the Tug Wajale has recovered all right. They flew him to Hargesia and put him in a house there. He had a tame cheetah and it is believed that the cheetah harbours a tick which carries it. I am always glad to get away from the fleas and ticks there. As a result the site of our camp was moved.

Tug Wajale, British Somaliland via Aden, 24 March 1936

We have been having the war at our front door during last week. I came along the Boundary on 19 March and heard a series of terrific explosions to the south in the Harradiguit direction, 79 miles off, obviously bombing.

On 22nd about 8.15am we heard loud booms from Jijiga direction in groups of three or four at a time. The same evening refugees came in and we got the story; the Italians had sent twelve planes in successive groups of three. They had plastered the town of Jijiga with bombs, hit every one of the big trading establishments, some two or three times and done virtually no damage; more than a quarter of the bombs were dead. The population were warned when news had come over the telephone from Dagghabur but they had so often heard the same that they did nothing; the old cry of 'wolf wolf'. No British Indians were killed but half a dozen Arabs and a dozen Somalis and sixty odd Ethiops including women and children. 150 people were wounded. Luckily there are two Red Cross outfits, Finnish and Egyptian. The hospital and Maltese Mission were not hit. Next morning at dawn two trucks with thirty-six persons crushed in arrived, all the wealthiest survivors. As I was questioning them, boom boom again and it was clear the Desperate Squadron were at it once more. Details got later in the day showed they had not done much damage. Five planes came and they only dropped four bombs in the town hitting the court house and an empty petrol store but they flew low all round the town shooting up the civil population taking refuge in the bush and any animals they saw. Luckily there were no casualties. They drop a lot of incendiary bombs on the Somali huts and Ethiop grass houses.

This morning again boom, boom, 8.20am to 9.20am but louder than before. I suppose we shall have another lot of refugees in. Most of the people had left the town last night I gather and slept half the night in the bush. They probably only demolished a few more houses. Somali villages outside the town were also bombed. The town is undefended and there appears to have been no firing at the planes. It is the headquarters of Jijiga district and a town on the road to the front. A German armoury is established there repairing rifles and machine guns [MG].

It is a new departure on this front sending planes in numbers. We could hear each time a group of planes released their bombs, as a volley of bangs went off; as many as nine, one on top of each other went off at times.

Refugees just in again. They reported that twenty-six planes bombed the remains of the town which was empty, all people having gone to the bush. They circled low firing machine guns at any beast or person they saw; killed three people and an old woman carrying firewood on her back.

All the merchants are moving their stuff back to Somaliland. One shop had three high-explosive bombs and fifteen incendiary ones in it.

[As Anthony Mockler says in *Haile Selassie's War*: 'Jijiga had been honoured with a personal and flying visit from General Ranza, the air force commander on the southern front, and reduced to a mass of ruins.'* This was in preparation for the advance on Harar which Graziani was aiming for.]

Mail late this week; won't get it till Thursday. The planes are patrolling from sea to sea all round the boundary except a small bit on the French side. Off on my beat again to start a new aerodrome on the way.

Can you ask Watsons to send me out a pair of spectacles of my type and specification. I have broken mine and it is rather glaring without any. In haste. Afraid rather a patchy letter but the Jijiga business has kept me at it.

Duruksi, British Somaliland via Aden, 1 April 1936

Many thanks for your letter and the parcel, first part of which has arrived. I enjoyed the Elves plums for dessert last night. I shall relish the caviar anon when it arrives. Many thanks indeed for the parcels; they add a little zest to the rather dull food. The spy stories are very good and just the thing for light reading. I am most grateful and they are passed around.

No more news about the bombing of Jijiga but all the thieves from Hargesia went through and did well but were caught for smuggling goods back without paying customs duty.

One of our agents, who had been sent out for news to Gurati, brought back proof he had been in the form of three lower jaws not too old with flesh still on them. Horrible relics of Italian native troops killed there.

Harar has been duly bombed and four persons reported killed. The Greek grocer's shop in the central square was hit. I see two Italian oil ships have caught fire in the Red Sea. It is heating up now.

I expect to be home in September or October. A year of this life without a break in all weathers will be more than I care for. Should have liked to do longer and come home for the family dig in the summer of 1937 but shall not try.

British Somaliland, via Aden, 10 April 1936

I had a front seat at the war so to speak this week. Last Sunday 4 April I was having breakfast at the Tug Wajale when there was a terrific 'Wumpp' and I dashed to the tent door in time to hear a couple more and see two columns of smoke shoot up in the air about 6 miles away. We saw and heard the planes. It appears it was the desperate dago squadron trying to bomb an empty truck going to Jijiga.

Rains have started and I am really very glad as I was with the OC Troops

* Mockler, Anthony, *Haile Selassie's War*, Oxford University Press, 1984, p. 127.

from 4th till 10th going round the Boundary. We had his Staff Captain with him; a Motor Transport [MT] expert from the Royal Army Service Corps [RASC] and we got properly stuck twice in the mud and they saw first hand what conditions were. They were quite good and very nice over it. I brewed them hot whisky toddy; best stuff there is to keep the cold out. Of course I am always self contained so that it really does not matter to me if I am held up anywhere.

I hear the Italians have sprayed gas on Dagghabur and killed a lot of men and stock. It will probably keep us busy as it may drive some of the tribes on to our side. I am off again down west opposite that fort so as to be on the spot. [It was mustard gas. The Somalis would bring in the empty bomb cylinders to Sandy, the Italians having put the gas down in the morning when it was cold. The people would go and do their business in the bush with the result that the heat of the body drew the gas up and their feet got terribly burnt. After the Italians started using the gas the population became 100 per cent pro British and volunteered any amount of information.]

The truck is waiting to go in with this so I am afraid it is a very short note.

12 miles West of Aran Areh, British Somaliland, Via Aden, 15 April 1936

I am once again back down the boundary after escorting the OC Troops up to Duruksi. I spent one night there and came straight back down to Wada Gumared where my summer HQ is. It is on a caravan track which leads from Dagghabur and is very handy for the collection of news from passing caravans. The Camel Corps camp and aerodrome are 2 miles down the road. I have got a grass and branch shelter here with a small tent inside it so that it is very cool. I have a garden with beans, potatoes and maize laid out in front inside the *zareba*.

It has really been very quiet indeed, not even the noise of bombing; sort of lull over Easter.

Jijiga is deserted and all the people have now left and reside outside the town in the bush; they are daily expecting it to be gassed.

We caught some more Ogaden stock coming across yesterday. They are upset by the bombing and envy the peace our tribes enjoy on this side.

I have an unburned incendiary bomb here; it lives up a tree outside the *zareba* till the RAF send someone to examine it. Four Mills Explosive bombs were also brought in but I was out and the Camel Corps Officer kept the people waiting so they just went off with their bombs and have sold them I gather to the local Somali ironworkers who are extracting the explosive to fill cartridges. Heaven help the chap who ever fires one. I am trying to get them back before any damage is done.

British Somaliland via Aden, 21 April 1936

Things look bad for the Ethiop; their morale has gone opposite us. The gas has had an appalling effect. The continual bombing, to which the wretched troops are powerless to reply to, also gets them down. I give them another month if as much and the whole army will be making for home and our work in the boundary will begin; impounding Ethiops et cetera. They have not used their anti-aircraft guns at all; they prefer to keep them to look at.

I am off again at once down to the west end in case the Italians make a push with mechanized vehicles.

The French now hold the key in the railway which if they close it will put the Italians in a bad position. [The French ran the railway]. They are furious over the bombing of Harar. The French Mission got twelve bombs from five planes in ten minutes; the dual purpose hospital and Consular Agency got hit too.

Neither of our Military attachés have the smallest opinion of the Italian troops; they both say they are useless. On the other hand they say that if the Ethiop had officers he would have won. They got round the Italians several times but when their leader was killed they just sat down and did nothing. [As Sandy himself found later on, the Ethiopians were excellent soldiers when properly led.]

One of the officers on the boundary is going mad; awful business. He gets violent fits of temper, chucks chairs and things about for no reason. He may with luck be all right in Burao when he is not alone. He suddenly picked up a chair the Doctor had been sitting on the other evening and threw it away for no reason. The Doctor came back to find it smashed so went for the fellow and we had a job to separate them. He got involved in three fights in three days and thinks himself he is going mad. They get some queer ones out but you only find them out when you send them out alone to do a job.

I have some excellent photos this time for market in due course. I have a letter of introduction to the Daily Mirror so that might help in selling some.

Tug Wajale, British Somaliland via Aden, 28 April 1936

The war seems to have really started at last. I was lucky and was able to get full news of the Italian attack from a Cypriot who was on the Habash section of the Boundary Commission working their transport and was running the transport of the Ethiopian forces in the Ogaden. The Italians are advancing in 3 columns of a 100 cars each with troops in them; guns and tanks also carried. They have by no means had things all their own way. At Danane, the Ethiop shot down two planes and put two tanks out of action while at Burkot they put four tanks out of action and more got bogged down. A big troop carrying plane was brought down in flames. But they have been driven back everywhere and our last word was that they were 31 miles this side of Dagghabur. That night there was a storm which probably held them up or else they are waiting for the European troops to arrive now the fighting is over to enter Jijiga. No one has seen the white troops yet. The natives did all the fighting and suffered heavily.

Can't think why we have seen no aeroplanes scouting round Jijiga at all. Must end now to catch plane which brings mail and takes this home.

In fact, on 9 May 1936, Mussolini announced to a jubilant crowd in Rome the annexation of Ethiopia. The King was to be known as Victor Emmanuel, King of Italy and Emperor of Ethiopia.

British Somaliland via Aden, 14 May 1936

I have had a very busy week indeed. First of all I managed to induce the Ethiop post opposite us to evacuate their place and so avoid any chance of an incident if they crossed in flight from oncoming Italians. They agreed to go on condition that I took over the kit of their Chief of Customs who I knew; so I took over a lorry load of stuff and they were happy and left this night. We sent over our Police to secure what they could of the stuff left behind: water tanks, petrol, rifles et cetera and in the morning I burnt the site.

The same day I went off to Borama to visit my forts on the boundary and found that several hundred Ethiops from Taffari Bah and Aw Berc were waiting 400 yards over the Boundary and intended to cross. I went over to see them and found several I knew as Aw Berc used to be the Headquarters of the Ethiopian Boundary Commission. I sent back for some more troops to deal with the situation. They were waiting to cross till the last minute and were cut off from the hills as Jijiga had been occupied for some days.

About 5.30 shots were heard 7 miles off in the town and the rush started; screaming women and children, old men, soldiery, priests – the whole boiling rushed for the frontier carrying what they could. I stood with a patrol and searched and disarmed them. Stafford [later Lieutenant Colonel Henry Howard] marshalled them in an open space nearby. The rush went on for about 4 hours. We got 63 rifles, 7 pistols, 2 brand new automatic guns and a sort of gangster weapon firing Spanish cartridges and thousands of rounds of ammunition of all sorts. They had broken open the ammunition boxes and filled their pockets. We got them calmed down for the night. Most of them came from the post opposite ours in the Tug Wajale. We got them all off into Borama by 6.30; my word they smelt and six of them had smallpox. The priests brought all their vestments, incense burners et cetera. I have got some very good photos I hope of the business. [Some of the refugees were later in the 2nd Irregulars with Sandy, in 1940. Headman Zaude Gabre Hiwat was one of his officers, later becoming a minister in the Ethiopian Foreign Service. Sandy took all the refugees from Aden to Tanga when Somaliland fell in August 1940.]

We also got some cars abandoned and hundreds of sheets of corrugated iron dumped our side of the border to save it falling into Italian hands as well as water tanks, petrol et cetera. The numbers were 257 including 100 men and 22 infants in arms.

I greatly enjoyed the caviar. We drink rum in the evenings now and we had it with that. Glad the garden opening to the public was a success.

No news now; a reaction after all the excitements.

Tug Wajale, British Somaliland via Aden, 18 May 1936

We have had a bad week of rain, all night long one day. Everything soaked and mud but we can't expect sun always. My gardens are in bearing now and carrots, French beans, lettuce and spinach are on the diet, also new potatoes. I am self-contained for vegetables and eggs, a great blessing.

We are busy trying to keep level with the Italian advance. They are going very slowly and showing no initiative. All the troops have left Jijiga and taken up positions in the hills, ideal for guerrilla war, so as to defend Harar from the Jijiga side and from the south as well. They had a hard knock at Danane and the two planes shot down was more than the Italian bargained for.

There is a pathetic post of thirty Ethiops opposite us. Every time you ask them the news they say 'The Emperor is victorious on all fronts'. They are in blissful ignorance that they are cut off and I have induced them to send somebody into Jijiga to get the news.

Must be back up the boundary tomorrow.

Enjoyed some raspberries and cream last night from the Fortnum and Mason box. Very good.

British Somaliland via Aden, 21 May 1936

Many thanks for your letter and the promise of a new Fortnum and Mason parcel. I shall look forward to it.

Things are quietening down here and my job is developing into the collection of military intelligence now that Italy has become a potential enemy or threatens to. The Italians have a force of 10,000 men in Jijiga at least with 1,500 motor vehicles. We are allowing trade with them but imports only and ten car loads of sugar et cetera went in yesterday; nothing is allowed to come out. They are doing nothing in the administration line till the winter beyond disarmament of the tribes. Bands of Ethiops are still being mopped up by them. They will have a devil of a job running the country and when they start taking land away from the people to settle Europeans they will have more bother. So far they have respected British Protected tribes and their rights.

Several Ethiopian families are settling down in Berbera, mostly people who were at Jijiga or had connections with this country.

I hear the Emperor got $960,000 out with him; they are worth about 2s each but that won't last him long. The Manager of the Bank of Ethiopia, an Englishmen, manages his private affairs and I have no doubt he is provided for amply.

[The Emperor had fled to Britain in early May realizing that the only hope was to appeal in person to the League of Nations. In spite of having been able to bring some money with him, the Emperor had to sell some silver.]

Many thanks for the offer to pay my expenses at Cromarty House; sounds the very place for me and just the sort of shooting I like. I am due to sail around 7 September. I spend some days in Paris and London at the museums in connection with my investigations into the old towns and when I have the data I want I shall come up home. [Presumably Sandy wanted to look at material in the Musée de l'Homme in Paris, which had been found by Revoil in 1882 at Salwayn near Heis in Somaliland. They dated from the first century BC to the first century AD and were of Graeco-Roman origin. Alas Sandy had not been able to visit the site but had seen it in the distance.]

British Somaliland via Aden, 28 May 1936

I have got some good museum pieces out of the Ethiop debacle; things left behind in a hole and found recently.

I have not been too fit lately; the eternal sun and always on the move in all weathers has got me down. I was having five days in one place or hoped to when we got on the track of some gun runners and that has kept me busy. I am going into Burao about the 14 June to stay with the Colonel for two nights and shall enjoy the rest and change to civilization.

One of my ducks was taken recently by a jackal so now I have two drakes and one duck; clearly not an economic egg unit but great possibility from a gastronomic one. Chickens are not laying well; the high wind which blows daily now is not encouraging for them. The clucking hen has left my grass hut at least.

Aunt Chrissie sent me an Italian anti-Fascist paper which I find most interesting and I pass it on to the Italian speaking officers.

I have joined the Sports Club in London, not a good club but one which caters for overseas Colonial Officers and KAR and means I have somewhere to go and stay in town. It is in St James Square and so is not a night club or anything of that sort and the subscription is good.

British Somaliland via Aden, 6 June 1936

I have been up and down my section as usual. The Italians are slowly administering their area and paying no attention to our grazing rights but are clearly going to adopt their usual principle of a closed frontier. I have met some of their patrols along the border.

With the Italians opposite us the whole problem of the defence of the Protectorate has altered and I expect we shall have more troops here soon.

The Italians continue to pour troops up into the interior of Ethiopia; they will need them as the whole place is infested with robber bands. The road from Jijiga to Harar is even unsafe except for convoys.

The whole system of supply is fearfully casual. Graziani himself tried to arrange a contract with an Italian to deliver 3,000 bags of rice a month, 2,000 of sugar et cetera. They could not get anyone to take the contract on owing to the fall of the lire. To our natives it is extraordinary that they should keep their forces supplied by such methods.

We are having a job disarming people who cross the boundary. The Italians have been carrying out a general policy of disarmament and as a result there has been an influx of rifles over here which we are trying to stop; a lot of the German and Belgian Mausers, new during the last year and abandoned by the Ethiop, have come over.

The dumdum bullets business is an affair with the Italian Consul in Djibuti who tried to bribe three fellows from the Red Cross to say they had fired on the planes. He offered them a 100 birr or £7-10s each and they all refused. [Dumdum bullets are hollow-nosed ones which fragment on impact and are illegal in war under the Geneva Convention. The Italians accused the Ethiopians of using banned dumdum bullets during the war. The Ethiopians said that these bullets were planted by Italian spies.]

British Somaliland via Aden, 11 June 1936

The Italian is having a hard time with the robber bands; sixty-six have been killed on the railway in the first month. Some of the best Ethiopian leaders are in the hills round Harar. Every night the bands come down and raid the villages on the plateau and shoot or ambush any small body of troops. Seven were killed on the Jijiga-Harar road last week by robbers.

One Italian clerk employed by G.M. Mohamedaly and Co., the big traders in Ethiopia, who I knew in Harar and Jijiga, reported to me that he had been approached by a middle-aged Italian Officer in Jijiga who offered him a fabulous sum if he would get them a touring car and petrol from Berbera as they said they wished to get to Somaliland as they were tired of the war and wanted a rest. They said the chief fear was not being able to get out of Jijiga;

they knew they would have no trouble in getting into British territory. Rather interesting and probably true as the clerk had no objective in making up a tale.

The Italians are allowing goods to pour in from Hargesia; British sugar, pineapple tins and all sorts of stuff regardless of the sanctionist origin simply because they need it. Their line of communication for Jijiga comes from Mogadishu.

British Somaliland via Aden, 21 June 1936

I have to get in touch with the Italians at once and start unofficial conversations about the boundary and our tribes. It will be interesting.

I am glad we are going to call sanctions off. It will create a much better atmosphere everywhere.

The Italians are taking strong measures to put down bands of Ethiopians who are still knocking about; there is a large party between Harar and Borama and our people saw them bombing and shooting up targets which turned out to be sheep and goats under trees. They rushed up troops but as yet can't find the delusive Habash.

I have applied to be transferred to Tanganyika. They have introduced people in above me, three in the last three years, and limited my chances of ever getting on as quickly. Also I have no chance of gaining any Secretariat experience here and thus turn to profit my Consular work; so I have started the ball rolling. Another factor too was that I have been specially employed on Ethiopian Political and Consular jobs; now that will end. I would sooner start afresh in a new country and learn a new job at the bottom than have to be second string in a district here. The leave conditions are not quite so good; one has to do two years but you get longer at home at a time.

I am going into Hargesia for a few days next month. The eternal high wind is most trying in tents. I shall be glad to see the last of Somaliland. I have had too much of it under bad conditions.

Wada Gumared, British Somaliland via Aden, 3 July 1936

I have had a busy week with Italian negotiations. The two fellows opposite us are Reserve Officers; one is a barrister and a charming fellow, Tassi, and we had an informal meeting one evening over white vermouth in my tent which was fairly satisfactory and we arranged to show him the boundary later. To my horror a fearful scruffy looking captain came who rejoiced in the most suitable if somewhat vulgar name of Peis. Tassi accompanied him and told me pretty plainly he didn't like him. We put up a lunch and they produced a bottle of Chianti and it was a very pleasant outing except that they were dumb when it came to any questions of politics or administration. I am quite sure they had been worried that I was at Walwal and figured in several documents on the Ethiopian side so to speak and they would say nothing; simply told us to write to Jijiga. They will be easy to work with if our government will only recognize the fact that they are there.

British Somaliland via Aden, 23 July 1936

Many thanks for your letter and the colour photo. I am amazed at the accuracy of the colours and the green is so true.

I am very annoyed now; they have given me the whole of the Esa country along the boundary to Jalelo where we join with the French in addition to my bit. The Italians are having such a devil of a time and have withdrawn all the irregulars from opposite us so that it looks as if their dealings with the tribes will be further delayed. All wireless transmitters have been closed down in Addis and the Ethiops have warned foreigners to keep to their Legations as there is a massacre coming off in Addis and Dire Dawa. The big rains are on and the Italians have no spare troops; no reserve of rations. The congestion in Djibuti is appalling I believe. Jijiga is practically empty; every available man has gone, not to Dire Dawa but south to cope with an outbreak in the Arussi country. The soldiers are of course fed up and awaiting repatriation.

The railway was recently cut and out of action for ten days. The Ethiops got a troop train coming from Addis. As a result of the derailing and firing, 150 were killed. Another train on the way up saw the mess so backed but it crashed too as the line behind had been cut after it passed. The Ethiops opened fire on it and the troops and passengers took to the hills; some are still missing. The Ethiop is at last learning something about how to conduct guerrilla warfare. The Italians now have five machine guns on every train and every station is surrounded with barbed wire. We get all the news from Djibuti; the railway headquarters being there, the Italians can't hush it up.

I am still travelling up and down but it is more interesting with the disarmament going on. I have rather upped the plans of the Government by getting over 123 rifles in 3 weeks and 7,000 rounds of S.A.A. They only anticipated 30 odd; we won't be far off 200 in a month.

Mails are more regular now. We have the Percy Company out near one of my bases and they send into Hargesia daily for water so I can get my mail.

British Somaliland via Aden, 30 July 1936

The Italians are prepared to let our tribes cross the border to graze, apparently if they are disarmed so I expect I shall be spending the rest of the year seizing weapons off people. Last week we reached 160 for the month, mostly French rifles of 1874 but got one hammer rifle of 1871, an Enfield. Others were German, Russian, Italian, Austrian et cetera and over half of them were at one time Ethiopian Government property.

I got rather a nice Ethiopian priest's cross in brass. Some Somali had stolen it thinking it was gold I suppose and I bought it for a few shillings.

I am having a few days rest now making up arrears of work. I have travelled on twenty days this past month. I hope to get into Hargesia for two nights for a conference. I am glad you are going back to Shetland. I only hope I may somehow be able to join the family party but can see little chance of it

British Somaliland via Aden, 12 August 1936

I enclose a 'Bouquet' I got from the OC Troops when he left. I suppose it is better than a bad report and will all help.

'The Political Officers are working most loyally and efficiently with the Somaliland Camel Corps. I should most especially like to draw your attention to the work of Mr A.T. Curle, MBE. He has been on the Frontier since the beginning of the troubles and has shown himself to be thoroughly efficient and a most hard working Officer.

Signed: J.W. Hornby, Colonel, Officer Commanding Troops British Somaliland'

We have had a lot of rain down the Tug Wajale area and the country is looking quite attractive for once; the rain continues to Harar and the hills I hope at the same time.

I have got a new Ford V8 Truck allotted to me; rather late but better than never. It has doors with windows in the cab in front so I at last can sit without a howling gale nearly blowing me out of my seat. I have reduced the seizure of rifles to a fine art in my section now. We have got 250 to date as compared to 16 in the neighbouring section. The Political Officer there is somewhat hidebound and afraid to act without the book as it were and as a result he gets no results. If a native runs away from a village with a rifle he looks up the book to see what he can do. I fear I put the whole lot under arrest till the man is brought in with the rifle.

At Borama, British Somaliland via Aden, 19 August 1936

I have now moved up the frontier a bit to the Esa and Gadabursi country and handed over the arms collection to another Political Officer. Tomorrow I go down along the frontier to the Esa country in my new truck to get an appreciation of the political situation; not that there is any but to see how things stand so as to give the Camel Corps something to base any movements over patrols.

I have just spent a day over at the Italian Post at Aw Berc where we used to go in the old days to discuss with the Ethiopian section of the Boundary Commission. We found the Italians in the same house as the Ethiopians lived in. We had to discuss about questions of the grazing rights et cetera with the Italians. The Colonel in charge was charming and a delightful man to work with. He had a Fascist Military Officer recording all the proceedings. I presume a sort of spy on him. They did us very well and entertained us royally. We got nothing settled as the Italian Government wish to restrict all transportation movement and our policy is to allow the tribes to follow their habitual practices.

The Italians have labour camps working at repairing houses and mixing cement et cetera. It seems curious seeing European workmen doing these jobs. They have cleared the place up no end and improved the roads and built culverts.

Borama, British Somaliland via Aden, 23 September 1936

Please let me have the Ormsacre telephone number so that I can telegraph cheaply if I want to. I cease to be under the Military on 30 September but continue to do the same work and be responsible to the DO till I go on leave. The idea is to bring the state of affairs back to normal by degrees.

In the Esa country I have discovered a series of stone carvings on graves with a phallic character. I have managed to extract one or two to take home. They are something quite new for Somaliland. [One of the carved phallic stones is now in the British Museum. Sandy had a note published on these findings in *Antiquity*, September 1937].

I had a very interesting time in Djibuti; the Italian stores there amount to 130,000 tons, the railway only taking 300 tons a day which is one tenth of their needs. So as you can imagine they are at their wits end to keep the show going. They have asked if they can build their own metalled road: Berbera to Jijiga and use their own labour and trucks and land their stuff at Berbera. Pretty cool. I don't know what our answer will be but I gather we shall say yes provided you pay full customs duty!!!

The Italians are expected to start a campaign of murder, arson, bombing and gas in October or November in the course of their pacification of

Ethiopia. A force is collecting in Jijiga now to deal with the Harar end of the country. Every day for the past ten days we have heard bombing from the Dire Dawa area and stories of wounded going back to Harar come through. I have had a most interesting letter from Taylor in Addis. About the beginning of August, 3 columns of 5,000 Ethiopians got to within 1,000 yards of the Legation on the outskirts of Addis. They of course were driven back by sheer weight of numbers but the Italians by no means had it all their own way. 300 Eritrean troops walked into an ambush and everyone was killed and one gun and two machine guns captured.There was another attack on Addis fourteen days ago, a very much more determined one but it did not succeed.

In fact the Italians have not improved the slightest bit since the war; they fall into every ambush and lack any military sense of defence or protection. They have no organization and cohesion.

The Italian motor transport however is wonderful I believe and shows a tremendous improvement on what was anticipated; it is that of course which won the show for them. Their supplies take fourteen days from Mogadishu to Harar, all done with five ton diesel tractors towing trailers. The supply route in the North has been cut and remains so, so that the railway and the Mogadishu-Harar road is all they have to maintain 50,000 men.

In Addis they have loud speaker vans which tour the town but as they broadcast in Tigrean no one can understand it. [The town was predominately Amharic speaking].

12 million lire in coins went up the railway recently. They are having awful bother with the lire notes.

Borama, British Somaliland, 20 October 1936

The fall in the Lire has badly affected Italian prestige. The financial state must be pretty bad; the Italian Consular cheques from Djibuti payable to the Governor for various sums in respect of money to the credit of Somalis killed in the war have all been returned from the Italian bank on the grounds that money cannot be sent abroad. You can imagine the effect on the native mind; the all-conquering bombast does not seem up to much when their money has depreciated by half or more out here. Desertions are becoming increasingly common among their native troops who find they are in arrears of pay. I hear that we are banking on Italy going bust at home, still the Communist movement is gaining under the outward display of Fascism. They are all out to make friends with the British at home.

We are also taking action through the British Consulate, Djibuti, to counter their refusals to grant British subjects a visa for Ethiopia but refusing all Italians a visa for Aden so that they are now compelled to wait in Djibuti for weeks sometimes to get steamers up or down the coast instead of crossing to Aden and getting a boat at once.

There is news of further revolutions, one led by Lij Yasu is supposed to be going ahead. [Sandy is probably referring to one of the Muslim sons of Lij Yasu.] Our natives are now prophesying that the Italians will be out of it by December 25th. I fear the wish has a good deal to do with it.

The food question in Ethiopia is getting serious; no one will import anything now and even if they want to they would have the greatest difficulty. No trader is allowed to hold more than 50 lire ready cash, any surplus he is supposed to bank. Food is scarce and expensive in Addis.

I don't think they will last very long; five years or so should see us rescuing them all from a horrible fate. Our prestige is enormous now in native eyes. We have no irksome restrictions and above all our money is good.

I shall be heartily glad to quit Somaliland after five years solid tent life. I have been trying to sort out my kit which has been in store in Berbera for five years. Some of it is a bit moth eaten and such things as spare blankets have all had to be shied away. Luckily clothes and linen were all right. The rugs also were intact and I have lent them to the wife of the Quartermaster of the Corps who is proud to have them and will look after them well and I can always get them if I want them.

I must also reclothe myself in London as I have had no suits for five years. I shall let Messrs Anderson have the honour of making me a new plus four suit; I bought the last in Aberdeen in 1922.

Hope to reach home Tuesday 15 December and enjoy the festive season in a house instead of a tent as I have done since 1932. My leave depends on the political situation as Plowman puts it: 'It is hoped that the next month or so will see a substantial improvement in the political situation across our frontiers. If that hope should not be realized, I fear that your leave will have to be postponed for some months since there will be no Officer available to take your place on the frontier.' However my passage has been booked and I live in hopes; but it is very uncertain.

CHAPTER **10**

Quiet Life as a District Officer in Tanganyika, 1937–9

In 1937 Sandy set off for pastures new when he got his transfer to Tanganyika, which had previously been German East Africa and is now Tanzania. It was handed over to be administered by Britain under a mandate after the First World War when the victors divided the spoils.

You can sense Sandy's boyish enthusiasm in these letters for a start in a new country. He had put the broken marriage behind him and most important of all, he had met and fallen in love with the girl destined to become his second wife. She was an archaeologist of repute and had been assisting her future father-in-law at an excavation where Sandy had been helping whilst home on leave.

Marseilles, 14 March 1937

I had a very good journey here and met an Ethiopian friend, Lorenzo Taezaz, who I had worked with on the Boundary and we travelled together to Paris. He is now attached to the Emperor's staff and is going to speak for Ethiopia in May at Geneva at the Assembly of the League of Nations just to show they still exist. [The Emperor was in exile in England at this time and living in Bath, having fled the country in May 1936 on Italy's successful annexation of the country. In June 1936 he had appealed to the League of Nations who did nothing apart from lifting the sanctions which had been imposed on Italy, which as Eden said, 'Were serving no useful purpose' – if indeed they ever had.]* He told me no Ethiopian is allowed to write a letter out of the country and most of the people with the Emperor have had no news of their wives and families for nine months. He says the policy is to wipe out the educated Ethiop. The Italian took all private deposits in the bank as well.

---

* Mockler, Anthony, *Haile Selassie's War*, Oxford University Press, 1984, p. 151.

British India Line SS *Madura* 19 March 1937

Here we are five days out from Marseilles and shall not
be at Port Said for another two. The boat is very slow and
somewhat dull after the P and O and nothing is either so
comfortable or so well done. The passengers are almost
entirely East African officials. I am lucky in getting in
with a nice party consisting of two ex-naval officers aged
about forty and a DC from Zanzibar and his wife.

We called in at Malta and went ashore for a few hours
to see the Island. The Fleet was out which was a pity as it
would have been a grand sight to see all the battleships
there. The government gardens in Malta were delightful;
a mass of flowers, daffodils and roses out together.

We met several naval people at Malta; they are fully
alive to the Italian menace. The local stone being porous is very difficult to
treat for mustard gas as it absorbs it. The Italians have one aerodrome 70 miles
away and four others within 90 miles, all in Sicily.

I am slowly gathering information about Tanganyika and most people
seem to like it. I understand from various other DCs on board that we have to
tranship at Mombasa onto a coasting steamer as the boat spends seven days
there.

SS *Madura* near Aden, Easter Day 1937

We spent two days at Port Sudan which is a wonderful port; ships tie up
alongside a modern equipped quay with cotton going out to Liverpool and
all sorts of things including cement coming in. [Port Sudan was in what was
known then as the Anglo-Egyptian Sudan and under the control of Britain
and Egypt.] Owing to the strict and efficient administration you are never
pestered by touts or beggars of any sort and can walk in peace. They have a
go-ahead garden even, which is in the form of a public park and considering
in summer the temperature rises to 125° one wonders how it can live. They
have a local Sudan handicraft shop which eliminates the swindling trader
on the quay. I was most interested in the 'Marine Gardens'. One went about
100yds from the quay in a launch with a glass bottom and you could see all
the fish and coral on the reef.

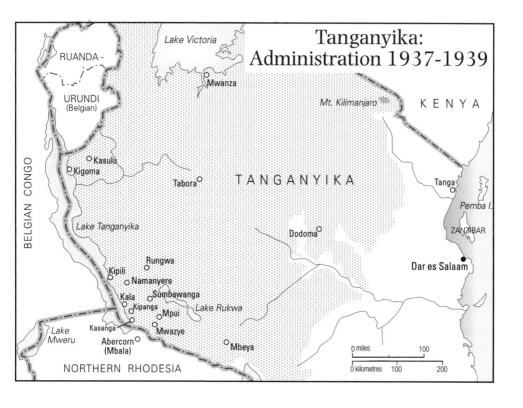

Tanganyika:
Administration 1937-1939

SS Madura off Kismayu, 3 April 1937

We are still dawdling along but hope to reach Mombasa tomorrow, Sunday afternoon; most inconvenient time to arrive.

At Aden, Campini who used to be Italian Consul at Harar, came out in his motorboat with a huge Italian flag and took me ashore for the day, motored me around and gave me a first class lunch with some 1886 Armagnac brandy. He introduced me to an Italian who had been in the campaign when Italy was invading Ethiopia who was sailing on our boat and who is trying to increase Italian export trade. From the two of them I got a lot of interesting news.

According to Campini, the attack on Graziani in Ethiopia in February was very serious; fifteen bombs were thrown, all Italian made, but luckily for him they were very poor and only a few went off. Simultaneously 4,000 men round Addis Ababa revolted and attacked the Italian communications but did not succeed. 500 Ethiops, practically all the educated ones, were shot after a summary trial. [Following the annexation of Ethiopia by Italy, in May 1936 Marshal Graziani had been appointed Viceroy as well as Governor of the new Colony of 'Africa Orientale'.] The Italians are pushing the construction of roads hard but you cannot even yet motor from Harar to Dire Dawa without being shot; one Italian a week is killed on this road. He told me that one

181

convoy of fifty lorries was ambushed and wiped out; all the troops had their rifles on the last lorry. In another case the men had their rifles tied on to the mule saddles and so could not get them off in time.

The Italian on the boat told me a lot of interesting facts too; he admits that the bulk of the troops are the scum of Italy and that conditions are far from peaceful, but according to Rome it is quiet and settled. He also told me that the Roman Catholic Church's attitude to the war was adopted because the Pope hoped to be able to get control of the Coptic Church in Ethiopia and the Vatican were still paying out money in bribes to the leading priests. [As early as the seventeenth century the Portuguese had for a short time succeeded in converting the court to Catholicism, this being only one of several attempts over the years.] He said he was ashamed of the behaviour of the Italians in Ethiopia. He further said that the Italian archaeological researches in the colonies were only actuated with the desire to prove that the Romans had been there first and one could not place much faith in them. He also blamed Mussolini for the way he behaved to Eden which was rather surprising. [The Fascist dictator, Mussolini, was head of the Italian Government from 1922 to 1943. In June 1935, Anthony Eden had taken a proposal involving the exchange of certain areas to Mussolini who had turned it down. See Chapter 8, page 132].

c/o District Office Tabora, Tanganyika, 14 April 1937

We had a pleasant trip from Mombasa to Dar es Salaam in the 3,000 ton coasting steamer via Tanga and Zanziber. Dar es Salaam is a beautiful harbour up a narrow creek; all very green and HMS *Enterprise* lying at anchor added to the view. The town lies along one side and is well built and kept. No one bothered to meet me and the customs arrangements can only be described as archaic. I put up in a Greek run hotel; the best in the place and went and did my duty calls. A very nice ex-Regular Officer also in the administration took me under his wing. I delivered my letter of introduction at Government House which is a nice building and was asked to lunch with Sir Harold McMicheal. He is a very nice man indeed [a former Civil Secretary of Sudan and a scholar of note].

Some of my kit from Somaliland has arrived alright and I was fixing up about it to come up country with me on the train when we heard there had been a washaway on the line and that only hand luggage could be taken. Anyway we got out of Dar es Salaam on Friday night. The trains are good with sleepers, bedding and Greek-run restaurant cars. We got to the washaway on Saturday morning and had to tranship everything to a goods train with flat trucks and open to the air which took us over the washaway and on for about 5 miles. Next we came to a bridge which was couped up at an angle and once more we had to tranship everything across on planks to a train on the other side which had brought passengers down from Tabora; they of course had to do likewise.

After another night in the train we reached Tabora about 8.00 am on Sunday. I am accommodated in the Rest House. As I only have part of my kit, I had to go out and buy a cheap household outfit so as to live till my stuff comes up. It is most annoying as I have to pay an exorbitant sum here for flour and the like. Now with the railway out of order and no heavy traffic the merchants are profiteering.

I duly reported to the Provincial Commissioner who is a nice old man of sixty retiring in September and I am posted to Tabora to learn the ways of the country and probably take over the District of Ufipa in about a month. I shall be stationed at a place called Sumbawanga. Tabora is a social sort of place with a club, 200 Europeans, schools, vets, agricultural officers, doctors, railways and the 1st KAR. It is nicely laid out with grass, trees, and an average temperature of 74°, maximum 84°, minimum 64°; mosquitoes galore and of course my net is with the baggage at the coast so I have a 2s one made in Japan. There are lots of English children here but the place is beastly unhealthy I should imagine. I gather it is a very expensive place to live in; people give each other parties and I am very lucky if I manage to get out of it.

The work here is far more interesting than in Somaliland and one has very much more scope. The Native Chiefs run their own shows, courts and treasuries in a way which I never would have believed possible. One has to supervise and check it all and arrange for the marketing of the native crops. Ground nuts is the principal one here. [As stated in *The Cambridge History of Africa*, vol. 7, 1986, 'The aim of the Mandate was to assure the primacy of native interest. In 1925 the Governor Sir Donald Cameron introduced indirect rule whereby chiefs became paid agents of local native administration rather than of the central government.'] I have got a boy and a cook; the latter a terrible looking old ruffian but good at his job. Wages are cheaper than Somaliland. Boys are not as good but the cooks better from what I have seen.

The Government apparently orders one to get a car if they consider it necessary and advance you the money to be repaid in instalments monthly up to two years. I have firmly refused so far and I gather there is a Government car at Sumbawanga so if I go there I shall be all right.

Tabora, Tanganyika, 20 April 1937

I am at last getting sort of settled in and most of my Somaliland kit has arrived; my rifles and two boxes are still considered too heavy to bring up the railway as long as the washaways continue. I suppose they will reach me sometime soon.

I am only attached to Tabora, learning the ways and spend the days in people's offices picking up the routine. It is really remarkable how the administration by the native has developed, the cash and treasury side of it especially. Although the local Africans are not nearly as intelligent as the Somalis they seem to have a much better money sense and with a little instruction can keep the accounts and books with only very remote supervision. Of course they are a far more servile race and being agriculturists they do what they are told.

I am caught out again; the Colonial Office people told me nothing about having to get a white full dress uniform so I have now to buy one out here with a sword et cetera; an infernal nuisance. The beastly thing costs me some £8 to £12. I asked for exemption till I went home on leave but they refused and said I could get one locally.

They had a cinema show, small size, at the local club on Saturday, films circa 1920. One local colour film taken by an ex-official in the railway was shown which was really excellent, with the colours wonderfully true. On Sunday they had a cricket match between European teams. I looked on for a few minutes at some very indifferent cricket; engine drivers, stock inspectors et cetera swiping about with brute force. However it gives the local inhabitants something to talk about. No European seems to be happy here unless he is rushing about at some violent exercise. Everyone has a car and I am looked upon as a sort of peculiar fish because I walk and refuse to buy a car.

The Club is the centre of social life. It appears to house usually about twelve corpulent, rather fly-blown, second-rate officials' wives who play bridge every day. It has a good library of novels, a billiard table and a bar with a selection of inferior brands of drink. I restrict my appearance to once a week as I can't afford to go every night. The local population get a tremendous kick out of the show and with a great display of ceremony I was introduced by the Provincial Commissioner and became a local member or something. Having seen many similar types of club in various parts of Africa, I am greatly amused by it all and mighty glad I am moving out of Tabora.

Tabora is very civilized indeed; a motor dust cart comes round to collect the ash buckets. There is electric light, water and WCs in all the houses but all the same I would much sooner be out of it. The whole place round the town is planted with mango trees and along all the roads during the season there must be a grand supply of fruit.

The ubiquitous Somalis have even reached Tabora; there are four halal butchers in the town and I talked to some on the train coming up. They are all in the stock trade but as there is an outbreak of renderpest sweeping the country, all movement of stock is restricted and they are not doing too well.

I went round to lunch with the KAR Battalion here yesterday. They have very nice lines and a very smart show with an excellent officers' mess. I have been asked to a guest night on Thursday. The Battalion is standing by to go to Somaliland at short notice on a peacetime posting. I suppose the Ethiopian refugees are proving too much of a good thing.

Here you get the South African and Rhodesian element among the European Officials; fellows who came up with the troops during the war and stayed on. Some of them have not been to England for years, always going on leave to South Africa.

Tabora, Tanganyika, 29 April 1937

I have at last got definite orders to proceed to Sumbawanga via Kigoma on Sunday week. I am to take over the Ufipa district as Acting District Officer. It is a long trip down Lake Tanganyika in the lake steamer to Kasanga and thence up 50 or so miles to Sumbawanga. There is only a mail once a month when the lake steamer calls at Kasanga. The telegraph does not even reach so it is really a grand place. That will suit me fine. [The Ufipa district was considered to be remote from the rest of the Territory.]

We had an excitement on Sunday when a big German Junker, all metal, three engined monoplane landed here and sunk into the waterlogged ground. It weighed 10 tons. No one was hurt but the propellers were all bent and they have been digging it out ever since. It was on its way from Berlin to Johannesburg.

The local club has an excellent library and I enjoy reading one or two good books. The drink they stock is perfectly foul. I can only conclude it is brewed locally! [At a later date Sandy discovered that the boy in the bar was caught buying local gin which he put into Gordon's Gin bottles and sold as such to members. The boy had actually swapped the good gin for double the quantity of the local muck and got a present in cash from the local maker. His stock of course looked all right. A Pole living in a hut near the club had masterminded the crime.]

I am getting down to my Swahili grammar now; although I can talk with great fluency I have no knowledge of the grammar. I find it hard to learn off the vocabulary words and memorize them now but it is only a matter of practice.

There is a dinner party tonight at the Provincial Commissioner's to which I am invited; it is rather nice of them as I shall meet several of the other Provincial Commissioners who are here for a conference on sleeping sickness. They have £300,000 to spend on it and are trying to decide how! After Somaliland such figures make one shudder. Government money is nothing here; people hire aeroplanes gaily and no economy labels are in use on envelopes as in Somaliland.

I must change for dinner now as I have to walk for about a mile.

Tabora, Tanganyika, 5 May 1937

I am at last getting ready to be out of Tabora and am going round the various departments: vets, agriculture, prisons et cetera to see if they have any points for me.

Yesterday I took the chance to go out to see a model peasant holding, established some 15 miles out; each holding has a whitewashed cottage and 10 acres of ground where they grow groundnuts, beans, maize and millet in rotation. It was quite interesting to see.

On the way we crossed some swamp land growing rice which I had never seen before. Grass was everywhere, about 8ft high; what a contrast to Somaliland. We also passed the house of a German who makes what he calls 'Tabora Wine' and vermouth and gin; he of course imports commercial alcohol in drums and adds flavouring and water and puts a pretty label on an old beer bottle. It is a dodge the Greeks used to do in Harar and Dire Dawa. I have not tasted and don't intend to. I have had the jacket for my white uniform made locally and tried it on; to my horror a huge cockroach fell out of the sleeve as I put my hand in.

The Governor, Sir Harold McMicheal, is very keen on all archaeological work and they have brought out no end of laws to schedule any monuments found and to warn off any amateur diggers; the remains to date include Livingstone's house, dinosaur remains, a meteorite and several cities. There seems to be nothing in the Ufipa area at all but then there was supposed to be nothing in Somaliland or so people said.

It will probably be a month or so before I can get another letter off to you as the lake steamer only does one trip a month. Communications are even worse than the NFD; in Kenya we at least had a fortnightly mail service.

Sumbawanga, via Kigoma, Tanganyika, 20 May 1937

I reached here without mishap after a very pleasant journey from Kigoma in the Lake Steamer and got off at Kipili. It was a nice vessel of 600 tons or so, built for the Elbe in Germany and taken out here in bits in 1914. She was sunk by the Germans to prevent her falling into our hands and salvaged some years ago. The scenery is delightful and one stops at several places on the way. Hills covered with woods come right down to the lake shore and a few villages on the banks add to the scene. The Captain, an ex-RN Officer, is a very nice fellow indeed. We celebrated Coronation Day by dressing the ship with flags. The catering is done by the inevitable Greek; this one had been in Ethiopia some years ago.

From Kipili I went up by district lorry. For the first part of the journey the road winds up hill through woods infested with tsetse fly. After a while one comes up onto a plateau and the scenery changes to rolling hills of grass with one or two higher rocky hills at the edges. I got soaked by rain and put up for the night at a White Father's Mission where they had a guest house. They had a fine place built rather in the style of the South of France. They grow wheat, coffee, peaches and all vegetables. They worked a water mill from a fall at the back. One of the Fathers had a wireless. [The White Fathers were a Catholic missionary society founded in Algiers by the Archbishop in 1879 explicitly for work in Africa. They adopted the white tunic. Tanganyika had a very strong missionary presence. One aspect was that converts were encouraged to abandon their old beliefs.] There are forty missions in my district, all White Fathers. They cause no bother and seem to have converted about half the district. They all held Coronation Day services and lectured the children on the King and Royal Family.

I came on the next day here; it is a delightful climate, never hot apparently and very fresh in the morning and evenings. One enjoys a lovely view from the house over rolling plains.

No sooner had I arrived than I was laid up with a temperature and a cold; being acclimatized to deserts, the damp and general mildness got me. I am now beginning to feel much better.

I have got my pictures up again, the first time since I was at Harar in 1932. Some of the talc has gone a bit yellow but otherwise they are all right.

There is a German with a small farm about 4 miles out. He supplies us with delicious butter at 4s a kilo. The only other farm in the vicinity belongs to an Englishmen called Bostock, a retired Gunner Major who is away at home at the moment.

Living is very cheap and I shall be able to save once I get my stores paid off and their freight met. All sorts of vegetables thrive. Roses, carnations, and dahlias et cetera abound in the garden round the house but long grass which is an infernal nuisance grows about 6ft high outside the roads and cultivation patches.

Can you please send out some flower seeds, the usual assorted packets and debit my bank account. I have vegetable seeds. Later I shall get you to send me some gladioli, red hot pokers and begonias when they are ready for sale towards the end of the year.

At Mto on Lake Tanganyika, Tanganyika, 7 June 1937

I was very glad to get out on trek again after nearly three weeks in Sumbawanga. I started off in the lorry down the road from Namanyere and tried to go down the track which branches off south and round Lake Rukwa but swamps held us up and I had to camp for the night near a village. When you reach a village, the headman always comes out to welcome you and the women come and yodel at you; a fearful noise. You always have to camp near a village so that your porters can get food. There are little huts for the Europeans at most villages on the route and they bring you water and firewood. It is all very different from Somaliland; the roads are kept up by the people who live on them. I turned back and went on down to Kipili the next day.

From Kipili I had a leisurely run down the lake on the steamer to Kala where I had to go ashore to see the village and meet the chief. I went and called on the Mission and met the Father Superior, Père Thomson, who is a great character. He had been a French Officer who turned religious and is fanatically anti-German. To his horror he recently bought a wireless and when he put it up it was broken and could only get Berlin, very loud; no other station. He was furious about it; '*Moi, ancien soldat de France*'. I was entertained with a bottle of wine and coffee. I spent the night at the mission and at dawn the next day set off with the Father in his motor boat to Kipanga. He was attired in a grey short overcoat affair, white shorts, black boots and sock suspenders. About 8.00 am, being the 14 July, he suggested a glass of sherry and produced a portable glass in a leather case with a cross on the outside. I can only presume it was part of his missionary equipment. We reached our destination up a narrow river which was most picturesque and he insisted on a bottle of beer at 10.00 am with breakfast to drink to '*La France*' and then off the old boy went about noon in his boat.

The DO before me had started a rice market so that people wishing to sell their rice bring it to the market where it is weighed under government supervision. A card with its weight is given to the owner who then goes to a merchant's stall and sells it at a fixed price which the merchant offers for the day. I had to start the one here today; of course the natives refused the price offered by the merchants which was a nuisance but I have hopes it may be going better tomorrow. They deal in kilograms while the names for the German coins are still used such as a *Heller* = 2 cents.

The ADO who was under me and the government lorry both go on this boat so I shall be alone at Sumbawanga with my flat feet to depend upon. I don't mind; in fact I prefer it. A new cashier has turned up for Sumbawanga, a very nice old man who was in Tabora; he has to take over the cash responsibility from the ADO.

I have had two rings from storks brought in, found dead near Sumbawanga; probably shot and both were from Rossiterm, Bavaria. I expect they were on their way home to Germany.

Sumbawanga, Tanganyika, 31 July 1937

I have just got back home so to speak after another round trip which was not without amusement.

I got my porters at Kipanga and trekked along the coast to Kasanga, a nice trip along the edge of the cliffs above the lake. Then from Kasanga I cut inland to Mwazye Mission, doing my 20 miles a day on foot. The Mission has a lovely site and must be something like what monasteries were in the middle ages. It has a mill stream off the local river, fields of wheat, plantations of coffee, orange trees and a large vegetable garden and cows. I spent the night there and moved on to Mpui the next day where I met a German who was trying to recruit labour. Thence I cut down to Lake Rukwa; all wooded country with here and there a lake. Next down a fearful escarpment into the valley where we are building a timber bridge across the Momba River so as to open the district up and let the European settlers come in to buy food for their labourers.

The climate in the valley is much hotter and not so infernally cold as the plateau. I then trekked down the valley and visited various chiefs on the way along. One old boy lined up all his wives, some dozen odd, to cheer me and all together said in Swahili 'Good morning Bwana', like a chorus.

I spent the night at the camp of the locust investigator from the Natural History Museum in London who is studying the locusts of one sort which originate from Lake Rukwa. He is a trained entomologist and goes all over the world.

Sumbawanga, Tanganyika, 14 August 1937

Clifford sent me a very anti-Italian paper called 'New Times and Ethiopia News' which gives all the details of the attacks on the Italians and their various actions. Even the women have taken up arms. [It was edited by Sylvia Pankhurst, the daughter of the famous Suffragette leader, Emmeline Pankhurst. Sylvia very much took on the cause of the Emperor and became a lifelong friend and supporter. Her son Richard is today one of the leading experts on Ethiopian culture and history.]

I had two Swedish missionaries here last week; one from Kismayu Mission, the other from Ethiopia. Both had been sent out by their committee in Sweden to look for a suitable theatre of operations under British control where they could carry on the work not allowed by the Italians in Jubaland, Eritrea and Ethiopia. Of course I knew a lot of their people at both Kismayu and Harar and we had many mutual friends amongst the Ethiops and the Somalis. I hope they will decide to start work here at Kasanga where the London Missionary Society is willing to make over their premises. It was funny that they should come to the one station in Tanganyika where they would be known.

The local Prison Commandant from Tabora and the Auditor arrived through by car last week and the latter is now going over eight years' arrears of work.

Sumbawanga, Tanganyika, 24 August 1937

I have had a week's rest so to speak since I wrote last and have been devoting my time to improving the station, planting trees in front of the shops and in the village, making small dams for water, making concrete pipes for the drinking water well, reroofing with tiles the clerk's house and a hundred and one odd jobs. We have just finished firing 2,000 roof tiles; we make them locally. The White Fathers' Missions originally introduced the idea; they are made from local clay.

The natives here are armed with the most miserable rifles: Tower muskets of 1856 and muzzle loaders with a great hammer. I can only presume the Somalis and Ethiops passed them on south when they got breach loaders. I never saw a muzzle loader in Somaliland.

My cook continues to do me well and thanks to the gardens I have three vegetables a meal.

Sumbawanga, Tanganyika, 28 September 1937

I have at last got back from my tour only to find the usual sea of paper awaiting as well as a murder to be investigated.

I visited Rungwa where the settlement is divided into two by a river; one old Sultan lives one side and one the other, both the same tribe but hated rivals and each accusing the other of bewitching him. One was drunk when I arrived so I hotted him up a bit and at least he was sober the next day, probably the only day in the year. There was a carved door at one of their houses, very interesting as it must have housed the tribal regalia, hoe, axe, bow, arrow and baton all of which were depicted in relief on the door. I am taking steps to have it scheduled as an ancient monument [later, in George Fifth Museum in Dar es Salaam].

On leaving Rungwa I struck off south west and then along the escarpment, rivers and falls coming down at regular intervals and very fertile indeed with lots of villages. I struck up and did the 3,000ft climb in a night between 9.00 pm and 12.00 pm and was able to move on by day to Namwele where there is a coal outcrop of very good quality coal but too far away to transport. An odd White Father, a Frenchman who went wrong, lives there with his half-caste family and looks after the claim. From there it is only half a day into Sumbawanga. I met no end of White Fathers going their rounds; it is the season now; in fact I saw more White Fathers than game!

No sooner was I back and hoping to enjoy a peaceful Sunday rest, than two Scots from the store in Abercorn came through; decent fellows, one very Glasgow and the other Dundee. Then first thing on Monday morning three lorries rolled up and who should get out but one Andrew Fowle whose brother was a Major in the 3rd KAR with me and who I knew in Kenya. He was taking an American round, collecting amnids for the Chicago museum. [Amniota was a term used collectively for categorizing reptiles, birds and mammals.]

Had a couple of White Fathers through recently, an American and a Canadian, both visiting other missions in their group. They were so used to talking French that they preferred to talk in that language. They are allowed to go home after ten years. They go to Algiers to the head mission for a year's course and then are sent back to the same part of Africa for another ten years.

There is a terrible German here who is recruiting native labour; he was a small clerk before the war but he has really excelled himself with his Nazi propaganda. He is going about saying that Germany will take over Tanganyika soon and that he will be the DO, Ufipa. He gave a recital to an Indian shopkeeper in the presence of a Swede who was passing who was much amused and reported it all to me. All the Indian said was, 'Well if you are the DO I will not pay tax.'

It is a fearful business with the labour recruiting; you have to explain to the boys all the conditions of their service and attest them. There are so many unscrupulous Greeks and people that the whole business is hidebound by regulations. The Ufipa people go down to Tanga to work on the sisal estates for a year at a time. They are famous as sisal cutters. The sisal growers are all making money now that the price has gone up and are extending their estates.

Sumbawanga, Tanganyika, 14 October 1937

I am still hard at it making up for the time I lost while out. The good harvest here means most of the villages are in a haze of beer for two months and the numbers of murder crimes go up. I have a manslaughter case and a murder on at the moment.

I got a wire today to say that the Provincial Commissioner is coming up to visit Sumbawanga on an annual tour on the next *'Liemba'*. I shall feed him well; that is always half the battle with these inspecting Officers. I am also threatened with the arrival of the Deputy Director of Medical Services. From his telegrams, he is one of those casual gents who expects to find motor cars everywhere. I gather he is going into the outbreak of Kala Azar in the Rukwa valley but as he will be unprovided I shall have to feed him. [Kala Azar was a malarial-type fever more prevalent in India than Africa].

The various labour recruiters, a Swede and the loathsome German, both got lorry loads of boys and duly left smashing some four bridges on the way; of course they must recruit one another's boys and have a row on the office steps. The German left his clerk behind in charge of all his goods; he got very drunk and borrowed his Master's automatic pistol and fired it off so I have the clerk in the jail and have confiscated the pistol. The German will be in a splendid rage when he returns.

191

Sumbawanga, Tanganyika, 3 December 1937

I went down last week to meet my friend Kametz who was coming up to stay. He is an excellent companion and is interested in so many things: beasts, flowers, building and furniture. His visit is very pleasant for me. He contemplates settling in Tanganyika. [He came from the town of Teschen in the old Austrian Empire and had been an officer in the Imperial Field Artillery on the Italian and Russian fronts during the First World War.] Just coming from Addis Ababa, he has very interesting accounts of the rotten time the unfortunate Italians are having. The Ethiopian resistance to the Italians is increasing daily and tribes who at first came over to the Italians are now active against them. There are bands of *Habash* everywhere who shoot any stray Italian, block roads and ambush convoys. No road is safe and no one dare venture out without an escort. The Italian casualties for the month are actually higher than during the war. They are having a bother with deserters from Native and European troops. The fields are all uncultivated and villages deserted. The Ethiopians are getting better organized every day and there is plenty of ammunition, mostly Italian from looted convoys. The bribery and corruption is appalling and owing to the financial question they are using Massawa Port and the Dessie road to Addis with the result that there is congestion there, accompanied by stealing on a wholesale basis. Everything has to be imported to Addis Ababa from Europe including flour; the price of living is appalling. Millions of lire a day are being smuggled out of Djibuti and they can't control it. Kametz fears a collapse of Italian rule in Ethiopia followed by a massacre and says it will not be long.

I have also had similar accounts of the appalling conditions from two Germans who had recently left. They confirm the stories of the fighting with which Sylvia Pankhurst regales us. They actually saw 2,000 out of work Italians demonstrate in front of the Fascist headquarters in Addis. They were rounded up with troops and sent off by train to Djibuti, put on a boat straight to Spain. Practically all foreigners have left. Prices rise, then are reduced by order to a level which makes it unprofitable to sell so Italian shops simply go bankrupt. The railway to Djibuti is not used as it means money has to be paid to France for all the handling. There was no petrol in Addis because the Ethiopians ambushed a convoy of petrol tank lorries using tracer bullets which set fire to them. It was weeks before they could get petrol up the railway. Robbers abound everywhere in bands. Italian influence has been completely ousted from the North West. The Italians themselves are losing heart. Rumours circulate of fresh trouble between Mussolini and the Crown Prince. The Italians themselves now say the former is not as strong as he was and now faces ever growing opposition.

Sumbawanga, Tanganyika, 18 December 1937

I was in Abercorn in Northern Rhodesia on a flying visit. It is a nice town with about sixty European settlers and an entirely different atmosphere to Tanganyika. It is interesting to compare with other Colonies; all their ideas and everything came from the south to whom they are allied having been colonized of course from there by Rhodes. The Chartered Company owns vast tracks of land all round Abercorn and the settlers are in some cases retired officials of the company.

The local natives here smelt bog-iron in smelteries; tall, cylindrical, chimney like buildings of clay construction. They put in charcoal, wood and iron in layers; rather more elaborate than the Shetland ones. After the smelting, they melt it still more in a crucible with the aid of a bellows. One German and one Austrian from Addis Ababa are on their way up here from Dar es Salaam to start in business; transport and a flour mill; the latter always a paying concern as the native women have to pound all the grain with a mortar and pestle. The people will soon realize the value of a mill. They are friends of Kametz and he may join in with them.

I had to sell up the effects of a deceased Polish Jew yesterday. At one time he had kept a shop in the Gorbals of Glasgow, a shop in Johannesburg, in prison in Dar es Salaam and gold mining in the Lupa area of Tanganyika; a strange career.

I have sent off to Mr Kerr today at the Royal Scottish Museum a parcel of local cotton cloth which is quite interesting.

It appears that I have unknowingly found or been the means of finding a new poison in Tanganyika and probably the world; tremendous excitement on the part of the Government Chemist because of this. It was a sample of native poison sent at their request.

The local village school in which I have taken an active interest came out top of several hundred schools in some examination. As a result they have sent some newfangled teacher down to try out adult education.

The cadet who is to assist me has now arrived. He is a very nice fellow, but as he has only three months' experience, he is virtually useless. These varsity people at twenty-three or twenty-four have no idea of managing men or controlling labour. You give them a job to do and they put no kick into getting it done. I have sent him out on safari to find his feet and learn about the African. He can learn more out than in the office.

They seem very pleased in this country if you do your job and they write and congratulate you which is nice. The thing which amused me most was to be congratulated on doing my job without grousing.

Sandy had now married Cecil Mowbray. Having got local leave he went down to Dar es Salaam to meet Cecil and her parents who had travelled out by sea. After a quiet wedding they spent their honeymoon on Zanzibar.

Sumbawanga, Tanganyika, 18 July 1938

We got back after a short trip in the *Liemba*. We spent a day on the road up stopping the night at Chala Mission where Cecil had her introduction to the White Fathers.

We had to start packing up and have now broken the back of it. Cecil is very pleased with the cook which is a great thing. [Sandy was shortly to move to another district centred on Kasulu].

I have had several very nice letters from the White Fathers saying how sorry they were that I was being transferred and thanking me for the many small kindnesses I had done for them; nice of them.

We are engaged in articles for the 'Tanganyika Notes and Records' on some local articles of interest: bells in tribal regalia and an old Bantu door.

On Manda Island, Lake Tanganyika, 31 July 1938

I have at last handed over everything at Sumbawanga. We left by lorry on Friday and reached the Lake shore on Saturday. The road down off the plateau is very attractive; one passes through forests of deciduous trees and across rivers. Suddenly you come out on the Lake which is just like an Italian one; deep blue with islands dotted about and very picturesque little villages with mango trees. We came out here to the island to camp till the steamer comes in which will take us up to Kigoma which is near Kasulu. The headman from the village who came over to welcome us took us over in a long dugout with ten paddlers and a steersman. Our servants and their wives and children were in another rather smaller boat. It was gorgeous paddling along in a canoe, with the men singing. The steersman directed the crew and set the pace of the strokes of the paddlers with singing and at intervals, after a long drawn out cry of '*Alla-aa*', the whole crew would join in the chorus. We heard at least five different songs on the way over and as a rule sung antiphonally. Our cook, who comes from the Congo, was in his element on water. He had soon seized the steering paddle and was urging his paddlers to race us.

Out here we enjoy pleasant breezes, feeding and camping under mango trees on the water's edge. A really delightful spot. Ducks are swimming about in the water a few feet away. We saw an otter while at breakfast this morning and our evening meal was disturbed by the gruntings of a hippo some distance off. A black and white kingfisher fishes round us most of the day. Dugout canoes pass up and down in front of us. At night they paddle out with a fire of burning grass in a projection in front of them to attract whitebait; very pretty sight seeing them go out and all the bay lit up. I counted over fifty. In the dark we look out across the water to the hills alight with the glow of bush fires.

Our camp is positioned between the two communities, one Mohammedan and the other Christian who all get on with one another. There is not much difference in their way of living. All the men wear a long white gown and either a scarlet *tarboosh* [red felt hat] or a little white embroidered cap. The women wear a big square of brilliantly patterned cotton wrapped round below the armpits. These used to be dyed locally with wooden blocks and home-made dyes but now they come from England or Japan. Phrases such as 'Kiss me Darling' in Arabic are sometimes printed in prominent places. These people probably have no idea of the meanings.

All life is centred around the water as it is predominately a fishing community as the soil of the island is too poor to grow much. Little houses with mud walls and thatched roofs are built close to the water's edge. Each house is surrounded by its mangoes, bananas and a few palm trees. The owner's canoe is drawn up on the beach and the great hooped fishing net is propped up against the wall. The sale of fish pays for millet, cotton goods, wood for boat building et cetera.

We have even had a social life. The headman of the village came on a formal visit accompanied by two elders and a poor relation as a retainer. They squatted on their heels and had a long talk with me. Another day a canoe arrived from the mainland bringing the leading Arab trader of the district again with the usual poor relation retainer. The Arabs from Muscat control most of the trade in the country districts. Often in small villages there will be an Arab shopkeeper selling varied wares which the Africans appreciate and can afford.

At first our visit caused great excitements. The villagers had obviously had visits from officials and missionaries but I think this was the first time that white people had actually lived amongst them.

Kasulu, Tanganyika, 21 August 1938

O'Hagan, the ADO, drove us out to Kasulu in his car; it is a nice drive through gradually rising wooded country. Kasulu itself is the most astounding place. The house is a square fort; very highly decorated with pinnacles everywhere and masses of pointed gothic windows with brass fittings. We are perched at the end of a spur half way up a long range of hills. We have a small 'Back Green' in the middle of the courtyard with roses and the remains of hollyhocks round a square of grass with a bird bath in the centre. The climate is hotter than Sumbawanga and the gardening possibilities not so good. The house being on a hill, water is difficult.

Cecil likes the house very much and with all the nice things she has brought out we can make it look very nice. We are hard at work unpacking now. [Things brought from home included silver, Persian rugs, pictures and knick-knacks]. Cecil is busy making curtains with the materials she brought out and unpacking the stores while I am at the office.

The Provincial Commissioner and the DO, Kigoma are due here next week and after that I hope to get out for a spell. We have an Agricultural Officer stationed here, quite a nice fellow whom Cecil travelled out with on the same ship, English but from Edinburgh University. His wife comes out later. There is an ADO here but he is in hospital at Tabora with appendicitis; he is I gather a nice fellow.

We have a weekly mail, in on Mondays and out on Thursdays. There are one or two people in Kigoma for Cecil and we are only 60 miles from civilization.

It is a curious show this; one spends one's time apparently taking inquiries into murders and safariing about.

Kasulu, Tanganyika, 28 August 1938

We have had various visitors during the week; one man called Clayton who is surveying in the area and aged about fifty. He has spent many years in Egypt and was concerned with a lot of those expeditions to the Libyan border. He is very interesting. He is measuring a base at present from which to carry on a triangulation of the north west area of Tanganyika. We also had a couple of visits from the senior sleeping sickness officer and his wife.

I have spent this morning and yesterday afternoon doing a variety of jobs about the house; fixing pipes from the kitchen sink to stop the water running down the outside wall; repairing the spring in the bed and fixing new pieces; putting wire netting over the loophole at the back of the dining room; putting new screws in the bedroom window; making an incinerator out of an empty cement drum; repairing the frame of the door of the store as the bottom had been eaten away by ants. Rats are a problem too. One has to be a jack of all trades here; luckily I have the tools.

I quite like this place now. I have rather shaken the police and the village conservancy gang as I always go round the police lines and the village in my station every Saturday and run it rather on army lines; if I give them an order and it is not obeyed I have the stick applied. My predecessors for some years have been young gentlemen from the varsity who go by the book of the laws in every respect and have not had much experience of direct dealings with natives.

We have a hospital here but no Doctor; an Indian is due sometime. Meantime an African dispenses medicine.

There is a school with about fifty boarders. They have a flute and drum band with an ex-KAR instructor, and four native teachers. It is not a bad show really. They march round the village every Saturday morning.

As round Sumbawanga, there are no end of missions in the district, White Fathers, Church Missionary Society, Dutch, German and others. So far we have only come in contact with the White Fathers who wasted no time in sending in a gift of vegetables.

Kasulu, Tanganyika, 5 August 1938

We have just finished with the visit of the Provincial Commissioner and the DO, Kigoma. They left this morning after two nights here. It all went off very well and I was congratulated on having cleared up the place.

I am required to do a number of 'Safaris' on foot in the hills round here; they want us to keep in closer touch with the local tribes. For years people have gone by car round the roads so that the interior has been virtually unvisited.

The soil here is all red laterite, very dusty and the erosion is very bad so they are spending several thousands of pounds on encouraging the native to terrace and ridge his plots on hill sides. They are fairly far advanced as they use cattle manure on their gardens but at the same time walk about in skins and bark cloth. The women are better looking than in my previous district but the men are poorer and not so well nourished.

We have got news of a stone circle in the district which Cecil is very anxious to visit; it is some way off to the east.

We went round to the Agricultural Officer's house to hear the news last night (6 September) as we had heard that France had mobilized and things were tense. No sooner had we got to the news time that the whole thing faded out and we heard not a word; most annoying.

Now this evening comes a note to say that a White Father missionary out with his rifle has shot a man, the old story of handing a loaded rifle to a boy; incidentally the missionary has no game licence and probably no gun licence. They will try to save paying for anything and then they get caught out good and proper. I am furious over it and particularly now that we are trying to stop the natives from killing each other along comes a careless white man and sets a bad example.

Cecil is in bed with a touch of malaria but as she has been taking her quinine daily it is not bad. The hospital dresser found the parasite in her blood.

Kasulu, Tanganyika, 25 September 1938

We have got further details of the Governor's visit. He arrives by air at 9.30 am and is met at the aerodrome by Mr and Mrs Curle; he inspects the school and hospital and then goes for a drive in the hills for the rest of the day. We have to turn out of our house completely and he takes it over [Cecil always told the story of him bringing his own dining room table]. He comes with two car loads of servants and all his own stuff. Meantime I am 'making hay when the Governor comes', getting all sorts of things renewed and replaced under the threat that HE is coming.

We had a funny show recently; £25 was stolen from one of the local chiefs, government tax money, by a cunning fellow or fellows who dug the wall away and crawled through a hole and took the cash box. The chief reported it and asked for a detective but at the same time got the local Witch Doctors onto it. They did their tricks and then, with gazelle horns on their heads and bells round their ankles, they led several hundreds of tribesmen on a hunt after the thief. They swarmed across all the fields and into the town, searched houses and then turned away in another direction. I was out at the time; needless to say the soothsayers did not find the culprits. The people are so primitive that the Witch Doctors still have a good deal of influence. Someone killed a thief early this year while he was in the act of stealing; the thief's body was dug up after burial and cut up in thousands of little bits and sold as charms against theft. The Government were in rather a fix as to what to do and eventually did nothing.

I have got over the bouts of fever alright and with the hard walking in the hills I am very fit. I have found a new type of medicine: quinine and stobvasol mixed for fever which does away with the necessity of having to take thirty grains a day for months after and the medical authorities approved of it alright.

Kasulu, Tanganyika, 28 September 1938

We are all waiting to get the news; an American Mission lets me have it each morning when I send a man out. It looks as if we called Hitler's bluff at last; if he does not climb down there seems to be little doubt that we shall join in.

I have been passed fit for the KAR Reserve and am just waiting to be gazetted to it as a Captain so if war does come I shall not have to come home to join up with the regiment. It means I shall have to do an annual training at least once in three years for a month.

Mussolini's attitude is best; he will have a time if he joins Germany as we shall send Haile Selassie out and Ethiopia will go up in smoke. Adowa won't be in it as with him back as a leader they would forgive the fact that he ran away and the effect would be tremendous. Anyway we hope there will be no war. You have a dugout in the rocks across the railway at least ready.

Kasulu, Tanganyika, 2 October 1938

We heard the wireless news from the American 'Glad Tidings Mission' and were very relieved to hear about the Munich meeting. Of course all the instructions arrived on 1 October 'What to do in the event of war' after it was settled. I am to join the KAR at Tabora if there is mobilization and Cecil is to be allocated a house at Kigoma.

We have at last got rid of the Governor and are enjoying peace again. We had a hectic time cleaning everything up, moving out of the house and of course it poured with rain towards the end of the week. We had nearly 2ins. It did the garden a lot of good and the roses are lovely now.

The Gubernatorial party arrived at about 5.30 pm which consisted of the Governor, Sir Mark Young, who started in the Ceylon Civil Service and has been in Palestine, Bermuda and Trinidad. His brother is head of the British School in Athens. He had a private Secretary, one Montague who is in the Administration here, son of C.E. Montague, the Author and Editor of the Manchester Guardian. Then there was the ADC who I had been at Sandhurst with, in the same company for two terms and had known quite well called Lloyd Carsin. The DO, Kigoma and the Provincial Commissioner were also with the party and the Doctor in charge of sleeping sickness. We gave them tea and then moved across to the ADO's house where we are staying. We have to wear a khaki uniform when the Governor is about which is a nuisance. We all went along to our house to dine with him; he gave us a fairly good dinner. He is a very nice man and asks endless questions and probes into everything especially prisons and hospitals. On the Tuesday he went round the station visiting the office, hospital, school et cetera. We then we went up onto the plateau and out for the day towards the Belgian borders, wonderful country, about 6,000ft with great ravines rather like parts of the Italian Alps with views of Lake Tanganyika between the gaps in the hills.

We went to dinner again that evening and then the next morning the whole cortège left. He seemed pleased with what he saw and all went off well. We locked up all our valuables when the Gubernatorial party came as the boys are known as thieves, nevertheless we lost one lamp and they broke the only glass we left out.

We also have a visitor in the shape of the Inspector of Schools who is up at the moment.

Alas, Cecil's first experience of a foot safari with porters, towards the Belgian border, was not a great success.

Kasulu, Tanganyika, 26 October 1938

We had a most unlucky trip. Cecil got a go of bad dysentery and luckily happened to fetch up at a German Mission where there was a trained nursing Sister who ordered her to bed on a diet at once and I had to leave her while I came on. They are very nice people who talk English and have been in England so I know she is being well looked after. I expect to go out with the lorry to fetch her in tomorrow or the next day.

The *michela* or hammock she was carried in worked well but appears to be a somewhat uncomfortable mode of progression.

Kasulu, Tanganyika, 30 October 1938

I have written to Plowman sounding him as to my chances of returning to Somaliland if we return Tanganyika to Germany. The general opinion here is, at least amongst the officials, that it will go back. No merchant is importing anything beyond his bare needs and the revenue is down to £30,000 on estimate and a great deal due to the uncertainty of the future.

In Dar es Salaam, the rumour is that when Germany takes over they will probably offer all Officers terms to leave; those with under ten years service will be offered gratuity and ten to seventeen years increased pensions and seventeen years full pensions. One will be transferred if possible. It just shows how insecure everything is here today; people going on leave are worrying about their kit if Germany takes over before they come back.

Kasulu, Tanganyika, 11 November 1938

I have been out to see Cecil and take some medicine which the Doctor had sent up. The dysentery has cleared up but as we are expecting that you will be a grandfather at the end of April, she has to take things very carefully. The Doctor comes on the 20th or so and will go out to see her; he is a very good man indeed. The German nursing Sister specializes in maternity work so Cecil could really not have fallen into better hands. [In fact, Cecil had a threatened miscarriage and at her age of thirty-seven in the wilds of Africa it can't have been funny.]

Cecil will be going home to Britain in January for the event and coming out to join me again in June. She is very comfortable with the German missionaries. The man is actually a Dutchman and his wife German. They live very simply and I send out a runner with extra vegetables and mutton now and then.

The Government have now decided that 'Plant More Crops' is the panacea for all the loss of revenue and so now we are trying to induce the natives to increase their area of cultivation; with locusts supposed to be on the way, prospects are not bright for next year. I am off tomorrow for the day up to the Highlands to distribute potatoes for seed. The potatoes at Kigoma come from the Congo and if we get the seed distributed in the high country there is no reason why we should not be self supporting.

The neighbouring areas in the Congo and Taka seem to be having a famine, mainly because they don't push the native to plant more.

We have a lot of bother with one or two of the White Father missionaries here; they are the most unscrupulous lot of Roman Catholics employing every sort of lie to attempt to get the natives into the schools. The Dutch ones are the troublesome fellows always. They of course are very frightened that Tanganyika will be handed over.

Kasulu, Tanganyika, 24 November 1938

Cecil is still out at the Mission and is very wisely waiting till the Doctor comes out to see her and I shall get him to bring her in; the bother is the road is so rough that the journey in the lorry would be absolutely out of the question and neither of the other cars in the station are even passably sprung. The Doctor however has a super American car.

Thank goodness the Agricultural Officer and his wife have taken the hint and no longer plague me to drink every night or dine with them; very kind of them but in a small place like this each must go his own way or else you become so sick of your neighbours. Once one starts trying to be sociable in small stations, it means bother. Sociability if it comes naturally not forced is very nice.

I have been out today in the lorry inquiring into a murder in situ so to speak. I find that if one does that on the spot you can get evidence which you would miss otherwise and you can get down to the motive as the neighbours always know who the victim's enemies were and what family quarrels there were.

Kasulu, Tanganyika, 16 December 1938

Cecil came in on Sunday. We had a good trip and she was none the worse for the journey. She is perfectly alright again but taking things easy.

The Royal Geographical Society have accepted a short article or rather a few pages of notes I wrote on some ruins in Jubaland at Clifford's suggestion. I have just joined the Society now.

A new grocer's shop has opened in Kigoma run by a Greek and we get the most excellent cherry jam there. They always make a good start these new shops; there is a certain amount of competition of course to keep them up to the mark.

Kasulu, Tanganyika, 6 January 1939

We have at last got over Christmas and New Year. Our chief delight here has been the new wireless. We can get Sydney, New York, BBC and Berlin, the last two very clear and no end of other stations with only a piece of wire along the floor to act as an aerial. It is a really excellent set. The husky voice of the Russian announcer from Berlin infuriates Cecil and Kametz who is with us at the moment.

I have five murders awaiting trial. There was a deluge of corpses over the festive season. They have given me powers of a First Class Magistrate now which enables me to deal with more serious cases myself. In addition we have had several subsidiary cases of chiefs who have robbed the murderers so we have had to sack them. The people here are so primitive that they put up with almost anything from their chiefs who are of a different race who came down from the north; they are the Watussi and more like the Galla of Ethiopia or the Somalis.

I have been out with the Agricultural Officer doing anti soil erosion banks across a gently sloping hill face where all the grass has been washed off with the result that huge ravines form with the water in the rains; we contour bank it. The native has to put in a day's work for a cigarette and a cup of salt. It is a big job which was started last year and it does stop the erosion. In addition we are prohibiting the burning of grass. If my successor continues the same policy it will make a wonderful difference in a couple of years; grass will seed and eliminate a lot of erosion.

Three out of four of us in the Kigoma district were at the Royal Military College. The fourth one, who wasn't military has disgraced himself by chasing after someone else's wife and has been exiled to the southern part of the district out of harm's way. University youths are not popular here now. In Somaliland we never got the same type of rather aimless youth, nicely mannered and sleek, quite good at his job and very nice but futile.

Sandy took Cecil down to Dar es Salaam to catch the ship back to Europe so that she could have the baby at home as she had been advised to do.

Kasulu, Tanganyika, 28 April 1939

Our continued state of tension has for the moment relaxed but I suppose we shall be standing to again soon. It is assuring to know that nothing has been left to chance here this time. The precautions for a crisis and war are perfectly amazing; everything seems to have been thought out down to the supply of cabbage seed, metal polish et cetera and even the telegraphic addresses of the various functionaries who will spring up if there is a war.

I hope all this European trouble will settle one way or the other soon; it certainly looks as if it would before May is out. We shall be cut off from mail for some months here I expect if a war does break out.

I should imagine that the Italians will think twice of being committed in Europe with Ethiopia in the state it is; there will be an immediate bust up there and it is the rainy season which begins in June which prevents any movements against the Ethiops. It will be unlikely that they will try much against Kenya with the festering sore of Ethiopia behind them.

I was very glad to hear of the compulsory military service for young men between twenty and twenty-one; it will be excellent and I can assure you some of the youths we get out here fresh from university would have benefited by it.

A series of daily rain storms with some wind has enabled me to get the battery charged so we can once again enjoy the wireless, not that the news is enjoyable listening. We are listening in to Hitler's speech today. We keep the clock at Greenwich meantime for the wireless always. [This was the date when Hitler tore up the 1934 naval treaty with Britain and denounced the mutual assistance pact with Poland.]

The local fruit season is in; guavas and tree tomatoes, both excellent stewed while the latter are also good as jam but it would have been better if the cook had not put cloves in. He as a horrid habit of doing that to everything, marmalade included.

Kasulu, Tanganyika, 11 May 1939

I got the telegram from the in-laws on Monday by the ordinary mail giving the great news of Christian Margaret's arrival [actually born on 5 May 1939].

Kasulu, Tanganyika, 26 August 1939

Here we are in the middle of this infernal crisis standing by with everything ready for the bang so to speak; eight hundred gallons of petrol spare for motor lorries amongst other things. I hope they will find a way out somehow. It could not be more disheartening at just the time I am due to go home on leave. Leave has not actually been stopped yet but I shall be lucky if I get home I fancy.

For some past time the native troops from Rhodesia have been massed ready at Abercorn while some Nyasaland troops have even come up to the more thickly populated German regions.

I gather German propaganda is not getting it all its own way. There was a meeting of ex-German native soldiers in Kigoma recently led by a missionary who told them all that the Germans were coming back and soon; one of the most influential natives just looked at the speaker and said 'Perhaps' and walked out. We have all these missionaries taped.

Kasulu, Tanganyika, 1 September 1939

Since sending off Cecil's letter yesterday, things seem to have taken a turn for the worse and the evacuation of London has begun. It looks now really as if I should be very lucky to get off on leave at all.

I still live in hopes that Hitler will negotiate at the last minute. You best expect me now when you see me.

And what of the war years and when was Sandy to see his wife and baby daughter again and in what country?

CHAPTER 11

Back to the Army 1939–40

S andy, having been a regular soldier, joined the King's African Rifles Reserve as a Captain.

2/6th Bn KAR, c/o Postmaster Dar-es-Salaam,
Tanganyika, 28 October 1939

Please excuse pencil, as I am writing in my hut, the mess being impossible and I am not fixed up yet. They have erected small huts for the extra officers, about 8ft x 14ft - very suitable for the purpose – much better than being crowded three or four in a room.

I am now a Company Commander in this 2/6th Battalion which is being formed. All the officers from the 2nd in Command downwards to the 2nd in command of companies have been selected from ex-regulars in the territory and the Lieutenants are all newly joined fellows. It looks like being a very happy show indeed as although the young officers are varied they are a very nice lot.

In the mess we have all ages from a boy of sixteen and a half, who has jacked his age, to men of sixty-five. Every sort of war and medal appear, South African 1897, Boer War, Russian Japanese War, Coronation 1918, Special Constabulary medal and everything you can imagine. The professions are even more varied – tin miners, gold diggers, engineers, prospectors, tobacco company agents, Shell agents, clerks in offices, bankers, men of affairs and sailors. Others include an advocate, a magistrate, and an agricultural officer, in fact every sort of trade. Most of the old men belong to the Garrison Company here.

My CO is a serving regular, a nice fellow and the 2nd in Command is a ranker from the Argylls. The other Company Commanders are a Gunner ranker, a Canadian and a retired Royal Scot from Aberdeen. The Adjutant is a retired Seaforth. It is far more amusing serving in a show like this as one has such a varied collection to serve with. One horror proceeded to comb his hair in the mess one day and cheese is always on the table at nights. I have been completing my uniform for the last few days as there was a large parade today. We wear slouch hats like the Australians – horrid things. Our badge is an Arabic 6 in brass on a piece of brown cloth on the hat.

An absurd censorship exists which I suppose is necessary. We have to post our letters open so that they can be censored at the orderly room. I must run down the town now to catch the post.

2/6th Bn KAR, Moshi, Tanganyika

Many thanks indeed for your letter with the description of the air raid.

We got here last week after a varied journey. We left Dar es Salaam for Dodoma at 10.25 am. Before we left one of the officers who was not coming, who had incidentally started his career as a private in the Gordons and was a gold digger on the Lupa River in Tanganyika before the war, appeared with the barman from one of the hotels in Dar es Salaam with bottles and bottles of brandy, ale and beer all iced. He put them in a carriage and dispensed free drinks to all the officers till the train started; an amazing show at 10.00 am. He had drawn his pay the day before and was just blowing it in the Gold Diggers way.

From Dodoma we came by lorry, through Kondoa and Babati to Arusha, which is a nice town right under Mt Kilimanjaro. There I met my friend Kametz and we drank some bottles of Moselle and ate Caviar. He is still employed by the Government on the survey job and getting on well. He has offered his services to the Government in any capacity. He is rabidly anti-Nazi now after his experiences as interpreter and censor for the camp at Arusha for a week or so at the start of the war.

At Moshi we are in KAR lines which were occupied by the regular battalions. I have a wooden hut with two rooms and a bathroom to myself. We have electric light laid on in our huts which is a blessing and water, but the huts are so draughty that one never needs the window open. We enjoy a continuous view of snow capped Kilimanjaro; it seems only a few miles away and is most picturesque. Mails from Dar es Salaam are hopeless. Nairobi is our nearest town really only nineteen hours by train. Mombasa is 201 miles by road.

I have to run the mess and do all the work of the 2nd in Command organizing the interior economy of the show. Later I will get some men I suppose for my Company. Our NCOs are all farmers et cetera from Kenya; very smart and keen but they don't know the routine of soldiering which one learns by experience. We are to have forty-three of them in all as compared with three in the old days in the KAR. We also have a Company of the Northern Rhodesian Regiment with us here, very smart men. We have a Turk as a Sergeant for our motor transport.

On Monday all the new officers have to go on the Square for a month or so's course.

It's a queer army; one gets a banker to keep your accounts and pay books and some of the commercial fellows to run the catering for the mess, so much simpler than the regular army.

We have no wireless and get very little news but it doesn't matter as we get no time off to worry about it. We hope to get a refrigerator and wireless out of one of the German houses on loan free.

I am as fit as a fiddle again and the new life with plenty to do and exercise keeps me up to the mark.

2/6th Bn KAR, Moshi, Tanganyika, 25 November 1939

Many thanks for your letter and the cuttings which I pass on to the Dutch White Fathers in Uha.

We have had a very rushed week, because in addition to our usual parades et cetera, it was sprung on us on Sunday morning that the General would be arriving that night. I was on parade from 10.00 am – 1.00 pm and then on the top of that I had to prepare for a cocktail party for thirty-five people for the General to meet the married ladies. It all went off well except that the port was overheated. With all the rush coupled with a go of fever for two days after, I am afraid I missed my weekly letter last week.

On Saturdays we go down and have a meal in the local hotel with wine for a change and go on to the club afterwards. The club consists of a bar and large lounge where there is dancing. There is always a cheery sing-song on Saturday nights as all the Sergeants belong to the club too. There is a far more colonial atmosphere than there is at home. We have one stupid pompous ass of an officer besides the schoolmaster and he took only three days before he put all the junior officer's and NCO's backs up!!

They are going to send back to Germany all the Germans and their women they can; I expect most of them will get off the Italian boat at Port Said if they can. They have in Dar es Salaam the biggest internment camp in the world which costs hundreds of pounds to run. About 400 of the Germans interned were sent back to Germany last week – no specialists only cannon fodder and useless mouths. I expect all our crowd from Kasulu will go.

I must say I am much happier back in the Army and am enjoying it. We expect to be here for about three or four months when we shall move on. According to a circular we, i.e. the officers who were in the KAR before the war, are permanently out here for the duration, not necessarily Tanganyika but Africa as a whole and we may even go to Egypt. We are not hampered by the hordes of soldiers' women like the regular KAR. All our men except the NCOs are young fellows.

We work very hard – 6.30am – 4.00pm if we are lucky but I like it and am very happy to be back again at a job I know the ropes of from A – Z. One appreciates the good training we got at Sandhurst and in the Borders. I am amazed how it all comes back to one again. We are all going to be doubled up soon as more troops are coming up from the South.

The news in the papers or rather on the wireless during the past week has been good and encouraging except for the magnetic mines. Poor old Shetland has been getting it. I wonder they managed to find the islands with the fogs. [The first bombs of the war had been dropped on Shetland on 13 November.]

2/6th Bn KAR, Moshi, Tanganyika, 2 December 1939

We have had the usual week's work which was harder than usual for me as my Company is just up to strength. The recruits have to be vaccinated and now with chickenpox amongst them it has made more complications. I have still to carry on and run the officer's mess and the canteens and games et cetera. The CO is particularly keen that I should continue with these activities so has given me a very good fellow as 2nd-in-command to my Company to enable me to get off. I had three quarters of an hour with the CO yesterday getting down to all the various questions my jobs entail including the supervision of the Sergeants' mess and the arrangements for the Xmas dinners for the Europeans.

Everyone gets the same reports of the evacuees from home. It must have been an eye opener to the country dwellers to see the 'rubbish' which live in our towns.

Poor Kametz had heard nothing about his family at all since August. I shall get you to try to get in touch with the International Red Cross to get news for him as to if they are alive or dead.

No one knows what pay we get as it is all based on service – if our service in the Reserve counts which it may do I shall be drawing £794 a year.

I have been bothered again by fever but managed to keep it under control; the cold winds I expect have brought it out. We have at last got a Doctor, the usual Scot who has been in Persia; a very good man who has got a move on in the sanitation of the camp.

Many thanks, I don't think there is anything I need for Xmas. As we are never finished before 5.00 pm we don't get much time for reading and we feed well in the mess. My only relaxation is a bottle of wine in the restaurant in the town on Saturdays.

2/6th Bn KAR, Moshi, Tanganyika, 11 December 1939

We continue to be worked as hard as ever and we seldom bother to go out of barracks now. Our world is getting smaller and smaller as it were.

One gets sick of trying to train recruits with no one and nothing and at the same time to run other jobs such as the officer's mess and the canteens.

It is very hot just now by day but at night at least it is cool and with the slouched hats we wear turned up on one side we get out faces fearfully burnt, while the dust on the parade ground is most annoying.

The Red Cross are giving the troops £30 for Xmas for a Beano – most of them want beer and sugar. They get lots of meat in the rations now otherwise they always plump for that.

2/6th Bn KAR, Moshi, 18 December 1939

Life has been going on as usual and my Company are now at their three weeks of training; they are not very good material – mostly a very mixed collection of labour from the sisal estates – all tribes from Rhodesia to Kenya. However they are not shaping too badly. I of course have so many other irons in the fire that I can only manage to devote about three hours a day to them.

The Rhodesians arrived last week and they are living in Company messes. They drag you in to have a drink if one is up near them so it's almost like a street of pubs. I have quite a lot to do with them one way and another over the canteens et cetera. They are a very nice lot mostly from the copper belt and about half regulars from home.

I am about to celebrate along with another fellow here my twenty-first anniversary of the day I got commissioned and do you know that I can still wear the same blue tunic I had made then which is not bad going. I have had my injection for typhoid again – we all have to be done.

All best wishes for Christmas and New Year and many thanks indeed for the Xmas present. I hope we shall be home for 1940.

2/6th Bn KAR, Moshi, Tanganyika, 2 January 1940

Life here is just work, work and work from 5.45 am till 4.00 pm and I am very lucky if I finish then. Now they have made us attend lectures two nights a week on various subjects. I have to give one on Ethiopia with reference to East Africa on 12 January.

My friend Kametz came over from Arusha for Christmas and spent two days with me. We went for a motor trip to a hotel some 25 miles out, Kibo Hotel, Marango, kept by some sort of Teuton with a Latvian cook. Kametz will soon be moving near here and I shall see more of him. He has at last got news that most of his family are all well but he has no news of his younger brother who was in the Polish army. He got the information through a friend in Switzerland who wrote to the Police in Teschen.

To add to our other troubles the General [Brigadier Gerry Easton, Royal Horse Artillery (RHA)] came up and we had to have a guest night for him. It means an awful lot of work but all went well – a good liebfraumilch 1937 iced in the refrigerator. The Colonel was very pleased and said it could not have been better which was something. He is a very nice fellow indeed and if you

209

do your job he gives you every help. I have a good deal to do with him as I run all the odd jobs.

The intervention of air in Finland is most depressing and opens up the prospect of a long war. [Sandy must have been listening to his wireless as it was on that very day that 200,000 Soviet troops launched a new offensive against Finland.] I shall be glad when we can all be together again and I can see my daughter whom I gather has a tooth.

It is cheering news to me to hear you are back on the wine diet again. I only wish I was home to join you in a glass but I fear there is little chance till it is over. I shall try to get home back to the Regiment if I can but I fear I am permanently out here.

2/6th Bn KAR, Moshi, Tanganyika, 14 January 1940

I have been bothered by this infernal low fever which makes one feel rotten but yet never gives one a temperature. At last the Doctor having knocked me off quinine has been able to trace malaria parasites in my blood so I have been undergoing injections in the muscles of my backside with Ateline which is one of the by-products of Aniline dyes. I have to have further doses by the mouth. I hope this will be the end of the fever.

I was kept busy last week by the audit board on the battalion accounts. As I run or am responsible for all of them, it took some time getting them ready and checked up.

A forestry officer has been posted to us as a Lieutenant so I have managed to make him responsible for the upkeep of the gardens and hedges in the cantonment. There is a variety of creeping grass which has been planted all over the place and does not need cutting; it gives the effect of a lawn and keeps the dust down.

My lecture on Ethiopia went off well. It is a good job over. Some people even thanked me. All the other regular officers here have to give a lecture on some subject which has been chosen for them by the CO and in addition the MO gives a weekly lecture on First Aid.

My Company is coming on well and have now got their rifles. I have quite a lot of work in connection with the regimental institutes which comprise the beer shop and dry canteen in addition to the Sergeant's Mess, all sports and the general welfare of the cantonment. It takes me an hour or so every day away from the parades as my British CSM is away for the moment and all the other officers and NCOs are in a class except one – it is difficult.

2/6th Bn KAR, Moshi, Tanganyika, 28 January 1940

Many thanks for your letter and cuttings. The latter together with King-Hall's Newsletter which Cecil sends out are passed round quite a lot of people. [The newsletter was founded by Commander King-Hall after he had resigned from the Navy in 1929.]

I was not allowed to go out with the Northern Rhodesians to the manoeuvres but however did manage one day out. It was very interesting seeing the developments which have taken place in recent years in various lines – the anti-tank guns and the vast numbers of motor cars. They had Field Ambulances, casualty clearing stations and the whole show of the supply columns et cetera. Rain damped the operations a bit. It was interesting to see how much better the KAR looked after their men and what a much better spirit we have. Of course Northern Rhodesia is getting towards South Africa.

A lot of young officers are going to a school of instruction in Kenya and my CSM is going for a commission so it looks as if we shall be short handed unless we get some more officers. O'Hagan, the ADO from Kigoma, joins us on 1 February.

There has been quite a lot of fever and a couple of officers have been down with it. I suppose the rain has brought it on. Flu has been going through the Company and I have had forty a day sick – only one got pneumonia.

I believe there is a chance that I may get home for two months' leave but nothing is out yet and there are several others who have done longer than me and being a new unit still training we shall stand less chance than the other battalions.

I have at last started reading again – feeling so much better now that I have got rid of the fever.

Could you please look in my kit and send out a map case and a service protractor as well as any army web equipment.

2/6th Bn KAR, Arusha, Tanganyika, 20 February 1940

We moved over to Arusha, 50 miles by lorry. We are comfortably installed in the old KAR Detachment Mess where we sleep and have some drinks in my refrigerator and a fire in the evenings. We feed in the local hotel which costs us 4/5d a day – not really a bad price. The 2nd Lieutenant who is attached to our Company comes in a lot too. He is a ranker and we will make a soldier of him yet. His father is head caterer in the Union Castle Line and worked in the Admiralty all the Great War at victualling HM ships and is back again at the same job this war.

We have a continual stream of troops passing through going up to Kenya.

I saw my friend Kametz on Saturday and he likewise turned down the proposition which was made to us [by Brigadier Sandford to be a spy in Italian occupied Ethiopia. Brigadier Sandford was raising personnel for his Mission 101 which was to become part of Gideon Force and was to enter Ethiopia from the Sudan and reinstate the Emperor.]. He thought exactly the same about it as I did so I presume the persons concerned will think again when they find that the people who know the conditions won't touch the job. [Sandy was 6ft 4 and Kametz was 5ft 6 so they would have been easily recognizable and both were well known. Sandy knew he was on Mussolini's black list due supposedly to his presence at Walwal.]

Arusha is much colder than Moshi and a much nicer climate. It is just south of Kilimanjaro Mountain which towers above us. The area round is all farms of Europeans.

I have been round and paid all my official calls on the various officials.

2/6th Bn KAR, Arusha, Tanganyika, 10 March 1940

We are still at Arusha firing our musketry course. So far we are the leading Company in the Battalion by ten points and it looks as if we shall keep it up. We are all very pleased as half the men started with us from the day they joined; the others were sent to another company and kicked out as duds and now we are only too glad we took them on.

I had a cinema show for all the men yesterday. The local hotel keeper, who runs the big game trips to the Serengeti plains, where they feed the lions and provide camera studies from cars, showed his films to the men who loved it. I think they enjoyed most of all a close up of a native gobbling bananas.

Leave has now been definitely approved by the GOC and Clark my Captain goes home first as soon as his leave can be fixed. I will follow about September or October and will have two months in Great Britain. I will then have completed a forty months' tour and be entitled to about eight months leave which I can always carry forward. I can't get away until my Company is trained as indeed I would not wish to and I shall probably have to do a short course at home when I am there. Later on I shall get you to send out my kilt and home uniform for when I come home. It will be cold and khaki drill will be none too warm. [Sandy finally got home in October 1945, after 100 months.]

I have been having injections for malaria from the local Hungarian Doctor who used to be in Addis. He was with Ras Desta in Southern Abyssinia. His wife embroidered a banner for the Ras which the Italians captured and it is now in Rome in some museum. The Italians gave out that it was a fine example of native work much to the amusement of the Doctor's wife who worked her monogram on it.

We are now part of what they call the 'African Colonial Forces' equipped for European conflict in every way. We seem to be slowly following the French in our ideas of utilizing Colonial troops for the Middle East.

I don't belong to the club here – indeed it saves money. It has a nice golf course and is a little more than a pub house. I much prefer my glass of wine in the mess.

Mushroom season has started. We had a huge plate for breakfast this morning.

2/6th Bn KAR, Arusha, Tanganyika, 22 March 1940

Well I have now well and truly put in for leave, also I have asked to do a course on the Bren Gun and to be allowed to be attached to a unit of the Gordons in France for a month so that I can see the modern ways of war. They can but say no but I can see dates are of course uncertain as it depends on Clarke's return.

A dozen or so new officers have just arrived; they have been at the school of instruction at Nakuru and just passed out. It is funny one can't get used to odd types for officers and at first glance one always thinks what horrors to be officers they are so unlike the Royal Military College types.

The Governor arrives here next week and I suppose we shall have to turn out something or other for him. He goes on to Moshi where he thanks the various chiefs who gave grain to the KAR as a present or war gift to the Empire. I hear he is being accompanied by the KAR band from Dar es Salaam.

No more wines or produce from countries, not sterling countries, are allowed to be imported into East Africa. I would have thought that France was exempt but apparently not. Our hotel where we feed ran out of wines and can't get any more.

I was out to dinner with the DO; his brother is Prime Minister of Southern Rhodesia. They had a good dinner with a very pretty table. They all seem to imagine that I would find it strange or not like being back in the Army and am quite taken aback when I say I much prefer it. There are a lot of the ADOs who are sitting tight and going home for their full leaves after thirty months and grousing if it is put off. They soon shut up when they hear that I am going home for two months after a tour of forty-one months. Some of them will get a shock when they get home and find people do not regard them as quite so indispensable as they are out here and all their friends are called up.

2/6th Bn KAR, Arusha, Tanganyika, 7 April 1940

Many thanks for your letters and cuttings also for the map case and protractor which have arrived safely and are just what I wanted. My greatcoat has also come out from my tailors so I am ready for all occasions.

General Headquarters [GHQ] Middle East have been worrying me again to take on that Mission I have already turned down [Mission 101]. I have again declined unless the war comes out to Africa when I feel it will be work worthwhile. My Colonel is backing me up and doesn't want me to go and says he thinks it is a very unfair to ever offer me the job.

Our CO came through last week on Wednesday and was very pleased with all he saw. We are staying here another ten days until our NCOs are trained and then we go back to Moshi.

The local ladies are all busy knitting or about to knit comforts for the African troops; the chief trouble being that the African is so well found and has so little wants that he will almost certainly sell any comforts he gets to the Indian shops or his friends.

Just been sent up to GHQ Nairobi in Kenya by train this time. Expect to be back on Saturday.

2/6th Bn KAR, Arusha, Tanganyika, 16 April 1940

I got back from Nairobi by train on Saturday after a damnable journey involving several changes and waits. I was met by a F.A.N.Y. with a large staff car and hurled up to Force HQ where I was offered a job as Intelligence Officer in Somaliland on the staff to sail at the end of the month. There is a lot more to it than that and it is a much bigger show than ever in peace time. [Sandy was to be based at Hargesia and not get mixed up in the fighting. He was to question deserters coming from the Italian forces and gradually get information about the force building up to invade British Somaliland. It turned out that on that same day Brigade HQ had also received an order for him to go straight to Khartoum, presumably for Mission 101. The Brigadier replied that Sandy had already left for Somaliland which he knew well.] I am sorry to be leaving the Company which I have trained up from the raw but Clark, the second Captain, who has been with me very nearly from the start, is taking over from me.

I had a little longer than before in Nairobi but spent most of the time fulfilling commissions for people. I met several old friends whom I had known in the 3rd KAR in the ordinance stores. They helped no end and enabled me to get what I wanted at once. I also met one of the other people who is going and I hope another friend will be included who was some years in Somaliland and left about the same time as I did.

There is a huge Libby's meat canning factory just outside Nairobi which one passes in the train, a new innovation. The trains are de luxe in the extreme – huge great engines with long trains and first class dining cars with good menus with the name of the steward and the chef on them, usually a Goan with a Portugese name. Every time I see Kenya I realize what a change there is in the fifteen years; how much money there must be in the country.

I lunched in Nairobi with a Rhodesian officer I knew at the restaurant Chez

Gabi. I enjoyed an excellent lobster but the rest was poor, imitation French. Wines are getting scarce and we had a bottle of horrid Alsatian Hock.

Mombasa, Kenya, 29 April 1940

I have had a fearful rush last week packing up. To start with my kit coming from Kigoma got upset in a river which did not improve it – indeed all my suits including my dinner jacket were in pulp so I had them dry cleaned and have sent them home to Cecil ready for when and if I come.

I had a very nice send off from the Battalion. The officers and the British NCOs all came down to the station and blew bugles, sang songs and presented me with a bottle of beer for the journey and a signed advertisement wishing me good luck.

We sail on Wednesday and I have the distinction of doubtful value, but all and sundry impress it on me, of being the first KAR officer to be sent out of the East African Forces this war – further up so to speak.

The rest of the staff are due to arrive here tomorrow; so far the only one down is the inevitable Scot from Dumfries who is in a departmental Corps. I have a most comfortable room in the Manor Hotel with a bathroom, reserved by the military, cool and with a constant breeze, very nicely done with cement floors in green and cheap but nice coloured Norman Wilkinson reproductions. [Wilkinson was a contemporary maritime artist and poster designer for the London, Midland and Scottish Railway.] It is a very well run place indeed and when I look back on what it was like in 1923 when I first stayed there it is amazing.

I shall be able to get a letter off to you when we land. I gather not many people are travelling these days.

I am going out sailing this afternoon with the manager of the hotel. One of our officers gave me a letter of introduction to him. It will be a grand change.

HQ Fortress, Mombasa, Kenya, 3 May 1940

As you have probably guessed I did not get very far on my trip as we had all joined up on Tuesday morning when the Mediterranean was closed and the boat we were sailing on went by the South instead. [As Captain Roskill RN said in *The History of the Second World War*: 'The threat of war with Italy was becoming more imminent. On the 27th of April all except the fastest shipping was diverted from the Mediterranean to the long haul round the Cape and, after a temporary relaxation of the order, it was reimposed on the 16th of May.'] I was at once attached to the local HQ and am living and working there in the Intelligence office chiefly doing the ciphers. It is most interesting work as you can imagine as Mombasa is an important point. We are tied to the office these last few days and are not allowed out at all but things are getting easier.

We have a very nice Mess indeed, a large villa on the edge of the sea. I share a room with another fellow. Brigadier Wilkinson of the Indian Army and half a dozen fellows comprise the Mess which is most comfortable and homely. Our office is another villa. My immediate superior is a very nice fellow called Gooch who has a farm in Kenya.

It is very damp now with the rains on but it is not sticky at all which is a blessing.

I expect if this scare of Italy dies down we shall carry on with our trip.

Attached Somaliland Camel Corps [SCC] (KAR),
Berbera, British Somaliland via Aden, 22 May 1940

Here I am back again where I started eleven years ago. We landed at Berbera after a voyage of record time I should imagine. [Sandy travelled with the 1st Battalion Northern Rhodesia Regiment in a BI boat. The CO was Bubbly Lyn Allen who had been a great friend of Sandy's at Moshi before he sailed.] We went ashore at once and with the help of a battleship they unloaded on the same day. It gave one an excellent idea of what a job it must be landing at Narvik or Gallipoli especially if it was under fire. Such a wonderful variety of stores is included – everything from machines to socks and tinned goods galore.

It is all very jumpy at the moment and one is rather confined. I spend all morning questioning people who have come in from the Italian side.

They have made quite a lot of progress here in the past few years I have been away – water laid on even in some of the houses and new roads – sanitation schemes et cetera. The people are much more settled on the whole I think.

The Italians have I gather worked wonders at Jijiga and Harar [both in Ethiopia which had been colonized by the Italians since 1935]. A first class road connects them and you can do the trip in two hours. It took me three days by camel safari ten years ago. Hotels and clubs have also sprung up everywhere. Needless to say they continue to have trouble in the interior.

I unfortunately can't tell you details about all the preparations. For the past six months things had been got ready. All the British and Indian women and children left last week for either Mombasa or Bombay whichever they chose – an evacuation.

I have not had a chance or don't look like getting one to study my ruins further, at least not yet a while.

They have had record rains this year here and all is greener than I have ever seen it with more grass about. Last year was apparently a good year too.

There are two new officials since I left, transferred from the Colonies. But on the whole they are the same old lot. There is a new Governor of course whom I met years ago in the NFD in Kenya who is very interested in the papers I wrote in Antiquity. Plowman the Chief Secretary is on leave and it is doubtful if he will return; I am sorry as I liked him.

I live in a small Mess with two Camel Corps fellows and a South African doctor – all very nice fellows. They have a lot of Southern Rhodesian officers and NCO's here to complete the Camel Corps – they are a very good lot.

Leave here holds good as pre-war so I shall try to get home as soon as I can. I am fed up with Africa but one can't see much hope with Amiens and Arras fallen and Italy on the verge. [On 21 May 1940, German troops had reached the Aisne River and Amiens on the Somme which was only 60 miles from Paris.] I only hope things improve in France soon and I can get home in the autumn. Over three years is too long a tour if one is an official.

Attached SCC (KAR), Berbera, British Somaliland, 31 May 1940

I think that at last it looks as if Italy will be coming in and that we shall get our share of the fighting. My job does not lead me into the fighting directly and my first duty is to get the information back where it can be of use.

I expect we shall get an aerial greeting one morning as we are fairly close to Jijiga.

About fifty British Somalis came across yesterday discharged from the Italian forces on the Sudan border. They had cheques to the value of a £1,000 payable in rupees in Aden – all their back pay and savings for years. It looks as if they would be unlucky. Incidentally the Italian Government cheques are frequently dishonoured in Aden for lack of funds.

The Italians are very short of sugar and paraffin so their idle boasts about paying their troops in Berbera don't carry much weight. The proverb 'The empty tin makes most noise' is particularly apt and I never fail to rub it in for propaganda. The Italians fully realize the predicament they are in and have already started buying meat supplies because they say the British and French have shut the sea. The native has already realized that the Lire will be worthless.

We are at last dealing with 5th column agents or spies and there are quite a lot in durance vile; it has made a lot of difference and had a good effect on the people.

I have been busy camouflaging my tent. They gave me a brilliant white one, also my lorry, paint with sand thrown in. I have the whole thing organized so that in the event of an air attack while I am on the road each person knows what to do.

Bad news from France but it seems to have shaken our people into a firm resolve to win the war at all costs. That blackguard Leopold will go down in our history books at least as a cad of the deepest dye. [On 28 May 1940, King Leopold of Belgium had surrendered to the Germans against the advice of his government.] My wireless is the only one in the place and works well. I can work it off my lorry battery if I am on the move.

We get very good army rations now here; tins of first class sausages, bacon, cheese, jam et cetera and crab now and then. They have a new line of damsons, I presume from Kenya but wherever they come from they are quite good, if one did not suffer from a surfeit of them. I have a large reserve supply in case I have to go off on my own.

The moment the war starts here we are of course under French Command. Hope he is better than Gamelin. [Gamelin, Commander of the General Staff in France, had been sacked on 17 May 1940 after the French Army was defeated by the Germans during the Western offensive. He was replaced by General Maxime Weygand.]

I am glad Cecil has moved to Taunton. Kent or South East England will be no place to be I should imagine nor would Edinburgh but I should imagine with Churchill that Berlin or Cologne would also be unpleasant. [Churchill had become Prime Minister on 10 May 1940.]

Attached SCC (KAR), Berbera, British Somaliland, 6 June 1940

Here we are still sitting waiting for the Italians to do something. We had a lucky coup last weekend and two native deserters came in with all their kit. They confirmed most of the dispositions I had already got hold of; one was a very intelligent fellow. The Italians dress their native troops in a very sensible way, khaki shirt and shorts of a greenish hue, a khaki turban with small tasselled fringe of the colour of the battalion and a cummerbund of the same colour. Their equipment is a cheap untanned leather belt with two pouches in front holding twenty rounds each; it is supported by a narrow strap which goes round the back of the neck. They are not hampered by boots or heavy equipment and must be very mobile. They were both from British tribes. They were followed a few days later by some very doubtful individuals, I presume sent over to see where they had gone. A haul like these two fellows saves one weeks of work and questioning.

I spend hours interrogating natives and it is extraordinary what one manages to collect. We have also locked up several of these spies, both men and women.

I had a trip for two nights down to my friends the Northern Rhodesians. I took the deserters with me and their uniform to show the Rhodesian troops what their enemy would look like. I also attended a conference. It was a nice break in the routine.

The windy season has started and in bivouacs it is awful especially as the troops do not know how to make themselves comfortable out here yet. I am all right in a house at present. The Governor [Sir Vincent Glenday] is up here for a visit but being under the Military it does not affect me in the least.

Officials who have finished their time are still being allowed to go on retirement. The RQM of the Camel Corps leaves in four days.

We have at last taken action against the virtual 5th Columnists and locked up all suspects. The Italians have been doing it for months – they had hundreds of homeless natives who had gone over to see relatives as spies.

We have quite a good mess – a Welsh Guards officer in the S.C.C., a Maltese officer, a South African Doctor with the Field Ambulance section from Johannesburg and a fellow who was in an English regiment for six years and has knocked round East Africa in sisal estates and was in Southern Rhodesia when the war came and joined up there. A good mixture.

The mails seem very bad, odd ones from home and not one from Mombasa since we left as no letters have been forwarded up at all. I don't know how they go, Cape or Suez, or whether they just keep them and wait for some steamer going to Port Said.

Attached SCC (KAR), Berbera, British Somaliland, 16 June 1940

Many thanks for your letters – two of which arrived last week and also for six lots of Spheres forwarded on from Kenya.

The long expected war broke out on Monday [1 June 1940].The first I knew of it was that the staff car which my friends the Northern Rhodesian Regiment had promised me when war broke out arrived in the middle of the night. I had not heard the 9.00 pm (for us) wireless.

The Italians made a poor start and have had a lot of bother with their native troops. Thirty have deserted to us and the French in ten days while the shortage of food has made others very discontented. Seven Europeans were caught trying to desert to us two days before the war. I expect they shot them.

Up on the frontier they captured five of our irregular scouts who did not know there was a war on. We have seized the initiative and last night attacked one of their small posts and killed three and wounded one. We retook a lorry which had had to be abandoned on the frontier when we drew back on the outbreak of war. We had no casualties. Tonight others are out and we shall keep them on the hop.

We expected we might get unwelcome aerial attention but only one of our planes has passed over to date. An Italian on the roof of their customs post at the frontier fell off in fright when it passed over and never fired a shot. Natives on our side watched it.

I had a lovely report in today which sums up the native point of view in a nutshell – it is quite all right to tell it. The Italian official at one of the small posts across the boundary called a meeting of all the local natives and traders on Monday and told them war would break out. He himself and many others did not want it but a few did and had got their way. Britain and France had control of the seas so they could get no more cloth or other goods into the country and they must make what they had go as far as possible. Traders must sell a little to each person till their stocks were finished. No one could cross to British Territory. One old Somali got up and said, 'I have lived with four Governments, the Egyptians, the British, the Ethiopian and the Italian. Under the Egyptian long ago we sent our caravans to Zeila for cloth and sugar and we had food. Under the British you have peace and plenty of food. Under the Ethiopians you have peace and plenty of food. The Italians came here with war. They have now brought famine and are bringing another war.' There was no answer.

Intelligence is coming on well and we are at an advantage. We know they can't get any real reinforcements and, as our tribes graze over into Ethiopia and nothing short of a wire fence will keep them out, there is a steady flow of information. On the other side we have the sea and can get reinforcements any time easily so we play on this and circulate tales of the arrival of tanks, hundreds of men et cetera which get where we want them and make them nervy.

I have an Ethiopian interpreter coming up to help me [Nagash Roba]. As part of my job in propaganda, I have already drawn up a pamphlet for dropping from the air on the Ethiopians, signed of course by the Brigadier and full of highfaulting terms and parables 'The empty tin makes the most noise'. One has of course to avoid any phrase which might say 'We are fighting to give you back your land' as it might be produced like the McMahon letters years later. [In 1915 Sherif Hussein after meeting with Sir Henry McMahon had understood that Palestine would be given back to the Palestinians after the end of the war. This claim was later disputed by the British Government.]

The local steamer actually did a special trip across and has brought our mails. Our Navy must have got control of the Red Sea. As the tub does about four knots, it would be a very easy target.

Now that there is war we have to walk about with revolvers on all day and have packed up our mufti [civilian clothes].

Attached SCC (KAR), Berbera, British Somaliland, 21 June 1940

Here we are now in the second week of the war and if it had not been for the French breaking their Treaty and suing for a separate peace we could be very well content with the way things are going. [On 17 June 1940, Marshal Pétain, who had become Premier the day before, asked for an armistive. It was this armistice which when signed gave Germany control of northern France and the Atlantic coast.] We had the initiative all along the frontier and had wiped out several posts by raids by night and day and kept them guessing.

As soon as this French business started the Italians got their tails up again and took up a fresh attitude of bombast – strengthened all their posts and put Europeans in. They now have four sentries in each one. Their posts are surrounded with *zarebas* now and are where roads cross the frontiers. It does not stop us raiding them anyway. We use rifle grenades on them. One which we cleared yesterday was quite interesting from the intelligence side; there were numbers of postcards of the sites of Rome which they give free to natives, the Forum, the Arch of Titus et cetera – also an Italian Field postcard which included a map of Ethiopia on the back so that the soldier could let his people know whereabouts he was. It was of course done for the Ethiopian war. We also got a number of military manuals and the statement of evidence against a poacher who had hunted without a gun licence near Naples – typewritten out – how it got out to the frontier I don't know.

They continually fly over Berbera but seldom drop bombs and if they do they land in the open – the same at Zeila. Four Italian bombers did a night raid on Aden; they dropped their bombs on the wrong point some miles away all together and then returned to Assab. On landing one blew up, another caught fire while the remaining two crashed. Our RAF going over in the morning saw them all on the aerodrome. Two fighters also crashed at Jijiga, I presume damaged in our raid on Dire Dawa. Some Somali, who suggested it might have been a British bullet and not magic, was put in jail.

I am kept hard at it questioning and now and then going out up to the forward areas to get fresh news. I was up on Wednesday when I saw a plane coming straight down the road only fifty feet up. We ran for cover only to find it was one of ours returning from a reconnaissance where he had spotted two crashed fighters and so was expressing his *joie de vivre*. [Sandy recalled how he did a Victory roll as he passed.]

We all hope the French out here will stick on. The General, who is called Le Gentilhomme, made all the defences round Jibuti. He is not the sort to give in and is of course in command of us here. It would be too much for him to surrender to the Italians all he had made without a fight.

We are getting more and more empire products – Australian matches with a warning on the box to put out the match to prevent danger of bush fires.

I went down to see my friends the Northern Rhodesians on Monday. I always land there when there is some depressing news. One time it was Leopold quitting. This time it was France and the death of a DC in Berbera [Horsley]. He was a fellow who had been twenty years out and was overworked. He was hit in the head in the last war. I went down in the Staff car the Rhodesians have lent me. It is rather annoying to get in and out with a chauffeur holding the door open and 'Simulating a General'.

I hope you have got a decent air raid shelter. I don't like the sound of the green shieling [a shepherd's summer hut] with turf on it.

Our mail steamer goes at irregular days now; it was feared lost last week as there was a submarine outside Aden but it turned up as so did the submarine which surrendered. They are no good in adversity these Italians.

Attached SCC (KAR), Berbera, British Somaliland, 29 June 1940

Goodness knows how long these letters take to reach you. I expect they go via the Cape and Bombay. We have had none from home since the war started here. I have had a very busy week. First of all our irregulars captured a large three-engined brand new service bomber intact. The plane came down, no one knows why yet, and the crew got out, all of them and only one with a revolver although they had rifles in the plane. They went to some native nomadic huts nearby and were given milk. The owner of the village had been in the Italian army and spoke a little Italian and he kept them talking and sent for the irregulars who by luck were close by. [Sandy recalled that the locals sent a letter in Arabic to the DC saying that they had captured an Italian aeroplane and had need of his technical assistance. The irregulars were close as they were guarding a ration and small-arms ammunition dump which could be used in the event of any unit retiring to the east that way.] They came up and stalked the plane to make sure there was no one in it and then ordered the Italians to stand up while they covered them with their rifles. The senior who was a Colonel fired his revolver at them and of course that was the signal and they were all shot down and killed. If the stupid ass had not fired they would have been brought in as prisoners. We sent out a party as soon as we heard and found the plane intact – all the papers including the ciphers, notebooks and notecases. They had six machine guns including two Lewis guns and they never thought of leaving one man to cover them while they got out. No clue as to why they came down at all.

Two of our irregulars on the coastal plain got another plane. They covered the crew and they surrendered; then one marched them off while the other guarded the plane. Aden captured one intact too and flew it back to their aerodrome.

We have had one setback at least to our prestige. The Italians have occupied Borama – it was untenable from a military point of view and the DO [James Walsh] got away with all the staff and the police.

The Camel Corps carried out one good raid and inflicted heavy casualties. The Italian native troops used hand grenades which burst with a bang and went off within a foot of the officer and did him no harm at all.

Two regular army NCOs from the Middle East arrived last week. One is a Hussar with the Household Cavalry, a pleasant change from the rather sloppy

Southern Rhodesians, one of whom always says 'Cheeribye' when he salutes and withdraws after talking to you.

The news is most depressing these days and it all depends really on what French Somaliland does. If they stall on we are of course well placed but if they lay down their arms then we can only do one thing or else get more troops.

No sign of hostile aircraft yet over us but I expect they will come. The RAF bombing Dire Dawa of course limits their scope. They also bombed Jijiga.

I am at it all day long – collecting reports and interrogating people and it is a strain without a break. One lives in a continual atmosphere of tension.

I have been able to replace my pyjamas and vests in a princely style out of silk from the parachute of the plane. It is first class stuff and very strong.

I still have my staff car lent by the Rhodesians. We don't use it much. [The car actually belonged to the CO, Lieutenant Colonel Bubbly Lyn Allen. Sandy recalled that he was a slow, stuffy-looking fellow who failed to impress senior officers but was however a first-class CO. He did a brilliant job but was never mentioned in dispatches or decorated.]

Attached SCC (KAR), Berbera, British Somaliland, 7 July 1940

Still no mails and not likely to be for another month or so to let them catch up round the Cape route – it will take four or five months to get an answer to a letter I reckon.

Here we are at our fourth week of war with Italy and so far it has gone in our favour. We have the initiative along the frontier and maintain it. Odd raids on posts once or twice a week keep them on the hop and especially as they put their sentries up the trees they fall ready victims. We bag about four or five a week with practically no casualties ourselves. In addition we have had very substantial reinforcements and can cope with all that comes now. All their posts are entrenched behind *zareba*s.

The Italians dropped some propaganda pamphlets on the native village last week. They were done for Arabia and Egypt and spoke in flowery terms of 'Rose Egypt' and how Italy and Germany were the champions of Islam. It was addressed to the Somali nation. We concocted a reply based on concrete facts which the natives here could see and knew about – the shortage of food, petrol and how the Italians themselves always wanted rupees. We read both out to the natives who said we have been under the British for fifty-six years and next to the Italians for five – it is addressed to us, we will answer this one and they are now concocting a reply which they want dropped on the Italians – of course they can't stand them. I was surprised in the change in feeling in the four years or so I was away how much more pro-British and anti-Italian the people had become.

Once a week we have a sort of fright – news of battalions massing opposite us; then they seem to melt away again. Deserters keep coming over, three last week and it is apparent that they hold them by a very delicate thread. It is only the bombastic lying saying they hold Djibuti and will soon have Berbera which puts the people off deserting. Once we can strike them a hard blow we shall be overwhelmed with deserters. They don't pay their men and let them run up large balances to hold them.

I expect you heard on the wireless how General Le Legentilhomme, the OC French Somaliland, told the Italian delegates sent to him, that he did not recognize any armistice and gave them a time limit to leave the territory.

We had a youth of sixteen who deserted last week and he said he was not the youngest – lots more were like him.

Christopher Consett, Russel's cousin, came back here today as a Major. I worked with him before and will be very glad to see him. He is a very nice fellow. These arriving all bring us news of the outside world which we are devoid of except for the wireless – no papers of course here. I have written to Nairobi to get the East African paper sent up; it will come quicker than the 'Times'. I will also get news of KAR units in it. It is curious to hear of Moyale, Wajir, Kismayu and places one knew well mentioned as the scenes of raids and fighting. [Moyale, in Kenya, fell to the Italians on 10 July 1940.] One gets quite accustomed to the wartime aspect of this country – road blocks against tanks et cetera all over the place.

16 July 1940

Another week of war past and we are still awaiting a visit from Italian bombers – beyond our proximity to the frontier it looks rather as if you are seeing more of the war than I am. We have had Italian reconnaissance planes over us several times but flying very high.

We continue to harass their posts. Last week we had a deserter in from one of them and acting on his information we attacked it the next morning. Apparently the moment our machine guns opened the Italian Lieutenant was seen getting away at full gallop on his pony – he chucked his revolver away and was in pyjamas. He led the flight when the troops took the post. They got all his clothes, uniform, pots and pans and camp bed and burnt 20,000 rounds of ammunition. I have his tropical helmet in the office now. He will cut a *'bonita figura'* if he managed to reach another post as he will be unable to replace any of his kit or uniform. They spared the garden with some lettuces he had. Of course we don't hold their posts. We killed two or three and wounded many more – it keeps them on the hop.

My friend the Colonel of the Rhodesians has just been up for a visit. We have a lot more troops here now – a veritable international African 'zoo' if you include Europeans too. I fancy we cover the world at least as regards experience – KAR, an Indian Army Battalion, Punjabis and East African Light Battery.

Two more deserters last week – a Corporal and a Colonel's orderly, both British protected natives. There is a constant stream of them which must be most annoying to the Italians. They only hold them by not paying them and lying to them.

At the moment things are very quiet here – the rains in the highlands of Ethiopia will show up things and encourage the Ethiops.

Forward Intelligence Officer, c/o Force HQ,
British Somaliland, 28 July 1940

I have been very busy since I last wrote and have been down to Berbera and Force HQ twice – luckily Berbera was not bombed while I was there. The place is crowded out with officers of all sorts and British NCOs – one hardly knows a soul now – so many have come in and are continually coming. It is remarkable how little damage has been done in the nine air raids. No house in the European quarter had a direct hit but most of the windows were smashed and the wind and dust just whistle through them.

I have now to deal with the propaganda side and the Ethiopian Patriots as far as Addis Ababa so it is a big job. I saw a lot of the Ethiopians who came across the border to me when the Italians took Jijiga. We also have many others who fought for two years in the province opposite us against the Italians and all they ask for is to fight again – pay is no object to them and all they want is rations. They say 'We fought for two years without pay for our country and that is all we want to do.' One of the leaders was at St. Cyr, the French Sandhurst [Colonel Asfau]. They are a truly remarkable people.

The Italians have now been very helpful to the Intelligence officers. When they come on a patrol into our territory, they leave bits of paper with their names on them and company rubber stamp on the top. The Camel Corps chase them; all that is necessary is for them to hear the Corps is on their track and they leg it unless they are in a trenched position. The Italians have at last evacuated the frontier posts they held at such cost. They must have lost about thirty killed and twenty wounded to our two killed and one wounded. A Mills rifle grenade fired into a post causes awful havoc apparently. Last week we just sent irregulars up to fire shots at the post by night and one small section to crawl up to the *zareba* and lob bombs in – the result was always a heavy fire all night at nothing because our people had all withdrawn; it showed their extreme nervousness.

[On 23 July 1940, General Germain had been sent by the new Vichy French Government to replace General Le Legentilhomme.] The new General was chased away at first but eventually wormed his way in and negotiated the new term. The French in Djibuti have signed an Armistice with the Italians on the basis of status quo – they do not lay down their arms and the Italians do not occupy Djibuti. It leaves our flank open and we can't hold Zeila but it does them no good, merely adds to their lines of communication especially as they have not got command of the sea [as recounted in the Supplement to the *London Gazette* of 4 June 1946: 'This collapse of French resistance released the whole of the Italian Eastern Army for operations against British Somaliland.']

We constantly have Italian planes over but they only dropped bombs the time I was away. They fell in the open and did no damage beyond killing one small bird. I have a couple of trenches alongside the house to which we all retire.

When more troops arrive I shall probably be a Brigade Intelligence Officer [IO]. Already I have nothing to do with the Camel Corps except that I live in one of their Company Messes. We are very lucky as we have all the pre-war organization and contacts. We have our gardens and can get eggs which the newly arrived units can't get at all. It is all bringing money into the country as all the troops have to be fed on fresh mutton – several thousand sheep a week not to mention the milk, eggs et cetera they buy as well.

I have asked Cecil to get some comforts for my troops. Having no civilian population the SCC are left out of all these comforts and cigarette schemes. The others coming from large colonies get stuff frequently.

On 21 August 1940 Sandy's father received the following telegram: 'Safe with what I stand up in.'

On a troopship heading SW, 25 August 1940

I sent you a wire from Aden – just to let you know I was safe. I fear we don't put too much faith in the honeyed words of the B.B.C. My wireless set of course went west with all my other stuff.

Here I am heading for East Africa again!

It is all a very pleasant reaction after the fourteen days of 'Blitzing' we had. I got out in what I stood up in and could carry in my haversacks. I lost all my uniform, my shotgun which annoys me most of all, rifle and all my notes on prehistory in Somaliland, crockery, cutlery, bedding, tables, chairs, tropical suits et cetera, all had to be abandoned. All the cookery pots we smashed with a pick – bed et cetera we cut up into little pieces – my clothes and two suitcases, one of which you gave me when I went to Sandhurst, the other one of Mother's I gave to my boy and cook so may get them back in years to come. I had a tin box in Berbera with all sorts of stuff including gold cufflinks the aunts gave me on my 21st birthday but I hope the navy put some shells into the store before the Italians got in. They blew up most of the houses.

It started as far as we were concerned at Hargesia after lunch on Sunday 4 August when three planes came very slowly over us and dropped bombs – mostly on the native town and outside. We were in a trench and had none within 400yds but it was most annoying the slow deliberate way they came over and round and round. They killed sixteen people in all including a gentleman who we suspected of being a 5th Columnist who had deserted us that day. [The slit trench that Sandy was in was just across the dry river bed from the Government offices in Hargesia.]

We had ample news of the advance down the road and two of my agents mixed with the advancing forces. The Camel Corps harassed them and knocked out three tanks, setting one on fire. When they were massing to attack Hargesia, I, according to my orders, left to join the Rhodesians but I heard the tale of what happened. [Sandy had to take the radio valves from the Hargesia wireless station and leave at midnight. Hargesia fell the next day, 6 August 1940.] It was the German method exactly – first of all down the road came four Blackshirts on motor cycles wearing black berets followed by two cars with officers, then medium tanks, then the light tanks. The cyclists and cars were destroyed. They also had artillery et cetera which we had not. The two companies at Hargesia held them up – twenty to one odds and at one time they were faced with eight tanks firing two machine guns each at their positions – artillery and infantry all firing and the troops got out without a casualty. It is incredible really – they had six men taken prisoner and the Italian Major took and wore the hats and boots of the first and had a fight with another officer over the man's bully beef. The prisoners escaped and told us the tale later. They all were dressed in only their shorts – all their other clothing had been taken. Our people must have exacted a heavy toll on the Italians and over fifty Europeans were killed not to mention natives. On the way back to reform, eight natives of the Rhodesians ambushed an Italian lorry of Irregulars and killed the twenty-five in it with a Bren gun at close range and broke up the lorry.

It was not long before the Italians continued their advance again down the main road and when they bumped the next positions the motor cyclists were there again, but not the cars this time. They met their usual fate. Then when the medium tank came along it stopped and out of it got an Italian and two Somali women who calmly pointed out where the mines were laid in the road block. They were all shot dead but not before the mines had been pointed out. We could not cope with the medium tank as our anti-tank Boyes rifles would not penetrate it.

At this time I was camped close to the main position held by the Rhodesians and was agreeably surprised one night to find a dozen or so lorries with the Black Watch at my camp. They had overshot their camp; it was good to hear a volley of homely Scottish oaths in a dialect one knew.

One day the Italians in their planes came over low as usual and spotted my car and let me have it all round. One fell less than 50yds away from where I was taking cover but did no damage – one was 20yds from the car – real big stuff but by great luck no damage was done.

I went down to Berbera for a day and had a grand view of an air raid – saw the anti-aircraft guns with their puffs of smoke all round the flames. [The bombing of Berbera was an almost daily occurrence.]

About this time I was posted to a Brigade which had been newly formed – the Brigade Major was none other than my old friend Rupert Murray in the Black Watch who was General Cameron's ADC. He asked kindly to be remembered to you. We shared the fortunes of the campaign together till the evacuation – getting bombed and machine-gunned and shelled and spent hours in the open or some beastly sandy trench taking cover. We have planned a real good meal at the New Club [a smart club in Edinburgh which was founded in 1787] when the war is over to laugh over our experiences. We had ten machines bombing one day – they came so low that the Black Watch got one with Bren Gun fire and it blew up before reaching the ground. I saw the remains – what a mess!!! [This was the attack on Tug Argan which was a gap 4 miles wide which had been held by the Northern Rhodesian regiment and the KAR since the outbreak of war on 11 June 1940. It was on the road between Hargesia and Berbera.]

I had to make several trips up to the Rhodesians' position which was being attacked and on one occasion got shelled by pack artillery and 4.5s. They must have seen me and as they were attacking apparently just below where I was across my line of advance they were protecting their flanks. Shelling is not bad – you hear them coming and can lie flat. There were quite a lot of duds that morning. When I came to go back I found several direct hits on the road.

In due course the Italians hammered the Rhodesians out of their positions – the usual odds sixteen to one and using fresh troops for each attack – they shelled, bombed and machine gunned the positions which were on rocky hills for four days and then never took them because we retired. The Northern Rhodesian Regiment put up a magnificent show and even captured two guns and killed a General but they could not get the guns out and with the numbers the Italians had they could infiltrate round the flanks. It was a hopeless position; there we were with no artillery, our air force chased out of the sky or at least we never saw them because they daren't appear for fear of losing a machine. The Italians then kept fighters up over the roads all day and used to dive down and shoot up any cars they saw or any people. At Brigade HQ we had our share of that – you can see the plane coming at you and firing live bullets which make a fearful mess of anything they hit.

After the Northern Rhodesian Regiment withdrew [from the Tug Argan and moved back to cover Berbera] we put in the Black Watch [at Barkasan] and also to cover our withdrawal to the coast and the evacuation. They were attacked by the usual column with motor cyclists at 10.30 am and fought till 4.30 pm inflicting appalling casualties on the Italian Ethiopian troops. They drove them back 900 yards with the bayonet when their ammunition ran short and officers saw the Blackshirts in the rear shooting the retiring native troops.

Andy Pitcairn's Company was on the flank and got the worst of it and I met him when I was up with a message coming out of action about 8.30pm with his Company. [Andy was from Edinburgh too.] While the Black Watch were fighting we were shelled continuously. It was a good sight to see the shells bursting on black hillsides and the white puffs. For some unknown reason they put down a barrage in front of the Black Watch about 5.30 am – it was an extraordinary sight to see – this drop curtain of smoke and bursting shells across the centre part of a gap about 2 miles wide – it was very clearly defined.

Brigade HQ had to retire and as we could not get our transport up we had to jettison all our stuff. I took a bottle of sparkling burgundy in my haversack and it about saved our lives. We had had no food all day. We legged it across sand to a new site. I was destined to cross that sand three times more with messages before we finally withdrew.

About 8.30 pm or so I did two trips up to the Black Watch and saw them coming out of action. It was moonlight and men were asleep either side of the road. The wounded were coming in and being attended to. They had their Bren Gun Carriers which are like small tanks which added to the scene. Luckily they had given the Italians such a knock that they never even tried to advance far less fire a shot after dark; if they had we would have been in the soup.

I had one exciting trip in a lorry along a road which was being shelled from time to time by mortar shells – luckily they put nothing over while I was going along. Coming back from the trip, I met an officer of the Black Watch called Fairlie who was wounded trying to get back. We found a box of their mess linen lying abandoned – napkins beautifully embroidered with 'The Black Watch' in blue sewing across the corner. We took a couple to mop up his wound which was not bad only a flesh one I fancy. I collected other walking wounded as well.

The 2nd KAR battalion also put up a fine show the same day. The Italians pushed on without a proper reconnaissance and relied on the air to spot our lines. They walked into the KAR machine guns while in fours all closed up and the attack never came. Many must have been killed while our losses were nil.

When the units were all out of action we got into lorries and ourselves into a staff touring car and left for Berbera to embark but we were a bit previous. Some fool took fright and blew up the road too soon so we were faced with over a hundred lorries trying to negotiate a sandy bypass and only four hours till dawn when we would be at the mercy of the enemy planes. [The officer who was stationed there had been given orders to blow up the corduroy across the dry river bed in the event of an Italian blitz of armoured cars coming down the road or something similar. The Somaliland Camel Corps had let loose their horses that afternoon who stampeded into the bush and the officer thought it was the Italian cavalry.] We had no course but to abandon the large lorries, a hundred odd, some brand new and to march the troops across the gap and get vehicles from Berbera. The lorries had food, clothing et cetera on them and we smashed up what we could. The photos of our rout and all those abandoned vehicles must make awful propaganda. I had to stay till the end here directing the traffic and left on one of the Black Watch Bren Gun carriers. We were met by odd cars coming from Berbera to see if there were any more troops to get out of it. The canteen and shops had been thrown open and they brought us drambuie, rum and beer galore – all were welcome in our tired condition. I came the last mile or so in a car with young Dick Lauder, a nephew or grandson of the one we knew.

Once in Berbera at dawn we went straight to the shore where men were being embarked on lighters. All the cars were parked on the front. You never saw such a mess – refrigerators, suitcases, champagne and beer. You could take it if you could carry it. The rest was to be blown up by the navy in order to render it useless to the enemy. [The people in British Somaliland who had been evacuated had taken all their cabin trunks down to the pier in case there was a chance of getting them off. There was champagne because Government House had been blown up to a certain extent. The Governor had gone and somebody had taken the champagne down to the ship.] There was no drunkenness in spite of the open house and cases of beer everywhere with bottles for the taking. Most people were too tired to bother.

We got on to a ship and I just lay down on the deck with my gas mask as a pillow and went to sleep. We all did and continued to do so all day long with intervals for meals. We were not bombed for some unknown reason and more and more stragglers kept arriving. Most of the Camel Corps got out but had a bad time. [The reason why the Italian planes never attacked the evacuation at Berbera would seem to have been that they followed their usual route, flying along the main road between Hargesia and Berbera. On seeing the line of abandoned lorries they launched their bombs on them and never continued to Berbera which was protected by AA guns and a warship.]

We got over to Aden where we were parked in the same lines and I managed to wrangle this trip back to East Africa with my own Intelligence Section as well so that I can take the field again at once but I shall try to get some leave to spend with Kametz at Moshi if I can.

[On arriving in Aden Sandy found a group of 700 Ethiopian refugees – one of the Somaliland DCs was delighted that Sandy should take charge of them. Before being shipped over to Aden there had been a delay and 'a scorched earth policy was adopted'. This involved devastating all land and buildings in the course of advancing troops so as to leave nothing salvageable to the enemy. The refugees had taken full advantage of this and carried off blankets and greatcoats before embarking for Aden. However Sandy asked for all this clothing to be handed back before they reached Mombasa, and it was – two lorry loads of it.

On nearing Mombasa the ship was escorted by a South African plane as an Italian submarine had been reported in the area. On arriving at Mombasa, Sandy got permission to take his refugees on a tour round Mombasa Island. He took the more important refugees round the customs godowns and showed them the produce awaiting export, including tea, coffee, skins, hides et cetera. One of them, on hearing that the British had been in control in Kenya for about forty-five years, remarked, 'Well, if they had been in our country how much richer we should be today.']

I hope to goodness they don't let us down again like Somaliland – put us up against artillery, aircraft and tanks while we were virtually helpless. [The East Africa Light Battery in fact did sterling work but was very heavily outgunned.] The reinforcements were of course on their way but arrived too late. Four days would have done the trick and what is worse they had been requested two months previously and repeatedly asked for. Someone in what we call 'Muddle East' and Cairo ought to be hauled over the coals or better still make him sit in a trench while slow aircraft bomb and machine gun him and artillery fires at him while we had not one gun to reply with or a plane to send up to drive off our oppressors. I bet he would not waste time then. [175,000 Italian troops were deployed against the four defending battalions.] Our casualties are really very small, while the Northern Rhodesian Regiment has the most [the casualties amounted to five per cent of the force].

We did see one of our planes at dusk coming back from the Hargesia direction and it was being shelled by an Italian anti-aircraft mobile battery. We saw the stream of illuminated shells going in its direction.

The French of course gave the Italians all the details of our positions and also our numbers, weapons et cetera which made the attack possible in the first place, that was after the good General there had been ousted. A French Staff officer told us as much ten days before the show and said the Italians would do it in eight days.

The Italian gain is nothing but moral really. He has no petrol to run the lorries and has a large population to feed.

I got 2,000 rupees to pay off the Irregulars just as the shelling started but they did not wait so I handed it to my Ethiops of whom I have three for Intelligence purposes and told them to look after it. [British Somaliland had been a colony of India until 1898 so the rupee was used and continued to be up to 1951.] They did and what is more I next saw them two days later in Aden with the money intact waiting for me – a very good show. When we counted it was 2,000 rupees. They had got a different ship and of course had to cross the blown up road and change lorries with other troops of all sorts about. I got them a reward I am glad to say. [For the next ten months Sandy was pestered by the Paymaster to know what he had done with the 2,000 rupees sent up to him, eventually managing to get a field cashier to put an end to the nonsense.]

I paid off my boy and took away the small Somali youth I brought up with me. He did very well and was awaiting me at the blown up road and again in Berbera although I was the last down. He had my haversacks all right and had been chased on board but managed to avoid actually embarking till I came.

We are due in Mombasa tomorrow so I must finish off.

As Moyse-Bartlett recounted in *The King's African Rifles*, published by Gale & Polden in 1956, p. 503: 'The Italian jubilation knew no bounds, and Mussolini trumpeted his victory to the world with the arrogant assertion that British Somaliland was henceforth for ever Italian territory. But General Godwin-Austin, telegraphing from Aden the news of his safe arrival with the Force, ended his message with the words "All in good heart". The final round was yet to come'.

Eight months after the conquest the British were back.

CHAPTER 12

The Raising of Curle's Irregulars, 1940–1

Att. Intelligence Dept. Force HQ,
c/o Army Postal Services [APS], Nairobi,
Kenya, 23 September 1940

I am still at large and at leisure. I finished up my stay at the Kibo Hotel, Marengo, with a trip up through the forests on Kilimanjaro. It was really lovely – huge trees covered with lichen and the upper sides of the trunks covered with ferns, some hanging ones. It was lovely in the sun which just gave it all a yellowish olive colour and as it was thick foliage it was wonderful. I got up to the area of giant heathers. There was plenty of fresh elephant spoor but very few birds about.

The natives round here grow coffee and it is wonderful soil. It is all marketed and controlled by a co-operative society supervised by the government so that they get good prices. Individuals could never manage to dispose of the small lots. It brings in to the natives £75,000 a year. There are also many European estates here on the foot of the mountain, mostly Greek and German owned; the latter are now leased to non enemy aliens.

My host, A.L. Bennett, who runs the Coffee Co-operative Society, takes me out every evening for a run in his car and we take two of my Ethiopians with us to show them the country. They never cease to wonder how fertile it is – maize, wheat, barley and all growing amidst the bananas which are 30ft high and coffee galore. The natives give them presents of maize et cetera because they are soldiers and have been in the war.

There is no shortage of food here, caviar, turkey, fresh prawns from the coast, ham, butter and cheese galore; a nice change after ration food and tinned damsons. You can still buy Hock at 9/- a bottle.

Rather annoying, if I had stayed on in the 2/6th Battalion I would have been able to go on leave to South Africa for two months and Cecil would have been able to come out. Both the officers who were down for it the same time as me have just come back. No hope of course now till the end of the war and being with Ethiopians we shall probably be kept busy after. Goodness knows what it will lead me into – I always keep going off on side lines.

I hope you have got a trench or an Anderson shelter now. From what we saw and experienced of air raids nothing would induce me to go to the 'Green Shieling'. It is a death trap.

After his leave Sandy had reported to East Africa Force, Intelligence Branch. General Dickinson, the General Officer Commanding, gave him the job of raising, organizing, training and commanding a unit of 300 men taken from amongst the Ethiopian refugees at Taveta who were to be known as the 2nd Ethiopian Irregulars. These were the refugees who Sandy had been in charge of on the troopship after the evacuation of British Somaliland in August 1940. Sandy had known many of them in 1936 when he had taken them over the frontier into British Somaliland during the Italian Ethiopian war, when he had disarmed them and sent them in lorries to Borama where a refugee camp was being prepared for them, where they they stayed until 1940. After being evacuated to Berbera they met up with Sandy yet again. Another coincidence was that some of these men had formed the Ethiopian escort to the Boundary Commission when he had been at the famous Walwal incident on 23 November 1934.

Sandy was thus in the enviable position of knowing many of the officers and men personally. He was given absolute 'carte blanche' as to how it was done and how it was to be organized; he could have any European as an officer provided he was not a regular soldier. The unit was to be trained and ready to take the field in a month.

The purpose of the unit was to counteract the Italian Banda, who were locals engaged by the Italians and were causing a great deal of trouble to the KAR in the northern frontier of Kenya towards the boundary with Ethiopia. These Banda were highly mobile, were well led by Italian officers and had even captured the paymaster's lorry. At this time the Italians held a great deal of the NFD. The unit which was to be highly mobile, was to operate in front of the regular troops and secure their flanks. In addition, they were to operate behind enemy lines to disrupt communications.

At the refugee camp the men had been organized into groups with leaders based on where they came from. Sandy selected six of the most suitable leaders and said, 'I want you to get me fifty men each. You will select them and they will be engaged as soldiers. There will be an Ethiopian officer, known as a leader, with each group and you who raised the people will be the leader of your group.'

When they had produced the men Sandy continued by saying, 'I will pay you, I will clothe you, I will feed you and command you. There will be one punishment of fifteen or twenty-five lashes of the whip. [The punishment was seldom used and was of course not countenanced by the

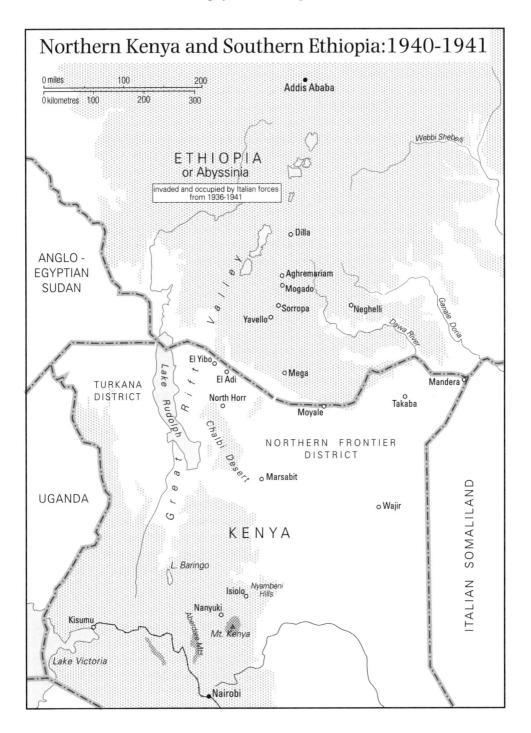

Northern Kenya and Southern Ethiopia:1940-1941

0 miles 100 200

0 kilometres 100 200 300

Addis Ababa

ETHIOPIA
or Abyssinia

invaded and occupied by Italian forces
from 1936-1941

Webbi Shebelli

ANGLO -
EGYPTIAN
SUDAN

Dilla

Aghremariam

Mogado

Sorropa

Neghelli

Yavello

Ganale Doria

Dawa River

El Yibo

El Adi

Mega

Mandera

North Horr

Moyale

Takaba

TURKANA
DISTRICT

Lake Rudolph

Great Rift Valley

Chalbi Desert

NORTHERN FRONTIER
DISTRICT

Marsabit

Wajir

UGANDA

KENYA

ITALIAN SOMALILAND

L. Baringo

Isiolo

Nyambeni
Hills

Nanyuki

Kisumu

Aberdare Mts

Mt. Kenya

Lake Victoria

Nairobi

235

army authorities.] War is serious it is not a game. It is a matter of life and death and I am the master. If you don't want to come, don't. No one is compelling you.'

All of them joined without any bother. Sandy had experience of Ethiopians, and knew that a firm hand was essential and was what they expected. Brigadier ('Fluffy') Fowkes, who was commanding the 2nd East African Brigade, said to Sandy at a later date, 'I thought you were playing with fire but I now realize you knew exactly what you were doing.'

Next came the selection of officers. Sandy needed tough men sometimes from an unorthodox background to complement the men. Amongst the more colourful characters was Sandy's old friend Kametz, who had served in the Imperial Austrian Artillery in the First World War and had been decorated. In addition he had been many years in Ethiopia and had been on the Ethiopian section of the British Somaliland-Ethiopia Boundary Commission. Another officer was Carl Nurk, an Estonian, who had joined up at the age of sixteen and fought against the Bolsheviks in General Alexander Rodzianko's forces in 1919. He had walked across Europe and North Africa to Lake Chad. He then joined the British contingent and fought in Finland against the Russians. To add to the foreign legion element there was a very amusing Free Frenchmen who kept a very good cinema and café in Addis (Monsieur Idot). There was Dugand, a Frenchman from Mauritius, who had deserted from a Messagerie Maritime boat at Mombasa in 1913, and King Magee who had fought in the Boer War. Kenyan farmers were represented by Bedford-Pim. Then there was Dalton who had started life at Osborne and Dartmouth, but decided not to go into the Navy. He had been all over the world, he was a gentlemen and his wife was out in Kenya with him. Sadly Sandy had to get rid of him as he had had polio and if he ran and fell down he could not get up; he had somehow been passed fit on his medical examination.

By early the following month, five companies had been raised. Though the unit had no bayonets or equipment, Mills hand grenades were given out with which the Ethiopians were exceptionally skilful, along with Long Lee Enfield Mark 6 rifles of pre-1914 vintage and leather rifle slings. After the personal intervention of General Cunningham, Bren guns were sent up by air for the unit.

Uniform consisted of part-worn khaki drill blouses, shorts, pullovers and slouch hats. Blue armbands such as umpires wear at manoeuvres at Aldershot were issued. These were worn folded as a wide lanyard on the shoulder and made a nice splash of colour. The horrid greasy slouch hats were embellished by a bunch of black cock ostrich feathers – two ostriches were shot to provide them. The men made their own Ethiopian-style cartridge belts, made from the hides of the oxen provided for the meat ration, which held up to a hundred cartridges singly. In fact these were a blessing as it discouraged charger loading and unnecessary blazing off of ammunition. Sandy himself elected to wear one and carried his sporting Mannlicher Schaeoner with hard-nosed bullets. To capitalize on the Ethiopian's natural ability to move at a jog trot with his rifle butt to the fore and over his shoulder, the men were not allowed to wear boots. Though issued with tyre sandals, the men preferred to make their own from ox hides. The Ethiopian Irregulars had a warrior look about them and an identification that all could see, greatly enhancing the esprit de corps of the unit.

The Ethiopians are great meat eaters so Sandy was authorized to buy meat on the hoof and was given Maria Theresa dollars for this purpose when they got into Ethiopia. These were still common currency.

2nd Ethiopian Irregulars, c/o APS Nairobi, 20 October 1940

I am now in command of my own army known to all as Curle's Irregulars and I am slowly getting officers. We are a very happy show indeed. I am getting a QM and a Doctor any day now.

The Ethiops are of course all old friends – they are wonderful as soldiers – very keen to learn and good shots.

We are now up at the front again and the other unit has already been in action and done well so we get better rations et cetera as a result.

Two of my Companies go out to work under the local troops tomorrow and they are very keen. We are left alone and allowed to run our own show and am given the best of food and stuff available because of our job of harassing the enemy and moving light.

We are camped in a lovely forest near Marsabit but once off the mountain all round is lava rock and desert – worse than the Esa country behind Djibuti. It is very wet now and as we have no tents it is no joke in the forest. Elephants and rhino are constantly prowling round by night. I shall be glad to get out of this existence living in huts and getting soaked with one's bed flooded but strangely it does not affect me as it would in civilization. I suppose one is fit; it is not so hard on me because I am used to it but it must be awful for some of the other fellows.

I have a Sicilian from the imperial kitchens at Addis who does us very well. He is a godsend here, and with only bully beef, he can turn out a palatable meal. When my eggs come up he can make excellent cakes using the crushed oranges we get against scurvy as filling. We get the crushed orange pulp as a daily ration; it is wonderful stuff I must say. It is a curious life.

The Italians are very quiet here; never a sign of their planes; they must be very short of petrol.

I am kept very busy doing all the internal economy involved as well as training, being the only officer in the unit with previous army experience.

We are the envy of the KAR. Hundreds of officers want to join but they won't let them go.

All the units are commanded by Scotsmen. Grant who was in the Camerons and one Buchanan from Edinburgh who is an explorer, a silly old stick and won't last long. When I get my Commands started I will get you to try to interest some of the ladies with working parties to send comforts out to Ethiopia. We are no one's children and do not belong to any colony so we get nothing but I will wait till we get started.

Still got nothing in compensation for my losses in Somaliland. I don't suppose I ever will but no harm in trying.

2nd Ethiopian Irregulars (Curle's),
c/o APS Nairobi, Kenya, 24 November 1940

I am having a very busy time indeed owing to some bother in the other irregular unit. [The 3rd Ethiopian Irregulars were commanded by Captain Buchanan who had served in the First World War in East Africa but had had no experience of Ethiopians. He tried to run it on outmoded British Army lines which just didn't work with his independently minded Ethiopians who mutinied.] I was sent for and have eventually absorbed almost all the men into my show which is nearly doubled. My new men all come from the Kenya border and are a very much tougher and older crowd than mine. I found that I knew some of them and chased them when I was at Mandera years ago so I have a link with them already. [The majority of them had been soldiers of Ras Desta and had fought on the southern front in the Italian-Ethiopian war. In civil life they had been retainers, poachers and bandits. Many of them knew the northern frontier of Kenya from their elephant poaching days and were more familiar with it than the guides provided by the Kenyan authorities. One confessed that fifteen years before he had been chased by Sandy with a patrol of KAR. Another had been at the Battle of Adua in 1896 when the Ethiopians defeated the Italians. Sandy had learnt many and very valuable lessons from commanding a platoon in the NFD in 1926. With his leadership these men became one of his best fighting companies.]

I have ten officers under me [the 2nd Irregulars now consisted of ten companies]. I have as Second-in-Command a retired Colonel of the Indian Army [Lieutenant Colonel Warton who had given up his proper rank in order to see active service in Africa]. It all means a great deal of work and running about and organizing with as yet no one to help me. Now to crown all, three officers have gone sick and been evacuated.

[By November the unit was sufficiently well trained for the first companies to move out to the Chalbi desert where they were attached to the 5th KAR.]

While I was out visiting a post the other day two ancient Italian machines came along and fairly peppered us with bombs – incendiary and then infernal anti-personnel. My orderly whom I knew on the Boundary Commission and who was with me in Somaliland was killed by almost a direct hit 20yds from me. He had also been Kametz's orderly on the Commission for two years. If the Italians had continued to throw them out they would have certainly got me and the Officer who were lying in a patch with stones round us, it being lava rock and impossible to dig.

It is funny that in the company of the KAR with us the Sergeant Major was a Lance Corporal in my platoon for two years and one of the men was also with me. They were very glad to see me.

One of the fellows, who was a Consul in Abyssinia at the same time I was at Harar during the Italian-Abyssinian war, is coming up to see me. He has some staff billet in the 'Muddle East' as we call it. [Andrew Chapman-Andrews who became Political Adviser to the Emperor. He entered Ethiopia with the Emperor from the Sudan with Gideon Force in February 1941 and was with him on his return to his capital in triumph on 5 May. A book, *Chapman-Andrews and the Emperor*, written by his son-in-law, Sir Peter Leslie, was published by Pen & Sword Books in 2005.]

The new GOC, who is called Cunningham, commanded a Brigade with three Gordon Battalions in it. He gave me news of Murphy who is Second Major in the 1st Battalion. He flew up here for a day.

I am having difficulty getting a MO for my unit; we had one appointed but he got rotten feet and has gone back to South Africa. Meantime the authorities take weeks to replace him. We had a man killed in action and two wounded in a small show recently.

Being right at the end of the line we get very poor rations et cetera. In a month between twelve of us we have had twelve bottles of beer each and half a bottle of whisky for those who drink it. We can never get anything out of the canteen – the usual game, the people at the base get it first. Somaliland was much better. I get fresh veg sent up from the base and eggs but the latter never arrive so I have stopped them. The veg takes ten days to arrive but is fifty per cent good.

A lot of young officers arrived out from home – shiploads – they cheered us up with their reports of England. [These young officers were known as 'Irregulars'.]

I was to go into the HQ at Marsabit with its forests for a day to interview two officer candidates for my unit, but the rain had turned the mud desert, one has to cross into a sea, and I was defeated and forced to turn back. I am trying again today.

The Weekly Times and Spheres are beginning to arrive again and are most welcome.

I expect this may reach you near Christmas so all best wishes and I hope I shall be home by next New Year. I am due now about 267 days leave in England having nearly completed 4 years. We get ten days leave away from the front every six months. I shall go and stay at Moshi in the hotel on the mountain.

No news from Cecil for weeks and I am out of touch with any wireless here so can't send messages.

2nd Ethiopian Irregulars (Curle's),
c/o APS Nairobi, Kenya, 12 December 1940

I expect you have been hearing about us on the wireless although you didn't know it. We are continually scrapping with the Italians. Our recent show was when eight men of mine were tackled by fifty Italian *Banda* on mules whom they drove off killing ten and wounding many others whilst we had two wounded. We got ten bodies. [On receiving the report of this action at El Adi, the Brigadier would not believe it and insisted on sending up the Brigade Intelligence Officer with a lorry to remove the bodies. Their Corporal got a Military Medal straight away for his bravery. This action by the Irregulars, against odds of seven to one, was an enormous boost to the unit's morale. After that the companies were posted to various posts in the NFD towards the Ethiopian Boundary and in front of the Regular troops. It was found it was not practical for the Irregulars to operate with the KAR as they advanced too quickly.] In other small scraps we have always come out best. Now we have some white South African troops with us. I can't say whom but it has made a difference. [They were the Natal Mounted Rifles and the Irregulars now came under them as the East African Brigade withdrew.]

I am kept very busy with continual coming and going from the outposts and working in with the troops behind us – sending out supplies and all manner of things which come to my HQ for forwarding. I make frequent visits to the posts myself but as I get more officers the work will get better and I shall be able to be out more. We permanently sit on this front while Brigades change. It is an awful nuisance as each time one has to start all over again.

I am going down to the area of shops for a day to draw pay next week. It will be a change to get back to somewhere where you can get a bottle of beer. I have had quite a lot of shooting for meat lately and am very pleased with the results. I got out my old rifle I had not used for years.

I am now a Major – war time rank only of course. Jane has done well being a Sergeant Major.

2nd Irregulars (Curle's), c/o APS Nairobi, Kenya 27 December 1940

Many thanks for all your letters. I have had a bag full dating from 9 June to 3 November with quotas of papers; I suppose they have been round Africa.

I had a flying trip down to HQ to fight the battle for equipment which is much harder to cope with than fighting the enemy. I had one night in a hotel, The Sportsmen's Arms Nanyuki, where I enjoyed a bottle of iced Hock in an armchair in front of the fire in an empty drawing room. A short distance away a mob were scrambling in the bar to get their beers and whisky. I found a kindred spirit from the Gold Coast and we added another bottle which was the last the hotel had. I enjoyed it to the full.

I got some more officers as a result of my trip and we now number well over a dozen. I refused a Belgian – Polish Jew – he was well known to all in Addis as a swindler. The local HQ at Nairobi thought he was most suitable for my unit. I fear I disillusioned them.

Next day I started back and spent Xmas on the road and lunch at Isiolo with the Divisional General, a South African [General Brink] whose hobby before the war was cultivating succulents and aloes.

The military roads are wonderful up here now; all done by machines – tremendous progress all over the country. It will teach Ethiopia how to tackle such jobs.

We are slowly becoming a centre – Generals of all sorts come and visit the spot where my HQ is (North Horr); perhaps the name intrigues them. One fellow who was a subaltern in a neighbouring Young Soldiers Battalion of the Regiment in Germany with me rolled up.

I have never refitted myself. I have two soldier's kitbags and an absolute minimum of clothing – an army hairbrush, blankets, towel, soap and shirts. Being Irregulars we don't wear tunics and as we are always in the line there is no need for parade kit. I have a pair of boots. I had plate boxes for my crockery and a bottle box for my drinks made.

Our Xmas Comforts sent off by the ladies of Nairobi on 2 December have never turned up yet so we had a rotten Xmas on the whole but saved by our late Doctor who sent us three grand boxes of luxuries from Nairobi as a thank offering for the time he had with us and to show as he called it his admiration for our show. [Sandy remembers him as an excellent MO who wore a flap down the back of his helmet like Livingstone.]

The Italian native troops opposite us have given up patrols to our areas – we hear they just sit down a few miles away and say they have been thirty and seen nothing.

I have just got an Ethiop boy from the Refugee Camp to have all the show the same breed. He is good. Most of us are trying them out.

Wind and rain make our life uncomfortable here.

Many thanks for the Xmas gift of War Savings Certificates. One never has to think about money these days and it just doesn't enter into our calculations at all – we can spend it on nothing. I actually spend about £5 a month on fruit, vegetables and eggs for my table but very little on anything else; otherwise one would get scurvy. All our men are bad with it according to the Medicos and have a daily ration of crushed orange.

I am sorry to have such little news but as CO my job is to co-ordinate all my outposts and keep the show going.

2nd Irregulars (Curle's), c/o APS Nairobi, Kenya 8 January 1941

We have had no mail since Christmas but expect mail any day now.

It is getting hotter and hotter and never drops below 85° and rises to 109° usually 102° every afternoon with sand blowing about – a most unpleasant climate – worse than Mandera.

We are moving forward as the water is developed. It is curious to see thousands of white troops in the places which we have held for three months and drove the enemy out of. We have cleared over 2,000 square miles of Kenya of enemy, not a bad record.

The delay was during the move and we had a scrap just after. I have to stay back with Brigade HQ as my Companies are out all over the country.

My men put up a great show at El Yibo. We had one killed and three wounded. The Italian casualties were forty-one including two officers and all bodies were found.

[In this encounter Major Drought MC, one of the officers, aged seventy-two, was wounded for the seventh time in the five wars in which he had taken part. El Yibo was a heavily defended Italian strong point. Carel Birkby, who was the South African Press Association's First World War correspondent with the Forces in the East African Campaign, praises the Irregular troops' contribution in this action, attacking on the flank. As he said in his book, *It's a long way to Addis*: 'The Italians always seemed conscious of the threat represented by the vengeful Ethiopians prowling on their flanks and forever fanning up the flame of revolt in their unhappy empire.' Sandy's comment on the South Africans in action at this point was erased by the censor.] Water in this country is the trouble. We get one and a half gallons a head per day for all washing and drinking. It will be wonderful to have a bath with unlimited water again. Our liquor ration is almost nil – one bottle of beer and one bottle of South African brandy in the past three weeks.

It is remarkable how little we have been bothered by enemy aircraft. We saw four the first two days after the recent small advance to El Yibo. They bombed the Divisional and Brigade Generals and their staffs on their way up to see the new position. It was the best thing which ever happened: as you can imagine various antidotes arrived within a few hours.

We saw our planes bombing the Italian position – nice change to see some after Somaliland but the positions were empty.

The Mission [the 109 Mission was controlled by Roy Whittet and Dewar] is going to be a great help to us and instead of my having to battle with the base for stores et cetera they have to do all that and they run a school of instruction too.

Our men are wonderful in action – they go like hell at the enemy and fear nothing. The trouble is to keep them back.

We got six machine guns in the last show, all abandoned by the Italians with lots of equipment but once we are in Ethiopia we can't expect such an easy show. Their defences are good but our superior armaments and our superiority lowers the morale of the native troops.

It took five weeks for a telegram from Cecil to reach me – awful, they play about with the things.

2nd Irregulars (Curle's), c/o A.P.S. East African Force,
Mega, Ethiopia, 20 March 1941

We have been having a busy time and are at last settled in a British Consulate. Do read 'Seven years in Southern Abyssinia' by Arnold Hodson published in 1927. It is a lovely climate, cold with green grass and no water shortage.

[Mega had been captured on 18 March 1941. The Italians had it well defended and there was a fine fort which stands to this day, sixty-five years on.]

The great feather in our caps was the capture of Moyale. One platoon of mine with an officer [Lieutenent. Brooksbank] pushed ahead and occupied Moyale 72 miles ahead of the nearest South African troops and twenty-three hours before them and our men were on foot. The 2nd South African Brigade had supplied two trucks and an armoured car but after 20 miles had refused to go any further. The South African forces arrived twenty-four hours later and were received with a Guard of Honour of Irregulars at the entrance to the village.The South Africans had been boasting that 'They would capture Moyale back for the British'.

[Sandy put Brooksbank's name forward for a decoration and he was awarded an MC. The leader of his company was awarded the East African Badge for Gallantry. In *Abyssinian Adventure* by J.F. Macdonald it is mentioned that 'The Irregulars to put it bluntly had walked them off their feet. However rough or broken the country, whether uphill or downhill, the Abyssinians had by all accounts moved along easily at a steady 4 miles an hour.']

Actually we have seen very little fighting this side. The Italians left lots of stuff behind here and Kametz who has been sick is playing with the guns. We are getting more and more stuff now. We never see an Italian plane these days at all. We have experts attached to us.

You have no idea how nice it is to live in a house, even though it is a native one, for the first time since October. Fleas are bad. We have fires in the rooms – drums of water cut in two and logs stuck in – cedar wood.

Our friends from the south have gone; they say political reasons – fighting for a black man to put him on the throne gives too much pull to the bad parties down there. [In fact Sandy and his troops considered them to be poor soldiers and unwilling to close with the enemy. General Cunningham too had been disappointed in them. In the abortive operation against Giarso, the South African Air Force bombed the 7th South African Field Battery and the Irregulars by mistake and wounded several South African gunners.

Sandy had witnessed two South African lorries loaded with oryx for their fresh meat supply. Herds had been annihilated by the machine guns of their armoured cars. One good thing was that when the South Africans departed they left behind a mountain of tins of bully beef which the Ethiopians really liked. A problem arose when Sandy found that the South Africans were selling their boots to the Ethiopians who would proudly put them on. This detracted from their mobility and raised a cloud of dust. Orders had to be given forbidding the wearing of boots.]

We are now under the 21st East African Brigade – Brigadier Ritchie of the Argylls is our Brigadier. He used to be at the Depot and knows your family. Much nicer crowd than these boasting men from the South. As CO I speak the same language as the various officers on the Brigade staff and the COs of other units. I realize the value of Sandhurst training and all has become so much easier as one is dealing with professionals again. From now on the unit will be employed in active operations in such a way that its fighting qualities and strengths will be used to the best advantage.

[The success of the unit brought additional officers and NCOs whose presence was somewhat of an incumberance. All sorts of equipment were offered but it was essential to keep the mobility of the unit which had been responsible for its success. It had become self-contained for transport with a large number of captured mules, their own trucks for each company and their own signallers. More uniforms and better clothing had been issued including web belts and leather bandoliers, but the Ethiopians had already made their own. There were now two QMs.]

I have an Ethiopian seal, made out of wood depicting an eagle with a sword – my Somali nickname being eagle. We have another official one. [Prior to the Italian occupation every landlord and important person had his own seal with which he signed his letters. These seals were carved from wood, the practice continuing until 1945 when education began to spread. Sandy happened to have one of these wood carvers amongst his troops who made him a seal using the Lion of Ethiopia for the unit. In addition Sandy had his own personal one showing a bird with outstretched wing. His family crest was an eagle. Whenever orders were sent to Ethiopians they were written in Amharic by an interpreter and stamped with the two seals. Sandy gave the two seals to the National Army Museum.]

I have carte blanche to increase my men to any number and take on prisoners.

We hope to get ahead but the Italians are so elusive we can never catch them.

Things are going well. I have been asked if I would accept the job of organizing all the Irregulars with the rank of Lieutenant Colonel but it all depends on the scheme materializing. Meantime I have put in to have a political job in Harar with my men as interpreters, police et cetera.

Hope life will be more settled soon and I will get time to write.

2nd Irregulars (Curle's), c/o APS Yavello, Ethiopia, 23 March 1941

Here we are at last well into the Promised Land camped in the buildings of an abandoned airport at Yavello. We are in front in touch with the enemy; deserters keep coming in daily and are in a bad way. We will be moving on soon and into the bush again but it is lovely country with cedars. What a nice change from the low desert. We all without exception got sick when we came to living in houses again.

The Italians left pretty quick and we have had a lot of pickings. I picked up in the bush a very nice copper bucket with a brass base. All our boxes are now Italian and most of our drugs.

You have no idea of the amount of stuff scattered all over the bush – brand new plane wings et cetera abandoned. The buildings are most extravagant but so rottenly built. The beams are of seasoned walnut and elm from Europe. We get wines still in their cases unpacked. We found a vegetable garden here with spinach and lettuce and a case of mineral water which was special mineral water against 'Air Sickness', both most welcome. You have never seen such a waste for a country like Italy – masses of stuff. We found a dump of Mustard Gas bombs the Italians had blown up and left all ready to fill in and hide when they retreated.

We have our own wireless sets and even engineers to cope with demolitions so we are very well equipped indeed; two demolitions and booby trap experts arrived as soon as we started to advance.

Our air force has made a mess of this place – every building is riddled with bullets. My hut has splinter and bullet holes all over it. All the furniture they left behind has splinter and bullet holes in it and the mess included.

The enemy are deserting hard – four or five Africans a day. It must be hard on the officers with their men drifting away and they dare not stop them apparently now. Most of them are conscripts. The only thing they do is to mine the roads. I was down at a crossing of the Dawa River. They had built a fort and a bridge and mined the approaches. One of my officers, Lieutenent Dugand, took out seventy-six mines.

My old friends in the Northern Rhodesian Regiment whom I travelled up to Somaliland with and saw a lot of there are also in the same Brigade. Thank goodness we are no longer in one of these awful South African Brigades. One gets so sick of their boasting and inefficiency.

My unit is splitting up now. Some of the Kenya men are garrisoning the newly captured towns and keeping order while the young Somaliland people are pushing on. I am for the moment with the latter.

We were on the BBC again last night in our proper names and not as 'Patriots' as they sometimes call us.

2nd Irregulars (Curle's), c/o APS East African Force,
Ethiopia, 14 April 1941

We have had a most successful show early this month and not only did I have a grand view of the battle on 31 March 1941 at Sorropa which was 28 miles from Yavello and was a strongly held Italian position, but my men in four companies, having moved out two days before, got in round behind and cut off the Italian line of retreat as the terrain had not been suitable for armoured vehicles.

I was with Brigadier Ritchie. We could see and hear our own guns firing and then see the shell bursts. The Italians were holding a ridge with their guns in front for use as anti-tank. They put over a few shells which did no damage. We could see the sun flashing on the bayonets of our troops. They took the ridge after we had bombed and shelled it. An aircraft, which was reconnoitering, reported that my men were in position 8 miles behind across the road and that they were short of water. Carl Nurk, who was the Estonian officer in charge, had written in cummerbunds from the Italian prisoners the word 'Water' on the road. I went out to them along the road back which they had not mined and found they had got the Colonel of the Brigade and his staff and 2 other officers and 140 men. Only two days before the Colonel had sent his car away or we would have got that too. [Moyse-Bartlett in *The King's African Rifles* refers to the battle 'As an excellent little action in which Air Force, Artillery, Engineers, Infantry and Irregulars combined to overthrow some of the best Italian colonial troops in strong positions of their own choosing.' Carl Nurk was awarded an immediate MC.]

My men did a 25-mile march on a water bottle with only biscuits and ground nuts. We got the Brigade flag. [It was given to Brigadier Ritchie and was last heard of in 1958 in the 4th KAR museum.] The captured position was a mess – food still cooking – bodies of horses, mules and humans all over the place. They had very good dugouts but a bomb landed in the entrance of one and killed all in it. It is extraordinary the amount of stuff there is – all the officers' cooking utensils, kit, saddlery, pack mules and all the Brigade office papers et cetera. We got the confidential reports of the officers.

The road, where my men had cut it, was strewn with clothing and equipment, dead mules et cetera. The air force got at them in their retreat and shot them up so they abandoned everything and ran for cover. For several days we got mules and deserters coming in.

My men are now in front again holding the forward position [near Mogado] 2,000yds from the enemy. When the next attack comes we will know the country all round the enemy and be able to cut him off.

We had a lot of fighting in the Neghelli area and lost three killed but got thirty Italian Somalis, captured two cars and wounded one of the occupants. My men won't take prisoners unless an officer is on the spot. [Sandy had the greatest admiration for the leadership and example of Captain Warton at Neghelli which enabled the Irregulars to distinguish themselves. Four companies under his command had carried out many patrols behind enemy lines as well as attacking isolated strongpoints prior to Neghelli being occupied on 27 March 1941 by the Gold Coast Brigade from Italian Somaliland.]

I had a nice trip by air to see the Divisional General (Godwin Austin at Neghelli) whom I knew in Somaliland. He is very keen on employing us in our proper role and we shall be kept busy. I went to the place where Graziani had his victory. [In 1936 Graziani had commanded the Italian army which advanced from Somalia and defeated the Ethiopians on the Juba River. In 1936 he had been appointed Viceroy of Ethiopia.]

The Italians had put no end of work and money into the country – shops, all Italian, electric light and good buildings with the usual fascist rubbish written up. All of course are empty except for heavy furniture. No one cares, and uses any chest of drawers et cetera for firewood.

The rains are on full now and it is awful out as we are in bivouacs – soaked to the skin – one's bed soaked but we never feel any bad results. If I had slept in sodden blankets in peace time I would have had rheumatism for a week. In the front line we can't have fires as much as one would like. My HQ is back a bit in an old aerodrome but the hut has suffered from bombs and bullets of our aircraft and leaks.

My QM has gone back to Somaliland and so have most of the Camel Corps officers.

At last for the first time in the war we have had a visit from a YMCA Canteen – a van like a coffee stall – what a blessing it is – one could buy anything in it from Keatings, tinned milk and sweets et cetera. It is now back at Brigade HQ but will be up again soon I hope.

I was interested to see two huge phallic stones, 8ft long lying in the aerodrome here. I presume found in the construction. [These were probably ancient stelae which occur at several sites in the south. On another occasion Sandy found himself in a valley with a dozen stelae.]

We had a funny show yesterday – there was a party of surveyors up in front, out with an escort of ours. I suppose they showed something which caught the enemy's eye and as a result a volley of shells and MG fire opened on them at very long range. One and all they downed instruments, rifles et cetera and fled. Our people, who were quite used to being fired at, collected up all the stuff and brought it in with huge glee [short of Mogado forest].

It is very funny now about the Italian push in Libya. No one believes it amongst the natives – they have told so many lies that now no one pays any attention.

We had a visit from three very fast fighters, aircraft I mean. They hunt out Italian aerodromes and shoot up the planes on the ground. They were unlucky down here but there is one about. As usual we got bombed at in a recent operation.

Kametz is in for the moment and it is nice to see him again.

Can you please ask Andersons to send me out a new Gordon Glengary and a pair of Gordon red flashes for stockings.

On 5 May 1941, Emperor Haile Selassie entered his capital from the north at the head of the triumphant Gideon Force, but there were still pockets of resistance.

2nd Irregulars (Curle's), c/o APS Aghremariam,
East African Force, Ethiopia, 10 May 1941

Many thanks for the papers. We have had no letter mail for months. I suppose it has been sunk.

Rain continues here getting worse and worse and the conditions of continual damp are appalling. The state of the roads has to be seen to be believed – mud above the knees.

We continue as always in front of the regular troops. Last show a few days ago brought us up to the forest area – wonderful huge trees [*Mogado*]. We only partially got round the enemy but captured two officers and ten askaris – the former were not Fascists. Now they have gone back further.

At the last battle we had another view from the stalls but we were just in front of the artillery so got blown out by the noise each time they fired. [The stalls were trenches beside the South African light battery.]

The Italians felled fourteen trees bigger than full grown beeches across the road in the forest so as to stop armoured cars. They mined the sides so as to blow up anything trying to get round.

I am increasing my force so have been back at the store. We are supervising the enlistment and training of recruits.

We are now getting a regular supply of comforts from the various organizations. There are cigarettes from the Overseas League with a postcard to be sent to the donor, chiefly Americans in our lot. We had one who rejoiced in the name of Miss Eleanor McFetters – I have never heard of such a name before.

We had a European deserter, a gunner, over a few days ago. Hope more will follow. If only the road was passable we would have them cleaned up by now. They are waiting for the long rains in June and that will beat us.

I don't think I shall ever worry about a damp bed again at home – one's bed is always soaking.

I have a Tommy gun now – a rotten weapon really.

2nd Irregulars (Curle's), c/o APS East African Force,
Dilla, Ethiopia, 25 May 1941

I have at last got a day's rest in a house. I have pushed ahead of the KAR and am installed in the town of Dilla level with the north end of a lake.

We had a most interesting trip through grand country with wild coffee and all hills and valleys. The road along which the Italians had retreated from Giabascire a few days before was littered with postcards, letters et cetera. Our air force had been at them successfully as several lorries showed. Why the Italian shies away all his photos of his pals and girl friends when he runs away is a mystery but he does. Also there were masses of letters. The stench of dead animals, shot or bombed or died is the worst of all and the car would always stick at a dead donkey.

The country is in an awful state of disorganization. Bands of the so-called patriots are looting everywhere at the point of a rifle. It will not take long to clean it up with a firm hand. Deserters also add to the fun. Why the Italians went as they did is a mystery. They left amongst other things ten lorries, two cars, a motorbike and an ambulance all with the batteries in and working. I think the RAF's good shooting had something to do with it.

The house I am in which was the Doctor's has most of its furniture even two clocks but without the weight for the pendulum, a large typewriter, a bath and an old dog. Tons of coffee and cotton are in store in the town. They bought it from the natives and could not dispose of it. It is a land of luxury, eggs and chickens and I even found a pig with some young and just eating size.

We are indeed lucky having no aircraft against us. My difficulty now is to get my men's rations forward quick enough with the rains on the roads. The Italian roads have terrific gradients.

I have at last, for the first time for some weeks, been able to get my clothes and blankets dried out. One laughs when one thinks of the fuss at home with hot water bottles in case the sheets should be damp.

This is the country where they still use obsidian flints. All over the place there are scrapers without any patina on them and they use it for cleaning skins or hides or shaving.

I found a typed book on the History of the Mijertain Somali country, a monumental work which is very interesting. It runs to over 200 pages and the author I suppose had to do a rapid flight and jettisoned his work. I found it in the kitchen roof. It is the work of a student who has spent much time and research on it. [The Mijertain Somalis lived in what had become Italian Somaliland.]

I have replaced some of the camp kit I lost in Somaliland.

The flowers here are wonderful – wild roses and some new varieties of things I had never seen before. The Italians had little gardens in front of their houses but all has been neglected for the past three months out of fear for our aircraft. Every European house has its dugout.

Yes, the Third Ethiopian venture of Italy has been a bigger fiasco than the first. They have left behind better houses and roads but that is about all.

Wondo, 17 June 1941

Had an awful rush round the last few days. I had to attend a conference at division and then buzz up to Addis to see the Emperor and the heads of the Ethiopian army. We have finished fighting as the Italians have run too fast, and we are now employed in policing part of the country.

In the New Years Honours list of 1942 Sandy was awarded a DSO. The following appeared in the *London Gazette* of 30 December 1941:

For Outstandingly Distinguished Services

Major Curle organised, trained and has commanded Irregular companies during the period under review. His success has been outstanding and the high standard of discipline, fine fighting spirit and pride in themselves which characterize his companies derive from his personal influence and incessant care.

Wherever his men have operated they have won the admiration of all. No situation has been too difficult and no enterprise too bold for Major Curle to tackle personally and it is his own example of courage and endurance that has produced such high efficiency in these invaluable troops.*

Sandy was also awarded the Military Medal of Haile Selassie the First.

Sandy was very proud that in only seven months of operating the following awards were made to some of his men: three immediate Military Crosses, four immediate Military Medals, three Mentions in Dispatches, three East African Badges for Gallantry and two Ethiopian Military Medals of Haile Selassie I. Sandy was particularly delighted that apart from the MCs, these medals were won by Ethiopians, and the MCs were won because the officers were so ably supported by their men. Major General Godwin-Austin, GOC 12th East African Division had the highest regard for the Ethiopian as a soldier in organized units.

* Supplement to the *London Gazette* of 30 December 1941.

The Irregulars had indeed played their part in helping Ethiopia regain her freedom.

Having experienced the thrill of raising and commanding his own regiment and being his own boss, Sandy was then caught up in the bureaucracy of post-war administration. There followed a short spell working as Staff Officer with the Occupied Enemy Territories Administration, during which he did not find it easy working under the smooth political officers from the Sudan who were in charge of the show.

In April 1942, Sandy was posted to East African Command to raise and command the Coast Irregulars, south of Mombasa in Kenya, who were to be in place in case of a Japanese invasion. Sandy, as he had done with Curle's Irregulars, gave his men small flashes of leopard skin as a distinguishing badge. He told his men that they were '*Askari wa Chui*' which means leopard soldiers, a term that referred to their stealth and bushcraft. Their arms consisted of captured Italian carbines, folding bayonets, Biretta automatics, pangas and demolition charges. In the meantime he was promoted to Lieutenant Colonel. In October, the GOC was ordered by the Foreign Office to release Sandy for advisory duties in Ethiopia, which in fact suited him as it meant that his family would be able to come out to join him. Sandy had not seen his wife since February 1939 nor had he ever seen his daughter who was now three years old. In the event, his family were not able to join him until March 1944.

In March 1966, in his retirement, Sandy was thrilled and touched to receive a letter from the Ministry of the Imperial Court inviting him to special ceremonies to celebrate the Twenty-Fifth Anniversary of the triumphal entry in 1941 of His Imperial Majesty Haile Selassie I, Emperor of Ethiopia, to his capital, and to commemorate and honour the men who participated in the campaign to drive out the Fascist invader.

'It would be most fitting if you, who played an active role in these events, were present in Addis Ababa on the coming Fifth of May to take part in the celebration of this day of victory.

'I am commanded by my August Sovereign, His Imperial Majesty Haile Selassie I, to invite you to attend these festivities as an honoured guest. Round trip transportation will be provided to and from Addis Ababa as well as accommodations during your stay in Ethiopia.'

It was an indication of the high regard and appreciation of these soldiers that the Emperor wanted to include them. The Ethiopians had gone to immense trouble to track down these former comrades who had taken part in the liberation of Ethiopia from all over the world. Twenty-five were able to attend, including Sandy's old friend Sir Edwin Chapman-Andrews who he had known since 1930, and who had come in with the Emperor from the Sudan with Gideon Force as Political Liaison Officer. Amongst others there was Wilfred Thesiger, Laurens van de Post and Colonel Sir Hugh

Boustead who had raised the Sudan Defence Force Frontier Battalion in 1940. Brigadier Sandford was there; he had played a pivotal role in going into Ethiopia leading Mission 101 in advance of Gideon Force to get in touch with patriots. With characteristic sensitivity the Emperor also invited the son of the late Major General Orde Wingate who had been responsible for creating Gideon Force. Similarly the young George Steer, whose late father had been Propaganda Officer for the campaign, was included. All the guests had individual audiences with the Emperor and were presented with silver and gold commemorative cigarette cases. A silver salver was presented to the Emperor from the guests. All agreed what a wonderful and extremely well organized show it had been. It was a real tribute to the campaigners. Victory Day itself started with a church service followed by a five-hour march past which included one of the Emperor's lions standing without bars on a steel plate fixed over the bonnet of a light truck. The day concluded with a stupendous state banquet for 2,000 persons. The following extract from the Emperor's speech conveys something of the depth of feeling:

> We have gathered today to pay tribute to the noble fighting men of Ethiopia and of many other nations who struggled here and gave their blood to this land. We salute the heroes both living and dead, men like the late General Wingate, Ethiopian and foreigner alike, who enabled our people once again to walk freely with heads unbowed upon the soil of their fathers. Present on this occasion are a few of the valiant officers who twenty-five years ago travelled the long and arduous path to victory.

Bibliography

Journals
Chapter 5
1. Chittick, Neville, 'An Archaeological Reconnaissance in the Horn: The British-Somali Expedition 1975', *Azania, The Journal of The British Institute in Eastern Africa*, vol. 11, 1976.

Chapter 6
1. Clifford, Lieutenant Colonel E.H.M., 'The British Somaliland-Ethiopia Boundary', *The Geographical Journal*, April 1936.
2. *International Affairs*, vol. 53, No. 1, January 1977, p. 120.
3. Dunbabin, J.P.D., 'British Rearmament in the 1930s', *The Historical Journal*, vol. 18, No. 3, September 1975, pp. 587–609.
4. General Staff Intelligence Khartoum, *A Handbook of Ethiopia* (Provisional Edition).

Chapter 7
1. Chittick, Neville, 'An Archaeological Reconnaissance in the Horn: The British Somali-Expedition 1975', *Azania, The Journal of The British Institute in Eastern Africa*, vol. 11, 1976, p. 119.

Chapter 8
1. Graham Ritchie, J.N., 'James Curle (1862–1944) and Alexander Ormiston Curle (1866–1955): Pillars of the Establishment', *Proceedings of the Society of Antiquaries of Scotland*, vol. 132, 2002.

Chapter 9
1. Barton, Lieutenant Colonal J.E.B., 'The Italian Invasion of British Somaliland 1st–18th August 1940', The National Archives, Kew.
2. Supplement to the *London Gazette* of Tuesday, 4 June 1946.

Chapter 10
1. Harper, H.G., 'Irregular Forces In East Africa 1940–1941', *The Bulletin of The Military Historical Society*, vol. 15, No. 59, February 1965, pp. 58–61.

2. *The Abyssinian Campaigns: The Official Story of The Conquest of Italian East Africa*, Stationery Office, 1942, pp. 71, 74–5, 77 & 130.
3. Supplement to the *London Gazette* of 30 December 1941.

Books

Birkby, Carel, *It's a Long Way to Addis*, Frederick Muller Ltd., 1942.
Brown, Monty, *Where Giants Trod*, Quiller Press, 1989.
Boustead, Colonel Sir Hugh, *The Wind of Morning*, Chatto & Windus, 1971.
Budge, Sir E.A. Wallis, *A History of Ethiopia*, vol. 2, Methuen & Co., 1928.
Cimmaruta, Roberto, *Ual Ual*, A. Mondadori Milano, 1936.
Deeds, W.F.R., *At War with Waugh*, Macmillan, 2003.
Dracopoli, I.N., *Through Jubaland to the Lorian Swamp*, Seeley, Service & Co., 1914.
Fage, J. D. and Oliver, Roland (eds), *Cambridge History of Africa*, vol. 6, c.1870–1905, Cambridge University Press, 1985.
Fage, J. D. and Oliver, Roland (eds), *Cambridge History of Africa*, vol. 7, 1905–1940, Cambridge University Press, 1986.
Glover, Michael, *An Improvised Campaign: The Abyssinian Campaign 1940–1941*, Leo Cooper, London, 1987.
Gordon-Brown, A., *Year Book and Guide to East Africa*, Robert Hale Ltd., 1957.
Leslie, Peter, *Chapman-Andrews and the Emperor*, Pen & Sword Books, 2005.
Macdonald, J.F., *Abyssinian Adventure*, Cassell & Company, 1957.
Mockler, Anthony, *Haile Selassie's War*, Oxford University Press, 1984.
Moyse-Bartlett, Lieutenant Colonel H., *The King's African Rifles*, Gale & Polden Ltd., 1956.
Nicholl, Charles, *Somebody Else: Arthur Rimbaud in Africa 1880–1891*, Vintage, 1980.
Pakenham, Thomas, *The Scramble for Africa*, Weidenfeld & Nicholas, 1991.
Roskill, Captain S.W., *The History of the Second World War*, HMSO, 1954.
Scott, Pamela, *A Nice Place to Live*, Michael Russell, 1991.
Shirreff, David, *Bare Feet and Bandoliers*, Radcliffe Press, 1955.
Steer, G.L. *Caesar in Abyssinia*, Hodder & Stroughton, 1936.
Tancred, George, *Rulewater and Its People*, T. & A. Constable, 1907.
Taylor, A.J.P., *Origins of The Second World War*, Hamish Hamilton, 1961.
Travis, William, *The Voice of the Turtle*, George Allen & Unwin Ltd., 1967.
Waugh, Evelyn, *Waugh in Abyssinia*, Longmans, London, 1938.
Wightwick Haywood, Captain C., *To The Mysterious Lorian Swamp*, Seeley, Service & Co., 1927.

Index

Addis Ababa 87, 89, 91-2, 94, 97, 99, 100, 102, 110, 129-30, 142-7, 164, 174, 177-8, 181, 192-3
Aden 9, 35, 37, 75-6, 82, 104-5, 108, 112, 114-15, 118-19, 144, 149, 151-4, 170, 178, 181, 217, 221, 226, 230-2
Ado 134, 136-9, 161
Adowa 146, 155, 158, 198
Aisha 123, 127, 129, 160
Allen, Lt Col Lyn 216, 223
Aran Areh 152, 160, 167
Arusha 206, 209, 211-14
Assab 154, 158, 221
Aw Berc 169, 176
Aw Boba 93-4

Baldwin, Stanley 155
Barjun Islands 33-4
Barkasan 228
Barton, Sir Sidney 91, 104-5, 125, 131-2, 144, 146
Bedford-Pim 236
Beitz 124-6, 128, 149
Bennett, A.L. 33
Bennet, Maj 125-6, 129
Berbera 76-7, 95, 100-1, 104, 106, 108-9, 112, 114, 118, 121-2, 147, 149, 151, 154, 156-7, 159, 161, 163-4, 171-2, 176, 178, 216-17, 221, 224-6, 228-30, 232, 234
Beyu Anod 127
Bohotleh 152, 154
Borama 95, 98-100, 117, 127, 129, 130-5, 142-3, 149, 152, 169, 173, 176-7, 173, 176, 222, 234
Black Watch 38, 227-30
Brink, Gen 241
Brooksbank, Lt 243

Buchanan 238
Burao 101, 137, 149, 152, 161, 168, 171
Burkot 168

Camel Corps 76, 80-2, 84-6, 107, 125-6, 129, 133, 135, 151-2, 159, 161, 163, 167, 171, 175-6, 216-30, 247
Chalbi Desert 238
Chapman-Andrews, Maj E 100, 239, 251
Cimmaruta, Capt 137, 148
Clifford, Col 117, 131, 139-40, 148-9, 158, 189, 201
Collingwood, Lt 80, 82, 133, 136-9, 143, 153, 201
Colonial Office 9, 44, 139, 142, 148, 171, 184
Count de Roquefeuil 93, 95
Cunningham, Gen 236, 239, 244
Curle's Irregulars 234, 237-52

Dagghabur 96-9, 107, 133-5, 142, 147, 160, 162, 164-5, 167, 169
Damot 158
Danane 168, 170
Dar es Salaam 182, 190, 192-4, 200, 202, 205-7, 213
Dawa River 25, 50, 56, 59, 62, 66, 69, 74, 76, 245
Dilla 249
Dire Dawa 99, 102, 105-6, 110, 125, 143-4, 149, 177, 181, 186
Djibuti 35, 118, 123, 132, 148-9, 149, 151, 164, 172, 174, 176-7, 192, 224, 226, 237
Dodoma 206
Drought, Maj 242

Dugand 236
Durham, Maj 10, 22
Duruksi 163, 166-7

Easton, Brig Gerry 209
Eden, Anthony 132, 182
Eik 152-3
El Wak 48, 50
El Yibo 242
Emperor Haile Selassie 54, 64, 91, 97, 99, 101-3, 105, 110-11, 126, 132, 139, 142, 146, 148, 150, 169-1, 177, 179, 189, 198, 212, 239, 248, 250-2
Erigavo 112-13, 115-16
2nd Ethiopian Irregulars 234, 237-2

Fafen 107, 153
Fowkes, Brig 236
Fowler, Maj 27-8

Garba Tula 38, 45, 47, 49
Gerlogubi 135, 137, 142, 153
Germain, Gen 225
Gobwen 12, 14, 16-24, 26-32, 71
Godding Maj 139, 143
Godfrey-Fausett, Maj 121
Godwin-Austin, Gen 232, 247, 250
Gordon Highlanders 1, 4, 8, 62, 206, 213, 239, 248
Gorrahei 153-6, 159
Grant 238
Graziani, Gen 155, 166, 172, 181, 247
Guimbo 17, 22-4

Harar 82, 89, 91, 94, 97, 98, 101-14, 125-6, 128, 130-1, 143-4, 164, 166, 168, 170,

172-3, 175, 177, 181,
186-7, 189, 216, 239, 245
Hargesia 76-92, 95, 99, 101,
104, 106-9, 130, 142, 164,
166, 173, 175, 214, 217
Harradiguit 134-5, 138-9,
153, 161-3, 165
Heis 113-14, 171
Hill, Capt 152, 156
Hitler 198, 203-4
Hoare, Sir Samuel 139, 158

Idot 236

Jalelo 117-19, 121, 123, 127,
129, 174
Jijiga 89, 91, 95-7, 99-103,
109-10, 133, 142, 154,157,
163, 165-7,169, 171-2,
174, 177
Jubaland 9-35, 39, 42 , 45,
48-50, 52, 55, 64, 71-2, 76,
189, 201
Juba River 12, 17, 66, 76

Kala 188
Kalicha 56-7, 59, 62-3, 69
Kametz 147, 192-3, 202,
205-9, 211-12, 230, 236,
239, 243, 248
KAR 9-74, 183-4, 198-9,
205-15
Kasanga 1, 85, 189
Kasulu 194-204
Khartoum 154, 214
Kigoma 185-6, 194, 196-7,
199, 201-3, 211, 215
Kilimanjaro 206, 212, 233
Kipanga 188-9
Kipili 186, 186
Kismayu 12, 16-17, 20-1,
23-6, 28, 30, 32-3, 42, 51,
71, 101, 149, 189
Kittermaster, Sir Harold 82,
84, 100

Lake Tana 85
Lake Tanganyika 185, 187,
194, 199
Lamu 16, 17, 33-5
Le Gentilhomme, Gen 224-5
Lij Yasu 105, 178

Lorenzo Taezaz 126, 128, 179
Lorian Swamp 39, 48, 52,
72-3

Magee, King 136
Mandera 41, 45-74, 76, 78,
238, 242
Marango 209
Marsabit 37-8, 40-1, 237, 239
Massawa 153, 192
Mathew, Padre 87, 146
McMichael, Sir Harold 182,
198-9
Mega 95, 243
Mersi 134-5
Meru 86
Mission 101 212, 252
Mitchell, Hugh 28, 30-1, 40, 61
Mogadishu 69-70, 110, 146,
153-4, 157, 162, 173, 177

Mogado 64, 133, 148, 155,
158-9, 161, 169, 182, 192,
198, 212, 232
Mordale 124, 126, 127
Moshi 205-14, 216, 230, 240
Moyale 37, 42, 47 -74, 224, 243
Muddo Eri 53
Murray, Capt G. 49
Murray, Rupert 228
Mussolini 247-8
Mwazye 189

Nairobi 9, 10-12, 14-16, 21-
22, 24-8, 37-40, 46, 48-9,
55-60, 65-6, 68, 70, 82-4,
95, 134, 206, 214, 224,
233, 237-8, 240-2
Nakuru 213
Namanyere 187
Nanyuki 241
Neghelli 247
NFD 18, 39, 47, 63, 74, 76,
88, 186, 217, 234, 238, 240
North Horr 241
Northern Rhodesians 218, 221

Ogaden 54, 92-3, 95-6, 98,
101, 106-7, 131-3, 143,
149, 151, 155-8, 161, 164,
167-8
O'Hagan 211

Pankhurst, Dr Richard 189
Pankhurst, Sylvia 189, 192
Pease 48, 62
Philipps 62
Phillimore Tony 154
Pitcairn, Andy 229

Rahale 121-2, 124, 128
Ras Haylu 105, 107
Ras Tafari 92, 98
Revoil 113-14, 171
Ritchie, Brig 244, 246
River Tana 63
Rukwa 187, 189, 191
Rungwa 190

Sandford, Brig 211-12, 252
Sandhurst 1, 80, 112, 199,
207, 225-6, 244
Sumbawanga 183, 185-94,
196-7

Tabora 182-6, 188-9, 196,
199
Taffari Bah 169
Taveta 234
Taylor 127-8, 130, 139, 143-
4, 146, 162
Thomson, Père 188
Tug Argan 228
Tug Wajale 91, 162-6, 168,
170, 175

Ufipa 183, 185-6, 191

Wada Gumared 167, 173
Walwal 131-43, 147-8, 154-5,
162, 174, 212, 234
Wajir 37-40, 42, 45-74, 86, 224
Wardair 131, 133-5
Warton, Lt Col 238, 247
Webbe Shebelli 107, 146-7,
161
Wondo 250

Yavello 245-6
Yonte 27, 30

Zeila 117-18, 129, 132, 149,
220-1, 226